Port and the Douro

Richard Mayson entered the wine trade as a result of living and working in Portugal, which he first visited as a child in 1970. He read geography at university where part of his degree was a study of the micro-climate of Port vineyards in the Douro valley. He entered the UK wine trade in 1984 and spent five years working for the Wine Society, the world's oldest mail-order wine club. In 1987 he was awarded the Vintners' Company Scholarship and spent three months in the vineyards of Iberia. Director of a family textile and investment firm, since 1989 Richard has also been working as a freelance wine writer and lecturer. His first book, the award-winning *Portugal's Wines and Wine-Makers*, was published in 1992, followed by a second edition in 1998. Richard has contributed to a number of publications, including the *Oxford Companion to Wine* and the *Larousse Encyclopaedia of Wine*. He writes regularly on Port and fortified wines for *Decanter* and lectures to students at the Wine and Spirit Education Trust and Leith's School of Food and Wine in London. Richard currently divides his time between his home and business interests in the Derbyshire Peak District, London and Portugal. In 1999 he became a *Cavaleiro* of the *Confraria do Vinho do Porto*.

Leo Duff was born in Belfast, educated at Victoria College, and subsequently studied at Brighton College of Art and the Royal College of Art Illustration School. She has exhibited in Britain, Ireland, the USA and Portugal. Her work appears in many public collections, including the Victoria and Albert Museum, as well as the private collections of, amongst others, Jean Muir and Sir Terence Conran. Her clients include the Arts Council, the BBC, the Wine Society, Saatchi & Saatchi and *Harpers & Queen*. Leo visits northern Portugal on a regular basis and has illustrated a number of wine lists with water-colours of Oporto and the Douro valley.

FABER BOOKS ON WINE

Series Editor: Julian Jeffs

PORT
and the Douro

RICHARD MAYSON

faber and faber
LONDON · NEW YORK

First published in 1999
by Faber and Faber Limited
3 Queen Square London WC1N 3AU

Published in the United States by
Faber and Faber Inc., a division
of Farrar, Straus and Giroux Inc., New York

Phototypeset by Intype London Ltd
Printed in England by Clays Ltd, St Ives plc

A CIP record for this book
is available from the British Library

ISBN 0-571-19522-9

2 4 6 8 10 9 7 5 3 1

To the late Jorge Maria Cabral Ferreira,
who first inspired my interest in Port and the Douro

Contents

List of Plates

━━━━━

List of Maps, Figures and Illustrations

MAPS

FIGURES

ILLUSTRATIONS

Acknowledgements

This book began on 24 March 1980. It was the day that I was invited to lunch in Vila Nova de Gaia by Jorge Ferreira, then a director of the Port house A. A. Ferreira. Fresh from school at the time, I vividly recall being in awe of the heady atmosphere in Oporto, Gaia and the Port lodges. With a glass of Ferreira's ethereal Duque de Bragança Tawny in hand (still one of my favourite twenty-year-olds), I remember thinking that it would be a good idea to take up an interest in wine. It was two years later that I really came to know the Douro when I was given free-run of Ferreira's *quintas* for a university dissertation on micro-climate in Port vineyards. Jorge Ferreira was killed in a tragic car accident on the way to the Douro in 1992. This book is dedicated to him.

I am indebted to a huge number of people who have helped me since I first arrived in Oporto over twenty years ago. The following roster of names, which reads almost like a wine list, is by no means exhaustive but I hope that all those who have assisted directly with the preparation of this book are included.

First and foremost I am particularly grateful to the late Armando Pimentel, formerly President of the Instituto do Vinho do Porto (IVP), for agreeing to support this book and to all those from the IVP who have provided information. Representing the IVP in London, Sue Glasgow has been both patient and diligent in response to my hurried requests for a crucial fact here or another there. My thanks are due to her.

In the Douro I am especially indebted to the Symington family and to Jorge Roquette (Quinta do Crasto) for regularly providing me with luxurious lodgings and replete information for this book.

I also wish to express my heartfelt thanks to: Fernando Alves (ADVID), Tim, Philip and Sophia Bergqvist (Quinta de la Rosa),

ACKNOWLEDGEMENTS

Adrian Bridge (Taylor and Fonseca), Miguel Corte Real (Cockburn), Nick Delaforce (Croft and Delaforce), Johnny Graham (Churchill Graham), David Guimaraens (Taylor and Fonseca), Antonio Magalhães (Taylor and Fonseca), Nuno Magalhães (UTAD), João Nicolau de Almeida (Ramos Pinto), Dirk Niepoort, Jim Reeder (Cockburn), George Sandeman, Christian and Assunção Seely (Quinta do Noval), Charles Symington and Peter Symington (Dow, Graham, Warre, etc.) for providing me with so much technical detail from *quinta*, *adega* and *armazém*. In the Douro and Vila Nova de Gaia, it goes without saying that they also provided some great hospitality. There are many others in Portugal to whom I also wish to express my thanks: Carlos Agrelos (Quinta do Côtto), Manuel Angelo Barros (Barros Almeida), Fatima Burmester, John Burnett (Croft and Delaforce), Iolanda Carneiro (Wiese & Krohn), Alberto Domingues (C. da Silva), Peter Cobb (Cockburn), José Maria Soares Franco (Ferreira), Jorge Guimaraes (Forrester), Anselmo Mendes (ex-Borges & Irmão), Vito Olazabal (Ferreira), Manuel Poças Pintão (Poças), Pedro Silva Reis (Real Companhia Velha), Guilherme Alvares Ribeiro (Quinta do Valado), Jorge Rosas (Ramos Pinto), Alistair and Gillyane Robertson (Taylor and Fonseca), Henry Shotton (Symington), Rógerio Silva (Cálem), Domingos Alves de Sousa (Quinta da Gaivosa), Francisco Teixeira (Osborne), José Teles (Osborne), Messias Vigario (Messias) and Cristiano van Zeller. Without their help and co-operation this book would not be complete.

Oporto and the Douro has always been something of a cultural melting pot and a number of Australian wine-makers have recently started to have an impact on the region. My thanks are due to David Baverstock, Dominic Morris and Krystina Gerkens, particularly for their help with the chapter on Douro wines.

In the UK I am grateful to a number of people who have been on hand when I needed information, in particular: David Delaforce, Joanna Delaforce, Manny Lewin, Euan Mackay, Patricia Parnell and Raymond Reynolds. I am grateful to William ('Bill') Warre MW for his input into the first chapter on history and to Dr Derek Bunting for supplying me with so much fascinating information on the Whitehead family. Leo Duff, whose work I have admired and collected for some years, has provided evocative illustrations of some of the icons from the Douro, Oporto and Vila Nova de Gaia. The series editor, Julian Jeffs, patiently read through the entire manuscript and saved me from making some embarrassing errors. I am indebted to him.

Finally, I would like to thank my parents and friends for being on hand when I thought this book would never be finished. No book is ever entirely finished. In a world increasingly dictated by fashion, views and opinions change. Any factual inaccuracies on the other hand are entirely my own responsibility.

Richard Mayson, London 1999

Preface
Setting the Scene

<hr>

Port wine, *porto, vin de porto, vinho do porto*; they all take their name from Portugal's second city, Oporto. It is a curious fact that nowadays very little wine even touches the place. Apart from being the home of the Port Wine Institute (IVP) and the august British-run Factory House, most of the action takes place on the opposite side of the river at Vila Nova de Gaia or seventy to a hundred miles upstream in the vineyards of the Douro valley.

Previous books on Port have tended to concentrate on the two cities of Oporto and Gaia; the atmosphere, the rather clubbable lifestyle and of course the wine. Authors, many of whom were intimately involved in the trade, naturally tended to recount their own anecdotes in a semi-autobiographical way. They looked upon the Douro as a distant hinterland and frequently examined Port in isolation, divorced from any other wine. This is partly a reflection of the times. The Douro was indeed a remote place and, despite many attempts to mimic it, Port was and remains a unique wine.

Written from an independent standpoint, this book seeks to redress the balance by putting Port wine in context. It is an opportune time to do so. Since 1986 Port producers have been able to export their wines directly from the Douro, bypassing the *entreposto* or entrepôt of shippers in Vila Nova de Gaia. Impressive mountain-breaching roads have made the Douro more accessible than ever before. Where as recently as the 1980s a visit to the vineyards in the Douro Superior used to be something of an expedition, it is now perfectly feasible to commute in a day. Over a slightly longer period, the term 'Douro' has found its way in to the wine lexicon, attached to an increasingly impressive array of unfortified wines made from the same grapes as Port. For the first time in over a century, these wines are brought together with Port in the same book.

In the last two decades of the twentieth century, the face of the Port wine region has changed more than at any time over the last hundred and fifty years. Those who remember and recount things as they were often do so with *saudades*, that uniquely Portuguese feeling of yearning, homesickness and nostalgia all wrapped in to one. But for all the startling changes, the atmosphere that first drew my family to the north of Portugal in the early 1970s remains much the same. It is shaped by the domineering landscape, the unpredictable climate and the genuine rapport of the Portuguese people. It was the latter that undoubtedly drew the English to Portugal in the twelfth century and set off the chain of events that eventually created Port wine.

Terraces, Cima Corgo

This book begins by recounting that story, bringing the history of Port and the Douro right up to date. It moves on to chart the Douro valley. The vines, vineyards and *quintas* that make up the region are given their due weight for the first time in a generic book on Port. The way that Port is produced is then covered in some depth with an eye, an ear and a nose for the tumult of vintage. The narrative then moves downstream to Vila Nova de Gaia for the ageing and blending processes that form the many different styles of Port. This is followed by a detailed appraisal of Port types from basic, bread-and-butter Ruby to venerable Vintage. All years are assessed back to 1960 and significant vintage declarations as far back as 1896. A directory of individual Port producers and shippers follows, combining historical background with a further appraisal of their wines. The unfortified wines of the Douro are brought in together with an evaluation of the principal producers. The book concludes with a postscript which examines the prospects for Port and the Douro in the twenty-first century.

I have set out to make *Port and the Douro* a 'good read' for interested consumers and wine-trade students alike. Individual chapters may therefore be read as a complete narrative but are subdivided for ease of reference. Technical information on legislation, viticulture and vinification has been included in an elemental form. Where Portuguese terminology or technical terms require a more detailed explanation, they may be found in separate glossaries at the end of the book. The appendix includes an explanation of the main legislative bodies governing Port and the Douro. For anyone wishing to visit the Douro or Oporto and Gaia, short sections at the end of Chapter 2 and Chapter 5 respectively provide general directions but with so many changes taking place they are not written as a comprehensive guide.

Richard Mayson, London 1999

I

Bringing Port Up to Date

TRADE AND TREATY

On the morning of Monday 12 May 1986, Her Majesty Queen Elizabeth II was joined by His Excellency President Mario Soares of Portugal at St George's Chapel, Windsor Castle. The occasion was a service of thanksgiving to celebrate the six-hundredth anniversary of the Treaty of Windsor, the oldest and most enduring alliance between two nation states. As the congregation rose to strains of the hymn 'All People that on Earth do Dwell', thoughts turned back precisely six centuries to when Dom João I of Portugal and Richard II of England put their names to this 'solid, perpetual and real league, amity, confederacy and union . . . on behalf of themselves and their heirs and successors'. After the service the congregation retired to toast the health of British and Portuguese heads of state present and past with a glass of Port.

The story of Port and the Douro is inseparable from Portugal's emergence as a trading nation, in which England, another rapidly developing mercantile power, played a crucially important role. Although the Phoenicians are credited with bringing the vine to the Iberian Peninsula and it is likely that the Romans produced wine in the Douro, it was at the end of the eleventh century that Portugal began the transformation from a small, obscure county in western Iberia to an independent nation state. Until that time, the Moors occupied the greater part of the territory, building minareted mosques in the south and strong castles in the north, the remains of which survive at Numão and Lavandeira above the Douro. The Douro itself was described by Moorish geographer Al Idrisi as 'a big river with a rapid, rushing current, full and deep' and he depicted the landscape between the rivers Minho and Douro as 'a populous land with towns, castles and many tilled fields'. It was in the tenth century that this small territory adopted its name from that of the Roman city of Oporto: Portucale.

This became the embryo of the nascent Portuguese kingdom when it was awarded to Henry of Burgundy, who married Teresa, daughter of the king of neighbouring Leon in 1094. Henry, a cousin of the Duke of Burgundy, was reputed to have brought the Pinot Noir grape to Portugal (a name which lives on in the Douro under the guise of a variety called Tinta Francisca) but otherwise made little impact on his adopted territory. It was his son, Afonso Henriques, who can be credited as the founder of modern Portugal. Taking over from where his father left off, he graduated from plain *Portugalensium princeps* to become the self-styled *Alphonsus gloriosissimus princeps et Dei gratia Portugalensium rex*. After expelling his seemingly rather flighty mother from the country he set about driving the Moors southwards, leaving them confined to the coastal strip of the Algarve by 1168.

Many of Afonso Henriques' military successes were greatly aided by English, German and Flemish crusaders. They already knew something of the coast of western Iberia from the time of the First Crusade but, by all accounts, early relations with the English were far from amicable. Rather like today's hooligans, these early pirate crusaders gained a distinctly unsavoury reputation as plunderers, drunkards and rapists. Afonso Henriques succeeded in redirecting their misdemeanours from the Christians in northern Iberia to the Muslims in the south. In around 1140, a fleet of seventy ships carrying English and Norman crusaders bound for Palestine, sailed into the Douro and agreed to join the Portuguese in a combined attack on the Moors. Induced to stay in Portugal with the promise of good, cheap wine and spoils ahead, they went on to ransack Lisbon, capturing the city for Afonso Henriques in 1147. The new kingdom of Portugal received official recognition from Pope Alexander III in 1179 with the final conquest of Faro in the Algarve taking place under Afonso III in 1249, over two centuries before the Moors were finally driven out of Andalusia in neighbouring Spain. Thus Portugal took its present shape: a long narrow country roughly 600 km long by 200 km wide, dissected by two great rivers, the Douro and Tagus (Tejo), rising on the central Iberian *meseta*. Portugal's borders have since survived virtually intact, making them among the oldest on the continent of Europe.

By the mid-thirteenth century, a good understanding had developed between the Portuguese and English monarchs, and various, albeit unsuccessful, attempts were made to formalise this friendship by marriage. Against a background of relative peace, trade began to prosper with English merchants selling wool and manufactured cloth in exchange for olive oil, fruit and wine. The status of Oporto under the control of its bishop was called into question by Afonso III (1248–1279) and the crown established a competing royal borough at Gaia on the opposite bank of the Douro. It was decreed that a third of all ships descending the river and half of those arriving from abroad should unload at Gaia. The Bishop of Oporto rejected this and appealed to the Pope but was unable to prevent Afonso from establishing the separate *conselho* (municipal council) of Vila Nova de Gaia in 1255.

As substantial English mercantile communities grew up in the Portuguese ports of Lisbon, Oporto, Gaia and Viana, the traders of both nations saw the advantage of securing concessions for each other. Letters from Portugal's King Diniz (1279–1325) to Edward I and II of England illustrate the intervention of the crown in an effort to obtain safe-conduct and protection for Portuguese merchants in England in return for reciprocal rights. A series of commercial treaties were signed, beginning in 1294 and concluding in 1353 when the merchants of Lisbon and Oporto led by Afonso Martins 'Alho' ('garlic') negotiated a treaty with England's Edward III that guaranteed the safety of the traders of both nations, allowing free access to each other's markets.

It took an invasion of Portugal by Castile to formalise the alliance between England and Portugal. With the Hundred Years' War raging between England and France and the French taking the Castilian side, first Edward III then Richard II of England plunged into battle alongside the Portuguese. An alliance between Fernando I of Portugal and John of Gaunt, Duke of Lancaster was sealed in 1373 with the express intent of defeating the usurper King Enrique de Trastamara of Castile. However, when Fernando I died in 1383 leaving his only daughter married to Juan I of Castile, the Castilians laid claim to Portugal. With the help of 500 English archers, the Castilians were soundly defeated at the Battle of Aljubarrota in Portuguese Estremadura, thereby securing independence for Portugal in 1385. In the meantime, Portugal's ambassadors remained behind in England, and after detailed negotiations put their signatures to a new military, political and economic treaty at St George's Chapel, Windsor on 9 May 1386. The Treaty of Windsor, as it became known, was reinforced when the new Portuguese king, João I, Mestre de Aviz, married Philippa of Lancaster, daughter of John of Gaunt, in Oporto the following year. It yielded the enduring special relationship between Portugal and Great Britain that gave rise to a flourishing trade in wine and ultimately Port.

THE ORIGINS OF THE WINE TRADE

The marriage of João and Philippa was a huge success. There were eight children, the most significant of whom was their third-born son named after his English uncle, later Henry IV. Born near the waterfront in Oporto in 1394, the Infante Dom Henrique became much better known by the English name of Henry the Navigator. He was encouraged by the scholarly Philippa and led a studious life. From the isolation of his observatory at Sagres near Cape St Vincent, Prince Henry instigated Portugal's golden age of discovery (and ultimately her impoverishment) with his courageous exploits along the west coast of Africa. His mantle was inherited in the fifteenth and sixteenth centuries by a long line of Portuguese explorers, among them Bartolomeu Dias, Vasco da Gama, Fernão Magalhães (Magellan) and Pedro Alves Cabral, who discovered Brazil for Portugal in 1500. Ships returned with sugar from Madeira, spices from India and gold from Africa's Gold Coast reinforcing Portugal's attraction to English traders. Under the reign of Manuel I, 'the fortunate' (1495–1521), Portugal reached the zenith of its overseas influence with the Portuguese flag planted on four continents. The Cantino map of 1502 shows that Portugal even laid claim to the barren wastes of Greenland, Newfoundland and Labrador as Portuguese ships ventured ever further into the cold waters of the North Atlantic in search of that most precious of Portuguese commodities: cod.

Cod (*bacalhau*) had become – and still remains – a staple in the day-to-day life of the Portuguese. From the time of Edward III (1327–1377), codfish from the waters around the British Isles (dried and salted to preserve it on the voyage home) was particu-larly highly prized in Portugal, and wine from the vineyards of the

Minho in the north of the country became the principal currency in this trade. With a taste for bigger, full-bodied wines from southern climes like the Spanish 'Lepe' – famous according to Chaucer for its 'fumositee' – these northern wines were never particularly well regarded by the English. In fact Chaucer's French contemporary, Froissart, records that the wines from north-west Iberia were so 'ardent' that the English could scarcely drink them. In his scholarly book, *The Story of Wine*, Hugh Johnson recounts how archers sent by John of Gaunt had already come across the wines of 'Ribadavia' and attributes them to Galicia rather than Portugal. The modern-day Ribadave is an area corresponding to the valley of the River Ave just to the north of Oporto and it seems highly probable that the first Portuguese wines to reach English shores in any volume were similar in style to the thin, rasping red Vinhos Verdes that are produced in the region today.

This lucrative trade – *bacalhau* for wine – was further reinforced by the English Reformation launched in 1536. With the majority of English eschewing fish on Fridays and saints' days, earning themselves the Portuguese nickname of *rosbifes* (roast beefs) in the process, Portugal became the principal market for British fish. English and Scottish merchants or 'factors' settled in the northern port of Viana do Castelo at the mouth of the River Lima sourcing and shipping wine from the hard granite country between Monção (called 'Monson' by the English), Melgaço and Ponte de Lima. Known as 'Red Portugal', these light red wines must have been inherently unstable and spoiled long before they reached British shores. In support of this, Sarah Bradford records in *The Story of Port* that large quantities of Red Portugal were supplied to the British naval commissioners as 'beverage for the sailors' and quotes a seventeenth-century order to dispose of 'the remaining wines which are spoiling'.

In the meantime, diminutive Portugal had stretched herself to the limit. Not for the last time in her distinctly chequered history, the overseas empire drained the country. As able-bodied men migrated to Lisbon or journeyed overseas, fields were left unculti-vated and Portugal was forced to import even the most basic foodstuffs. With all the salt-beef used up, the hapless citizens of Oporto were forced to eat offal, gaining a taste for tripe which continues to this day. The dish, *Tripas à moda do Porto*, features prominently on the menus of most Oporto restaurants and the city's inhabitants are known in jest as *Tripeiros* – tripe eaters!

The crisis-point in Portugal's fourteenth century over-expansion was reached when the hapless King Sebastião, 'the regretted', was killed fighting the Moors at the Battle of Alcazar-Quivir in 1578 leaving no heir to the Portuguese throne. After a brief interregnum under Dom Henrique, the somewhat decrepit cardinal-king, Philip II of Spain marched into Portugal initiating sixty years of national humiliation. Despite England's bitter antipathy towards Spain, English and Scottish merchants (Protestant as well as Catholic), continued to live in occupied Portugal, albeit without any of their former privileges. Lured perhaps by the security of the larger city or possibly as a result of the silting up of the port at Viana, it was during this period that the majority of English merchants began to move south to Oporto.

Portugal's second city was already home to a well-established English Factory of merchants engaged in selling cloth and *bacalhau* to the Portuguese in exchange for oil and fruit rather than wine. The term 'Factory' needs some clarification. The Portuguese had their own factories or *feitorias* in India by the end of the fifteenth century and the expression subsequently came into common usage to describe a body of merchants or factors carrying on business in a foreign country. John Delaforce in his book *The Factory House at Oporto* explores the origin of the term in some detail and concludes that the English use of the term derives from the Portuguese. Certainly by the mid-seventeenth century there were English Factories in India as well as in Portugal at Lisbon, Oporto and Viana.

Following the restoration of the Portuguese monarchy in 1640 under the Duque de Bragança, João IV, the English and Scottish position in Portugal was considerably strengthened by a one-sided treaty with Oliver Cromwell in 1654. In return for supporting the Portuguese in their wars with the Spanish and the Dutch, Cromwell exacted enormous privileges for the English and Scottish merchants, which made them more powerful and prosperous than the Portuguese themselves. The colony in Oporto boasted its own consul, Church of England chaplain and Factory, which fought fiercely for its independence from a parallel institution in Lisbon. Their special status was further reinforced following the restoration of the English monarchy when Charles II married Afonso VI's sister, Catherine of Bragança, in 1662. In another treaty concluded in 1661, the English bound themselves to defend Portugal 'as if it were England itself'.

FROM WINE TO PORT

The defining moment in the evolution of Portugal's wine trade came as a result of England's deteriorating relations with France. In 1667, Louis XIV's minister Colbert instituted a protectionist policy that eventually closed the French market to imports of English cloth. In a tit-for-tat trade war, Charles II then prohibited the importation of all French goods, including wine. Only 120 tuns (about 120,000 litres) of Portuguese wine had been imported to London in the mid-1670s but during the embargo between 1678 and 1685 recorded annual shipments rose sharply to 6,880 tuns (6.81 million litres). But the English continued to favour the refined taste of claret over the wines of northern Portugal and much of the wine that reached London during this period was almost certainly French masquerading as Portuguese.

However, when war broke out between France and England in 1689, it became virtually impossible to buy French wines. This sent the Oporto merchants scurrying around for all the 'Red Portugal' they could find. Although the early shippers were not in the habit of visiting vineyards, their quest probably sent them upstream into the Douro valley. Job Bearsley, whose shipping firm was subsequently transmuted into Taylor Fladgate & Yeatman, is thought to have been the first English trader to venture upriver. Hard as it is to imagine today, the steep terraced slopes of the Douro were mainly producing cereals. Although vineyards had been planted in the region in the thirteenth century during the reign of Dom Diniz, 'the Husbundman', wine was still very much a secondary product. Vines grew from *pilheiros*, small holes specially constructed in the vertical terrace walls, thereby leaving all the available flat land for essentials like corn. Writing just over a century later, F.P. Rebello de Fonseca remarks that 'in 1681 there were no large plantations of vineyards', adding that they mostly comprised small plots of land scattered amidst the scrub. The region was 'one of the poorest in the kingdom, as is shown by the wretchedness of the buildings'. The Visconde de Villa Maior, writing in 1876, adds that with 'the English taste inclining to sweet wines' growers were obliged 'to rear vines in choice seats on the banks of the streams more exposed to the solar action, these comprising small areas scattered here and there in the woods'.

Wine-making conditions in the Douro must have been extremely unhygienic, and the first wines to be exported known as 'portoport' were a poor substitute for claret. An oft-quoted ditty written by Richard Ames in 1693 went:

> Mark how it smells, methinks a real pain
> Is by the odour thrown upon my brain.
> I've tasted it – 'tis spiritless and flat,
> And has as many different tastes
> As can be found in compound pastes ...
> But fetch us a pint of any sort,
> Navarre, Galicia, anything but Port.

Derogatory tasting notes aside, in the last decade of the seventeenth century England's drinking habits became less a matter of personal whim and more a symbol of political loyalty. In the years that followed James II's expulsion from England in 1688, the Jacobites would toast 'the king over the water' in claret whilst the loyal Whigs raised their tankards of Port to King William and the Glorious Revolution! Thus the Scots who remained loyal to the exiled Stuart king recited a sad ditty:

> Firm and erect the Highland chieftain stood,
> Sweet was his mutton and his claret good,
> 'Thou shalt drink Port,' the English statesman cried;
> He drank the poison, and his spirit died.

South of the border, even the English Tories needed some persuading by a patriotic Jonathan Swift:

> Be sometimes to your country true,
> Have once the public good in view;
> Bravely despise champagne at court
> And choose to dine at home with Port.

But in the same year Swift probably came nearer to the truth when he wrote: 'I love White Portuguese Wine more than Claret, Champagne or Burgundy; I have a sad, vulgar appetite.'

It was in the latter part of the seventeenth century that the foundations were laid for some of the great Port-shipping firms that continue to prosper today. One of the first English families to be mentioned among those gathered at Viana and Oporto were the Newmans. Based in the English west country port of Dartmouth they began trading in *bacalhau* in the fifteenth century. By 1679 they had their own fleet of ships bartering Newfoundland cod for Portuguese wine, which was found to have been greatly improved by the long sea voyage. This suggests that their wine was already of considerably better quality than the light, run-of-the-mill reds from the Minho which spoiled so readily. The Newmans' wine shipping company went on to become Hunt Roope (now owned by Ferreira) and the family still owns an important Douro property, Quinta da Eira Velha.

The English Port shipper with the longest continuous lineage is Warre & Co., which was founded in 1670, followed by Croft, which dates back to 1678 under the name of Phayre & Bradley. However, the oldest of all the Port shippers is the German firm of Kopke & Co., which was founded in Oporto in 1638 by Cristiano Kopke, son of the Lisbon consul for the Hanseatic towns. Like many of these firms, it began as a general merchant and only started specialising in wine a century later. Kopke is now owned by the Portuguese Barros Almeida group.

Hugh Johnson ascribes the opening up of the Douro to the Dutch, who began buying wine from Oporto after going to war with the French in 1672. They sourced wine from the monastery at Lamego on the south-western margin of today's Douro region. Certainly the best wines (so-called 'priestport') seem to have been produced by monastic foundations. A number of modern day *quintas* were established on land leased from monasteries like the Convento de São Pedro das Aguias near Tabuaço, now owned by the firm of Vranken.

Portugal's favoured status as an alternative source for wine for both the English and the Dutch was firmly established by the Methuen Treaty of 1703. Somewhat confusingly there were two Methuens; father and son. In an effort to ward off Portugal's brief flirtation with France, Sir Paul Methuen (envoy to the King of Portugal 1697–1705 and Ambassador to Portugal 1706–8) concluded a military treaty in which England promised to defend Portugal in the War of Spanish Succession. In the meantime his father, diplomat and cloth merchant John Methuen (Lord

Chancellor of Ireland and envoy to Portugal in 1691 and 1703, and Ambasador Extraordinary to Portugal in 1703), succeeded in securing preferential treatment for English textiles in Portugal in return for a duty levy on Portuguese wines that would be a third less than on those from France. Rather like Cromwell's treaty fifty years earlier, Methuen proved to be a rather hollow deal for the beleaguered Portuguese. Wines from Portugal already enjoyed lower rates of duty in England than those of any other country and the importation of French goods was in any case severely restricted. The influx of English cloth practically destroyed Portugal's textile industry centred at Portalegre and Covilhã but Methuen's provision for a preferential rate of duty did survive for over 150 years until it was finally dropped by Gladstone in 1866. As a result, the Methuen Treaty greatly advanced the cause of the Port trade.

The early years of the trade are well documented in the letters and diaries of Thomas Woodmass, who arrived in the north of Portugal from England in 1703, the same year as the Methuen Treaty. He landed at Viana and met Job Bearsley. Woodmass was taken to see the vineyards at 'Monson' before making for Oporto. He wrote: 'O Porto is much larger than Viana and here are more English and Scotch families. The wine of the Duro (*sic*) is much praised by Mr Harris and others.' (Mr Harris was presumably a member of the Harris family who settled in Oporto in 1680 and whose firm subsequently became Quarles Harris). Woodmass came across a number of early merchants, among them a Mr Clark (probably John Clark, a forerunner of Warre) and Mr Phayre of Phayre & Bradley. During the vintage at the end of September he wrote 'the heat is so great that breathing is difficult. Wine is at 13 *millreas* [i.e. 1.3 escudos] the pipe, but of this vintage there will not be abundance'. With the exception of the price, it could almost be an extract from a modern day vintage report.

Those pioneer travellers to the Douro must have suffered appalling privations. There were no roads over the mountains of the Marão and the inns and taverns were apparently so flea-infested that travellers preferred to sleep on tables. The River Douro itself became a means of communication but it was an unpredictable torrent. Floods were commonplace and in 1727 the Douro swept away over 100 people along with boats, vineyards, *lagares* and buildings at a cost of millions of *cruzados* (see page 49).

Portugal remained at war with Spain until the Treaty of Utrecht was signed in 1713. Apart from the local highwaymen who attacked Thomas Woodmass near 'Villadecon' (Vila do Conde) there were also Lord Galway's interfering troops, who went on a drunken rampage in Viana forcing the English merchants to shut themselves in their houses. However, as the century wore on life improved greatly for the growing British community in Oporto supported by their black, English-speaking servants. The wines also began to improve and demand steadily increased. Queen Anne placed an order for ten pipes of Port and farmers began to command ever higher prices for their wines. 'Red Oporto' was described as 'deep, bright, strong, fresh and neat' and in 1712 a merchant advertised the wine at 5s 6d a gallon. 'Red Barrabar Lisbon' ('very strong, extraordinarily good and neat'), however, still commanded 6d a gallon more than Red Oporto.

Most of the Ports shipped to England in the early years of the eighteenth century were dark, austere reds, fermented to dryness which earned them the name 'black-strap'. In a determined effort to make sure that the wines arrived at their destination in good condition, many merchants would add a generous measure of brandy probably raising the level of alcohol to around at least 15 or 16 per cent by volume. An early wine-making manual handbook, *A Agricultura das Vinhas* published in 1720, recommends the addition of three gallons (13.6 litres) of brandy to each pipe of wine although this rose to between thirty-six and forty-eight litres per pipe during the eighteenth century. (This compares with the 100 litres per pipe added to arrest the fermentation to produce Port today). An uncorroborated story suggests that as early as 1678 two Liverpool wine merchants found the abbot of Lamego monastery adding brandy during the fermentation thereby killing the active yeasts and conserving some of the natural grape sugar in the wine. No names are recorded for if they had, the abbot at Lamego would surely be as famous as Dom Perignon, the monk at Hautvillers who is credited with fixing the natural sparkle in champagne.

BAGA AND BULLOCK'S BLOOD

Such was England's control over Portugal during the first half of the seventeenth century that she treated it like a colony. Thomas

Woodmass reports as much at the turn of the century warning of 'bad feeling against us . . . as the principal trade of the country is in our hands, but that the treaties of commerce are in our favour'. As annual shipments rose to around 25,000 pipes, in 1727 an association of shippers was formed to regulate the wine trade and control the prices paid to growers. This led to accusation and counter-accusation as experimentation led to adulteration. The use of elderberry (*baga de sabugueiro* or merely '*baga*' for short) became widespread. This controversial practice crops up time and again in the history of the Port industry (see page 136). According to John Croft, who wrote a *Treatise on the Wines of Portugal*, it began in the early 1700s when Peter Bearsley (son of the aforementioned Job) found that elderberry juice greatly enhanced the colour of the wine. But by the 1730s sugar was also being added and *baga* came to be used to bolster both the colour and flavour of wines overstretched by poor quality spirit. Worse still, wine from Spain ('like bullock's blood') and raisin wines mixed with British spirits extracted from malt were passed off or blended into Port. Villa Maior quotes Rebello de Fonseca who blames the English merchants for having 'ruined the purity, great reputation and credit of the wine of Alto Douro enjoyed in the north [i.e. England], by blending with it weak, raw, colourless and inferior wines of Valle de Besteiros, S. Miguel do Outeiro, Anadia and other places' [i.e. Vinho Verde and Bairrada], making up for the 'lack of natural goodness with elderberry, pepper, sugar and other admixtures'. These wines arrived in England 'devoid of taste, body, colour or goodness of any kind; so that having gained preference over all others for strength, colour and delicacy of flavour it came to pass that not every other wine was preferred to it, but every other beverage'.

This unprincipled over-production brought about a slump in the trade and prices came down dramatically. A pipe of wine worth sixty escudos at the turn of the century fell to forty-eight in 1731 and just 6.3 escudos after 1750. With supply outstripping demand, the farmers could not find buyers for their wines. In September 1754 the shippers didn't even bother to visit the Douro, contenting themselves with a circular to the growers accusing them of adulteration and threatening to expose the culprits. The wines were described as having fiery spirit like gunpowder alight, the colour of ink, the sweetness of Brazil and the aromas of India. Provided that the 'aromas of India' referred to spice, the tasting note doesn't seem too derogatory. But the residual sweetness in the wines of the day was clearly controversial for the Factors wrote that growers were 'in the habit of checking the fermentation too soon, by putting brandy into them while still fermenting, a practice which must be considered diabolical'. They clearly didn't use enough brandy for 'after this the wines will not remain quiet, but are continually tending to ferment and to become ropy and acid'.

Over the preceding years, the small Douro farmers had clearly done well from the wine trade for as John Croft invidiously observes, they strutted through the streets of Oporto 'like so many peacocks . . . and thus vied with each other in gaudiness of apparel'. Now they came down to Oporto cap-in-hand pleading with the shippers to buy their wines. Needing no more, the British shippers refused and repeated their accusations. The Douro growers, desperate at the loss of their livelihoods, took their complaint to the highest authority: José I's autocratic Prime Minister, Sebastião José de Carvalho e Melo, subsequently ennobled as the Marquês de Pombal.

POMBAL AND THE EARLY REGULATIONS

Pombal already had a reputation for ruthlessness when he was appointed to the post of Minister of State following João V's death in 1750. The royal secretary Alexandre Gusmão, who coveted the position himself, exclaimed 'the people will suffer for it'. Pombal had been Ambassador to London from 1740 to 1744 where he had been thought of as 'busy and pettifogging'. But during his time in London, Pombal seems to have developed a certain jealous respect for the British and had formed the opinion that their ability to provide goods cheaply stifled the Portuguese.

The ineffectual José I (1750–77) steadily entrusted more power to Pombal and shortly after the catastrophic Lisbon earthquake of 1755 he became Prime Minister. Pombal acted to quell the problems in the Douro with characteristic decisiveness. In 1756, with the backing of a number of significant Portuguese growers, he created the Real Companhia das Vinhas do Alto Douro. The new Companhia or Company was all-embracing. It was empowered to fix prices, protect the authenticity of the product, raise taxes and even to grant rights as to which taverns could sell Port wine in the city of Oporto and three leagues beyond. It had exclusive trading rights with Brazil and all other Port wine for export had to be bought from the Companhia. A decree dated 10 September 1756 fixed prices at twenty-five to thirty escudos a pipe for Port of primary quality and twenty to twenty-five escudos a pipe for secondary wines. Pombal's Companhia was effectively a state monopoly that seems to have been constituted like a rather bureaucratic co-operative. The board of directors was made up of a president, twelve deputies, a judge conservator, a fiscal attorney, a secretary and six advisers all of whom were linked to the industry. A grower named Dr Frei João da Mansilha became Pombal's right-hand man. Needless to say, the British shippers were totally excluded.

The foundation of the Companhia provoked howls of anguish not just from the British Factory but also from the tavern owners who blamed the government for the steep rise in the price of wine. On 23 February 1757 (Ash Wednesday) a protest took place in the streets of Oporto, which quickly descended into a bloody riot. Christened the 'Tippler's Revolt', it ended with the arrest of 407 men and women, around twenty of whom were hanged and over a hundred banished.

The British, who were blamed for inciting the revolt, objected to Pombal and their own Prime Minister, William Pitt. Pombal told them in a high-handed manner that he refused to recognise the British Factory and that their circular to the growers treated Portugal as though 'it was not a Kingdom that had an indisputable right to make its own domestic laws'. If it had not been for the Seven Years' War with France and Spain, the Anglo-Portuguese alliance so carefully nurtured over the past four hundred years might have come to an abrupt end. In the event, Pitt was far too anxious to remain on good terms with Portugal to pick a fight and he turned a deaf ear to the shippers' complaints.

The establishment of the Companhia was accompanied by a series of measures to regulate the production of Port. A commission was set up to draw a boundary around the Douro region, restricting Port production to vineyards within the demarcation. Like most subsequent legislation in the Douro, this was not without controversy and three demarcations were proposed before the scheme finally came into effect in 1761. This was marked out with sturdy granite posts (over a hundred of which still stand) setting out two zones: one producing wines merely for home consumption (*vinho do ramo* or 'branch wine' after the tradition of indicating a tavern by hanging a branch outside*), and another for high quality wines for export. The latter could be sold at higher prices and were known, perhaps in deference to the British, as *Vinhos da Feitoria* or Factory Wines. This is still a source of considerable pride to the present-day owners of the Douro *quintas* that fell within the original *Feitoria* demarcation.

Noble house, Vilariça

In a concerted effort to stamp out the fraud and adulteration of earlier years, Pombal ruled that all elderberry trees were to be uprooted and every vineyard should be registered. Production quotas were issued based on an average of the previous five years' yields. On top of this, Pombal handed the Company the exclusive right to supply the spirit or *aguardente* used in Port production, fixing the price according to quality.

*A branch was also used as the sign for a tavern in England, hence the 'good wine needs no bush'.

Pombal's dictates had implications for Portugal's wine industry well beyond Oporto and the Douro. He ordered that vineyards in regions as far apart as the Ribatejo and Bairrada be grubbed up both to protect the authenticity of Port and to boost the production of cereals and rice. Any contravention of the rules would be met by stiff penalties ranging from six months in prison to deportation to Angola. But there is no doubt that the Real Companhia das Vinhas do Alto Douro proved to be a lucrative exercise for Pombal himself, who often flouted his own regulations. The prime minister had a country residence at Oeiras just to the west of Lisbon and he stipulated that grapes from his Carcavelos vineyards could be blended into Port. The Companhia also became corrupt and many of the officials used it as a means of lining their own pockets. Villa Maior writing in 1876 describes them as a 'true oligarchy' adding that 'to this day their *quintas* in the Alto Douro are distinguishable on account of the magnificence of the buildings and by the escutcheons proudly displayed over the principal gates of the mansions'. Many of the fine eighteenth-century houses which can still be seen lining the streets of Mesão Frio and Provesende were built by officials working for the Companhia. None the less Pombal's measures were as far-sighted as they were far-reaching. They continue to have an impact on the Douro and in other European wine regions two-and-a-half centuries later.

POMBAL'S DEMISE

Pombal's draconian measures were certainly successful in the short term. Exports to England immediately began to rise from a low of just over 12,000 pipes in 1756 to an average of around 17,000 pipes just four years later. Prices also began to pick up reaching around forty escudos a pipe in 1765. Two years earlier the Companhia had intervened to buy up wines 'preferably from the poorest farmers' in order to prevent a collapse in price due to the huge stocks of wine sitting at London docks. In 1766 a number of Port shippers failed, among them Adam Standard, Ricardo Tisuel and Estevão Heraut, but the majority weathered Pombal's legislation.

Pombal himself continued issuing decrees and dictates including, in 1776, a complete ban on exports of wines from Viana, Monção, Bairrada and the Algarve in order to protect those from the Douro.

He exceeded the powers vested in him until his royal patron, José I, died in 1777. José was succeeded to the throne by his rather more proactive daughter, Maria I, whose first act was to dismiss Pombal from office. On the day after the king's funeral, the prisons were opened and 800 victims of Pombal's reign of terror emerged. Reminded of a resurrection of the dead, the Spanish ambassador wrote that 'Pombal deserves the general hatred of the public for his cruelty'.

With Pombal's demise, many of his measures were either relaxed or abandoned. By order of the new queen, Frei João da Mansilha was exiled and although the Real Companhia das Vinhas do Alto Douro continued to exist in name, the company lost its monopoly in a royal decree dated 9 August 1777. In the same year a free market was declared and the wines of Monção could once again be exported although only Port wine itself could be shipped over the bar of the Douro.

THE EXPANSION OF THE DOURO

Up to this time the majority of Douro vineyards were located in the westerly reaches of the region, particularly around Régua, Godim, Lobrigos and Cambres in the area known today as the Baixo Corgo (meaning 'Below the Corgo'). The town of Régua, well-sited on a broad curve in the river, became the undisputed centre of the wine region having been the administrative head-quarters of Pombal's Companhia. The building, painted lurid pink, continues to be used as a wine-making and administrative centre by its privately owned successor, Real Companhia Velha.

Relatively few vineyards were to be found upstream from the River Corgo (the Cima Corgo) and almost none beyond Pinhão which marked the easternmost limit of quality wine production. Apart from those vineyards around Cambres and Pénajoia opposite Régua, the south side of the Douro was virtually uncultivated. Beyond the River Tedo the landscape was described as 'wild scrub inhabited by wolves and wild pigs which sometimes cross to the other side of the Douro causing considerable damage in the vines'. The one notable exception was Quinta do Roriz, which was leased from a religious order, the Tresminas da Ordem de Cristo, by a Scotsman named Robert Archibald. Villa Maior, writing a century later in 1876, says that 'being very much addicted to field sports and used to scouring the hills and glens of Scotland, [Archibald] found the savage wilds and rugged steeps of the Douro very well suited to his tastes. His sporting excursions having carried him to the place of Roriz, it came into his mind to build a shooting box . . . This lodge was the beginning of Quinta do Roriz'.

Further upstream, the rapids at Valeira were considered to be the natural limit of the eastward expansion of the wine region. Compressed into a narrow white-water torrent by huge slabs of granite, the Douro ceased to be navigable. Beyond Cachão de Valeira, the Douro Superior formed a distinct region in its own right. With its agriculture based on cereals and cattle-rearing, the hardy populace had traditionally looked towards Spain and the fairs at Salamanca as an outlet for their produce. Some Portuguese from the towns and villages near the border had even gone to study at Salamanca University. But from the mid-seventeenth century onwards, successive skirmishes between Portugal and Spain had led directly to the isolation and impoverishment of this once prosperous region. It was the need to integrate the Douro Superior that motivated the Companhia to begin the monumental task of clearing the Valeira rapids.

Work began in 1780 and lasted twelve years. It was financed by a tax of 400 *reis* for every pipe of Port, *aguardente*, vinegar or 'any liquid' transported by river. As the work progressed, so more vineyards were planted in the Cima Corgo upstream from Régua. The English preference for stronger wines was reflected by a significant increase in the production of Port from the hotter, more arid parts of the region around Pinhão and Tua. Whereas during the Pombal era the Cima Corgo had produced barely a quarter of the wines considered to be of first grade, by the end of the eighteenth century the Baixo Corgo had been overtaken as the main source of premium quality Port. Pombal's vineyard registration merely recorded the name of the owner of the vineyard and not the name of the property itself but by 1800 it can be supposed that a number of now famous properties as far upstream as the present day Quinta da Tua and Quinta dos Aciprestes were already well established. Indeed Villa Maior attributes the foundation of nearby Quinta dos Malvedos to his maternal grandfather who began planting vines on the site at the end of the eighteenth century. The great but remote vineyards above Cachão de Valeira like

Quinta do Vesúvio and Quinta de Vargellas were only planted in the early 1800s.

THE ORIGIN OF VINTAGE PORT

The rapid expansion of the Port trade in the second half of the eighteenth century had much to do with the science of the bottle. The first bottles had merely been used as a convenient vessel to convey the wine from the cask to the table. Short and squat in shape, they were totally impractical for laying down. As the eighteenth century wore on they began to be more elongated in shape with a longer neck until by the 1770s a bottle could be cellared on its side without too much difficulty.

This brought about an entirely new approach to wine in general and Port in particular. Instead of being acclaimed as 'new' as it had been earlier in the century, it was now possible to age Port in bottle, the cork providing an effective seal against oxidation and bacterial spoilage. The cylindrical bottle was available for the great 1775 vintage so, claims H. Warner Allen in *The Wines of Portugal*, 'it seems a fair guess that the best Douro wine of 1775 profited by it to become the first great Vintage Port in history'. However, the first mention of a Vintage Port appeared in a Christie's catalogue of 1773 when a wine from 1765 was sold. Certainly by the beginning of the nineteenth century, the Douro could boast a number of fine vintages. Sandeman claims to have produced their first Vintage Port in 1790 and George Sandeman, dining with the Duke of Wellington at Torres Vedras in 1809, declared the 1797 to be the finest Port year within his experience. But it was not until 1810 that the first shipper's name – Croft – appeared in a Christie's catalogue.

These wines were clearly nothing like today's Vintage Port. They were certainly lighter in style and probably aged for longer in cask before being shipped and bottled. According to T. G. Shaw, who wrote *Wine, the Cellar and the Vine*, published in 1863, it was common for the wines to be fined and racked a number of times before bottling, a process which would have stripped the young Port of much of its body and character. The first vintage about which there is any real certainty is the so-called 'Waterloo Vintage' of 1815, and it is apparent that by 1820, Vintage Port was eagerly sought by the British wine trade. Contemporary advertisements from the London wine auctioneers Christie's indicate the 1820 Ports were bottled three and five years after the vintage, and T. G. Shaw describes a wine from the same year as having 'plenty of crust and plenty of colour'. It seems probable that most of these wines were, in effect, single-*quinta* Ports sourced by shippers from a single estate and bottled bearing the name of a British wine merchant. The brand names of individual shippers only became prominent towards the end of the nineteenth century.

THE BRITISH COLONY AND THE FACTORY HOUSE

By the 1790s Oporto was in a social whirl. Port shipments to England alone had increased to 55,000 pipes and the British merchants could afford to live 'much better than the same persons would do in London' according to one visitor. In complete contrast to Thomas Woodmass, who described the privations of the English and Scottish eighty years earlier, Captain Costigan writes in 1778 of a civilised lifestyle of dancing, hearty eating and drinking and playing at cards. But he goes on to say that they 'are certainly no great attraction to the generality of Englishmen; neither have they time, even if they had any inclination, to study the country they live in'. The British families in Oporto intermarried with each other, keeping their distance from the Catholic *fidalgos* or Portuguese nobility. Such was their isolation from the local population that by all accounts the British merchants spoke the most execrable Portuguese. The Portuguese pronunciation of many British shippers is still a matter for mirth and mimicry two centuries later!

There was, however, a certain amount of migration in the opposite direction. According to Charles Sellers writing in *Oporto Old and New*, there was at the time a Portuguese community in almost every major city in England. Some were political refugees from the Pombaline period but others were traders and entrepreneurs. One such individual was Bruno Evaristo Ferreira da Silva who, through contacts in his native Oporto, obtained consignments of Port wine along with other Portuguese produce and quickly built up a thriving trade in England. According to Sellars, like the British in Oporto, Mr Silva 'was not able to master the language of his adopted country' but it did not prevent him from setting up a firm in 1798 which subsequently became Silva & Cosens, better known as the producer of Dow's Port.

Back in Oporto, the contemporary social gap between the British and the Portuguese is represented by the building of the Factory House. This gaunt but handsome building standing on the corner of the then Rua Nova dos Inglezes and Rua de São João was initiated by John Whitehead, Consul to the Factory, in 1785–6. Whitehead must have been a remarkable character: a dilettante diplomat, geographer, astronomer, and above all, architect. He was born in 1726 at Ashton-under-Lyne in Lancashire (coincidentally the birthplace of the author of this book, who also stood there as a parliamentary candidate in 1997), and came to Oporto with his father in the late 1750s. Whitehead's sister, Elizabeth, had previously married William Warre, then one of the leading members of the British community in Oporto. Warre was no doubt instrumental in arranging John Whitehead's appointment. Inspired by buildings in the north of England (and possibly helped by John Carr of York 1727–1803), Whitehead drew up grandiose plans for a club house which was completed, albeit somewhat scaled down, in 1790. Much of the exterior architectural detail is similar to the Santo Antonio Hospital, Oporto, also designed by Carr, and the interior arrangement resembles English spa town architecture of the period, with communicating reception rooms and a ballroom. Although on a much larger scale, the Crescent at Buxton in England, designed by Carr and completed in 1784, shares a certain affinity with the Factory House. Certainly, as James Murphy observed in 1795 in *Travels in Portugal*, the Factory House is decidedly 'anti-moorish' and still looks curiously at odds with other buildings on the Rua Infante D. Henrique. At the time of its completion at the end of the eighteenth century, the solid grey granite façade symbolised the confidence and permanence of the British Port shippers in Oporto. It nearly proved to be short-lived.

WAR AND UNREST

In the first half of the nineteenth century, Oporto was shaken by invasion and rebellion. In November 1807, the French marched into Lisbon under Marshal Junot, reaching Oporto under the command of Soult two years later. The British, sworn enemies of the French, packed their bags and returned home leaving their firms in the custody of the Portuguese. But thanks to the British, Marshal Soult didn't remain in Oporto for long. Less than three months after taking control he was surprised by an attack from Sir Arthur Wellesley (later Duke of Wellington), who approached the city from the Serra de Pilar convent in Vila Nova de Gaia. So swift was the recapture of Oporto that Wellesley apparently ate the meal that had been prepared for Soult in the Palácio dos Carrancas (now the Museu Soares dos Reis) a few hours earlier.

When the British merchants returned some months later, the city was in a state of some confusion. The French had briefly occupied the Factory House, leaving it to a Portuguese citizen who ran it as a coffee house until the premises were returned to the British in 1811 devoid of most of the contents. A celebratory ball was held on 4 June for which chandeliers, cutlery and chairs were hired, followed later in the year by a dinner attended by eleven members of the Factory House on 11 November 1811. The 'factory' itself had ceased to exist as an official entity following a treaty between George III and João (subsequently João VI), the Prince Regent from 1799–1816, who had left Portugal for Brazil when the French invaded. In 1812 the Factory House became the home of a new body, the British Club. The name was altered two years later to the British Association, the preserve of a select number of British Port shippers who form the membership of the Factory House today.

Although Oporto had been recaptured for the Portuguese in May 1809, the Peninsular War continued to rage in Portugal until May 1811 with a long stand-off north of Lisbon around the town of Torres Vedras. Wellington's officers drank the local wine and were well supplied with Port. As a result, in the years that followed the war, Portuguese wines like Bucelas, Carcavelos, Lisbon and Port became popular in Britain. The shipping firm of Sandeman, established in Jerez and Oporto in 1790, set up cellars at Cabo Ruivo near Lisbon, and new firms with established names began to appear, among them Cockburn (1814) and Graham (1820).

Another British military man of the time also enjoyed more than a glass of Port. Six weeks before fighting his last battle at Trafalgar in 1805, Vice-Admiral Viscount Nelson bought three pipes (1,150 litres) of Port for which he paid a total of £308 2s 0d. This seems like a small fortune as forty years later, the finest Vintage Port was only selling at £63 a pipe. Port also featured in Nelson's battle plans. Shortly before the Battle of Trafalgar itself, Lord Sidmouth was visited by Nelson, who apparently dipped his finger in a glass of Port wine and sketched a plan of action on the table top.

In the power vacuum that followed the Peninsular War, Oporto had become a ferment of radical politics. Inspired by Masonic Lodges and Portuguese Jacobinism, a revolt broke out in the city in 1820 in an attempt to persuade João VI (now enjoying a self-imposed exile in Brazil) to return to Portugal. This was accompanied by a demand for an assembly or *cortes* and liberal constitution, which was reluctantly acceded by the regents in Lisbon. João eventually returned, leaving his heir, Pedro, to govern Brazil where he became the constitutional emperor in 1822. However, following João VI's death in 1826 and Pedro's accession to the Portuguese throne, the country was pitched into turmoil by his younger brother Miguel, who led the absolutists in revolt against the liberal constitution. Under the absolutists, Pombal's old monopoly Companhia came to enjoy a new lease of life. However, the citizens of Oporto supported the constitutionalist Pedro against the usurper Miguel and in 1832 the city erupted into violent civil war. Although Pedro's troops held the centre of the city, the Miguelites bombarded Oporto from Vila Nova de Gaia. Caught in the midst of the fighting, the British Port shippers, who tended to side with the liberal constitutionalists, did their best to visit their lodges which were located in Miguelite territory on the opposite side of the river. There were few casualties among the Port shippers (many of whom rather enjoyed the diversion) but the Rua Nova dos Inglezes and the Factory House were frequently shelled. A Mr Wright of Croft & Co. lost an arm when a shell penetrated the ceiling of his dining room as he was enjoying a post-prandial glass of Port. But as the siege wore on, the situation deteriorated and the poorer inhabitants of Oporto lived in the most intolerable conditions. Even tripe became a luxury and many resorted to eating cats and dogs in order to survive. When the supply of pet animals was exhausted, large numbers died either from starvation or cholera.

There was also considerable upheaval in the Douro with armed militia terrorising the towns and villages. As the constitutionalists gained the upper hand, properties belonging to the clergy and absolutist nobility were seized and auctioned off, one such property being the huge Quinta dos Frades (Monk's Quinta) at Folgosa. Much as in the French Revolution some forty years earlier, the whole structure of Portuguese agricultural society changed. In the Douro, medium-sized landowners and bourgeois merchants picked up *quintas* expropriated from religious orders and with the suspension of the old Pombaline demarcation, more vineyards were planted upstream from the mouth of the River Tua.

Back in Oporto, after eighteen months of continual siege, the Miguelites finally retreated under attack from Pedro's troops supported by the British. In a final desperate act of defiance, the Miguelite Conde d'Almer ordered that the lodges belonging to the Companhia should be burnt and over twenty thousand pipes of Port were lost, much of the wine flowing into the Douro which turned a rather murky purple. Pedro VI duly arrived in Lisbon in July 1833 and shortly afterwards his daughter, Maria II, became Portugal's first constitutional monarch. In a final characteristic act of liberalism before his death, Pedro extinguished all the remaining 'privileges, authorities and prerogatives' of the Companhia proclaiming that from henceforth it was to trade on a level playing field with all other Port firms.

FORRESTER AND THE DOURO

There are few characters anywhere in the wine trade that equal Joseph James Forrester. Born in Hull in 1809, he joined his uncle's Oporto-based firm of Offley Forrester in 1831. Forrester was a bluff Yorkshireman who, like many from 'God's own county', became known for his blunt, forthright opinions. Forrester mixed on equal terms with the Portuguese, keeping company with everyone from the noble *fidalgos* in Oporto to the farmers in the Douro. Unlike most British shippers, he spoke fluent Portuguese.

In fact, Forrester is the first 'man about the Douro'. At a time when few shippers ventured upstream from Oporto apart from during the vintage, Forrester travelled considerably and came to know every twist and turn in the river. He frequently based himself at the Barão de Viamonte's Quinta da Boa Vista (see page 100), but in his biographical book, *Joseph James Forrester, Baron of Portugal*, John Delaforce records evidence that Forrester either owned or rented a number of other properties in the Douro and had a house at Régua. Delaforce comments that 'there is no doubt that he was more interested in the production side of the Port trade than in the marketing of the wines'.

Forrester's arrival in Oporto coincided with the height of the civil war. In a letter to his uncle he describes the scene in Vila Nova de Gaia with Portuguese lodges or *armazéns* raising the British flag in an attempt to distance themselves from the conflict. He adds 'in consequence of events Vila Nova is in such a state of anarchy that I find I cannot remain in the lodges nor go to them with any degree of safety. My life has twice been threatened and it was with considerable difficulty that I escaped yesterday from seven exasperated soldiers who were inveighing against the English, their government and their flag which is now so grossly abused with impunity and flying over the doors of many *armazéns*.'

Once the civil war was over, Forrester turned to drawing and painting and in 1834 (just a year after the end of the conflict) he published a remarkably detailed water-colour of the Rua Nova dos Inglezes with a key identifying thirty-four British and nine Portuguese merchants. The original painting was destroyed in the London office of Offley Forrester during the Second World War but a number of engravings survive.

Forrester's most enduring achievement is his detailed survey and subsequent maps of the River Douro and the Douro wine region. In spite of many frustrations over the quality of the engraving and copyright, Forrester produced two detailed maps, the first of which, a relief map entitled *The Wine District of the Alto Douro*, was published around 1845. His second, larger map is dated 1848 and charts the course of the River Douro from the Salto da Sardinha ('Sardine Leap') on the Spanish–Portuguese border to the mouth of the river at São João de Foz, 'a short league from Oporto'. He describes the river as 'for the most part a fine stream, of considerable breadth, but impetuous in its course and abounding in obstacles which render navigation difficult and dangerous. These obstacles are of very various kinds – some are shallows, some rocks, projecting from the banks, or rising in the stream, many are sudden falls, in some cases of several feet and continued during reaches of 80 to 200 yards, causing powerful and dangerous rapids'. Forrester goes on to state the case for improving the navigability of the river 'as an effective means for the amelioration of the ... whole agricultural population of the District of the Douro and the province of Trás-os-Montes'. At the time he records that 'the voyage from Oporto to Barca d'Alva [on the Spanish border] occupies, on an average, fifteen days'.

In some earlier observations Forrester records that the Douro 'is very unwholesome and thinly populated' and that 'the soil about the vines is turned and the grapes are trodden entirely by Gallegos of whom 8,000 are employed each season ...' Indeed Galicia in Spain, immediately to the north of the Minho province of Portugal, was even poorer and more down-trodden than the Douro, and the Gallegos who came for the vintage were also responsible for building many of the fine stone vineyard terraces, some of the best of which can be seen at Offley Forrester's Quinta da Boa Vista.

Forrester also records the difficulties of travelling in the Douro region, something which he must have experienced first hand. On his 1848 map he comments on the excellent roads around Zamora, Salamanca and Valladolid but in comparison 'the roads in northern Portugal are so bad that it takes eight days to go from Oporto to the Barca d'Alva, a distance of 120 miles!' He adds in a well-intentioned but characteristically forthright manner that 'of course in such a state ... it is impossible for the Portuguese farmer to compete with the Spanish smuggler'.

FORRESTER AND FORTIFICATION

These observations on the problems in the Douro are nothing when compared to his outspoken views on Port in general. In 1844 he published an anonymous pamphlet entitled *One or Two Words about Port Wine*, the author being described as being 'A Resident in Oporto for 11 years'. Needless to say it wasn't difficult to uncover his identity. Forrester was seemingly obsessed by the adulteration of wines in the Douro region, advocating wines that he termed 'pure' or 'unloaded'. Writing with the 'British public' in mind, his main criticisms were twofold. Firstly, just like Pombal a century earlier, he railed against the use of elderberry (*baga*) which he claimed was being added in amounts of at least 28 lb per pipe. This was no doubt true as the liberalisation of the Port trade following the constitutionalist victory of 1833 had led once more to the use or abuse of *baga*. But Forrester's second criticism was much less easy to justify for he condemned the addition of brandy to the wine 'when it is half fermented' and the use of *jeropiga* (grape must muted by the addition of brandy) to sweeten the wines before shipment.

The pamphlet caused a furore both in Oporto and the Douro. A circular from farmers and a number of shippers described his accusation that elderberry was being added as 'false, vague and unfounded', almost certainly a hypocritical statement which John Delaforce notes would have given Forrester some satisfaction. However, Forrester clearly favoured lighter, unfortified wines and at one stage even suggested that if the region's boundaries were removed, 'a good wholesome light Port might be produced' from outside the legal demarcation.

In his campaign for 'pure' unfortified wine, Forrester claimed that he had the support of 102 of the 121 parishes in the Douro region but in response his opponents produced a document with 208 signatures accusing him of 'subterfuges and sinister motives'. Accusations and counter-accusations flew back and forth for some time and Forrester received no support from his fellow-shippers, who were more concerned with supplying the British and north European markets with the sweet, fortified Port wines they demanded. Perhaps in response to some of his criticisms, the old monopoly Companhia was reformed in 1848 only to be abolished again a decade later. Forrester's idiosyncratic views on Port died with him and unfortified wines from the Douro received little or no attention until Fernando Nicolau d'Almeida revived the tradition with Barca Velha a century later. The subsequent history of the Douro's unfortified wines is taken up in Chapter 6.

FORRESTER AND DONA ANTÓNIA FERREIRA

Although Forrester had married in 1836, his English-born wife died in 1847 shortly after having given birth to their seventh child. Forrester never remarried but sought female company from Antónia Adelaide Ferreira. Born at Régua in 1811, Dona Antónia, as she became known, was born into a Port-shipping family whose business had been established since the middle of the eighteenth century. Over the course of her life she became the largest landowner in the Douro with an empire stretching from Régua in the

Baixo Corgo (where she lived) to the legendary Quinta do Vale do Meão high in the Douro Superior. By the time of her death in 1896 she owned a total of twenty-four *quintas* including famous estates like Quinta do Porto, Quinta de Vargellas and Quinta do Vesúvio. Charles Sellers, writing in *Oporto Old and New* just three years later, records Dona Antónia as 'the richest of landed proprietors, but there are few ladies in the land who had seen so little or knew so little of the world. Her thousands of acres of mountain land covered with vines were her chief thought . . .' The nature of the liaison between Forrester and Dona Antónia will always be open to speculation but there is no doubt that they both supervised the planting and cultivation of their vineyards together and spent a considerable amount of time with each other. Dona Antónia was clearly a strong and single-minded character and this side of her personality must have appealed to Forrester. She was married twice, firstly to her cousin António Bernado Ferreira II and, following his death, to her estate manager Francisco José da Silva Torres. Sellers records that 'there were never two men who spent more money in the Douro than the two husbands of Dona Antónia'.

Forrester was accompanied by Dona Antónia on 12 May 1861 when they left Quinta do Vesúvio travelling downstream by boat. At Cachão de Valeira, a narrow and forbidding stretch of the river which was then a white-water rapid, the boat capsized. Forrester was said to have been wearing a money belt laden with gold sovereigns which must have weighed him down as he struggled to swim to the river bank. He apparently reached the side and grasped onto a rock but was pulled down by the fast-flowing current and never seen again. Dona Antónia and the other members of the party survived, the ladies apparently buoyed up by their crinolines. There are a number of versions of this tragic episode and the circumstances surrounding the incident will never be precisely known. His son William was said to have been told that the corpse was found downstream at Pinhão, robbed of the gold by a local who subsequently confessed to the crime on his deathbed. One fact, however, is indisputable. A notice in the deaths column of *The Times* dated Thursday 23 May 1861 read: 'On the 12th inst., accidentally drowned while descending the River Douro by the upsetting of a boat at the Ponto do Cachão, Joseph James Forrester Esq. Baron de Forrester in Portugal, in his 52nd year.' Ironically, a small engraving of the Ponto do Cachão appears on Forrester's

1848 map. Denied a place in the British Cemetery in Oporto, a plaque mounted on the granite rock above the rapids is his only memorial. The river has subsequently been tamed by a series of dams built in the 1970s and Cachão de Valeira, now calm, feels dark and forbidding.

THE GOLDEN DECADES

The middle decades of the nineteenth century proved to be something of a golden age for Port. Production in the early 1840s reached 100,000 pipes of which around a quarter was exported, mainly to Britain. Port, mostly drunk young and often mulled, became a commonplace drink at all levels of society. At Oxford it was known as 'Bishop'. At one stage the Companhia intervened in order to stem over-production, purchasing 20,000 pipes of lower quality wine from Douro farmers. But at the opposite end of the spectrum, the practice of declaring wines from exceptional years gained momentum with 1851, 1863 and 1868 proving to be some of the finest vintages of the century. These wines came to be appreciated not so much for their youthful vigour but for the character and complexity that they gained with age. An auction catalogue from Christie's dated 3 December 1860 lists one hundred and twenty dozen of 'Rare 1820 Port Wine' from Burmester as well as wine from 1847.

Under the constitutional monarchy of Maria II, life became easier for the British community in Oporto and they began to mix much more freely with the Portuguese. With the demise of the *ancien régime*, society became more open and much less inclined to the extravagances of religious devotion that had affronted the foreign mercantile community in the past. According to a visitor at the time, the British 'moved in the higher circles of Oporto society' and 'inhabited some of the best houses in the most airy parts of the city'. In the mid-1840s firms like Sandeman, Martinez and Quarles Harris were regularly shipping well in excess of 1,500 pipes of Port a year.

DISEASE AND DEVASTATION

This prosperity was not to last. In 1848 oidium or powdery mildew first made an appearance near Régua spreading rapidly throughout the Douro. It first reached Europe from North America and according to Henry Vizetelly, who visited Portugal in the 1870s, began by imparting 'a strange bitter flavour' to the wines. By 1851 vineyard yields had begun to fall catastrophically with production at Dona Antónia's Quinta do Vesúvio being cut from an average of 313.5 pipes in 1853 to 69 pipes of mostly poor quality wine in 1856 at the height of the epidemic. Spurred into action, James Dow wrote a treatise on the subject in 1855 entitled *An Inquiry into the Vine Fungus with Suggestions as to a Remedy*. He issued a farsighted 'warning' to the Portuguese people reminding them that 'we hold no production of the soil by fixed tenure' and that 'apathy . . . must be the worst fungus of the two; for while *Oidium tuckeri* may be converted into a friend, the other must be for ever a deadly enemy'. Although oidium could never in future be described as 'a friend' it was brought under control fairly quickly by the use of sulphur.

However, worse was to come. The advent of the steamship meant that hitherto unknown pests and diseases were able to survive the voyage across the Atlantic. By far the most devastating of these was phylloxera, which was first discovered in a Hammersmith greenhouse in 1863. In his book, *The Great Wine Blight*, George Ordish records that an academic interest in plants and insects combined with the improvement in transportation unwittingly helped to disperse this tiny, almost microscopic, aphid. In ten years phylloxera spread throughout Europe, feeding on the roots of *Vitis Vinifera* vines. At first yields were merely reduced but eventually the vines just withered and died. Phylloxera reached the Douro at the beginning of the 1870s and, having first been detected in vineyards around Gouvinhas near Sabrosa, it was probably spread further by the construction of the railway (see below). According to a contemporary map by Rodrigo Morais Soares, by 1877 phylloxera had arrived in the Douro Superior. Growers went to extraordinary lengths to save their vineyards. In his book Henry Vizetelly describes how 'the Baron Roêda has tried, among other remedies, phosphate of lime, coal tar, sulphate of potash, natural magnesium and sulphate of carbon, all being applied to the roots of the vines, but with little effect'. Yields declined dramatically with Vizetelly commenting that 'the ravages of the phylloxera ... have very far surpassed any damage done by the oidium'. Facing a shortage of *aguardente* for fortification, firms either resorted to using grain spirit or imported quantities of highly rectified spirit from England.

Lacking any knowledge of how to combat the plague, the people of the Douro appealed for Divine Intercession to survive. The *Jornal de Régua* of 10 July 1880 reported on 'a procession of atonement, organised by the residents of Cambres, to implore Divine protection from the damage caused by phylloxera'. Facing financial ruin, many smaller growers simply abandoned their vineyards. An unnamed British wine merchant visiting the Douro in 1874 compared the effects of the disease to 'the nature of that which destroyed potatoes in Ireland' such was its impact on the local populace who had nothing else to depend on for their livelihood. Despite extensive replanting programmes in the 1890s and 1980s, huge swathes of abandoned terraces known as *mortórios* still provide powerful evidence to the extent of the phylloxera catastrophe.

TRAVEL IN THE DOURO: 'STEAM HORSE' AND SAILING BOATS

It would be hard to underestimate the impact of the railway on the Douro. Construction began in 1873, just twenty-five years after Joseph Forrester had complained about the paucity of communications in the region and a mere twelve years after he met with his death trying to navigate the river. The railway arrived at Pinhão in the heart of the Cima Corgo vineyards in 1879 and at Tua in 1882. By the time it reached Barca d'Alva on the Spanish border in 1887, it had become a lifeline for the remote communities of the Alto Douro, cutting the journey time to Oporto from days to hours. The small steam train became known to all as the *paciência*, such was the need for patience with its frequent stops for loading and unloading. But anyone who has visited the Douro will appreciate that the railway, following the river for most of its course, is a considerable feat of engineering and its construction during the years of the phylloxera crisis must have helped to alleviate some of the suffering among the local populace. In fact, one of its first major uses was to deliver large quantities of copper sulphate and carbon disulphide, heavily subsidised by the government, in an attempt to control oidium and phylloxera.

In spite of the obvious benefits, the railway had its detractors. Writing ten years after its completion, Charles Sellers complains that the 'steam horse has not added to the beautiful though wild scenery of Tráz-os-Montes' (archaic spelling), adding that it has 'diminished the number of picturesque flotilla of wine boats so familiar to all those who know the region'. Nevertheless, the long, Viking-inspired boats known as *barcos rabelos* continued to ply the Douro until as late as the 1960s. Screeching bullock carts brought the wine down from the *quintas*, many of which maintained their own riverside quays. Some of the larger *barcos rabelos* could ship as many as seventy or eighty pipes of wine at a time. Ropes were used to drag them on board and the pipes were stacked three high. The journey by boat was hazardous in the extreme. Depending on the flow of the river, a fully laden *barco rabelo* would take about two days to travel downstream from Pinhão to the quayside at Gaia. During the voyage, the crew would converse to each other in song improvising their own chant as they went along. This would occasionally be interrupted by a yell as they approached some rapids. The helmsman standing on a high poop above the main deck would grip the tiller and look ahead for half-submerged rocks while the remainder of the crew sounded the bottom of the river with long poles. The hardest task of all was the return journey to the vineyards, ascending the river with a boat-load of empty pipes. This could take anything between eight and fifteen days with navigation completely impossible during the winter floods. Making use of the Atlantic westerlies which funnel upstream, the mast would be raised and a square sail billowed forth. Oxen were tethered to the boat to drag it up through the rapids. Some *barcos rabelos* have survived, powered incongruously by little outboard motors while the skeletons of others can be found rotting on the river bank. A small fleet of *barcos rabelos* has been mothballed and moored alongside the quay at Vila Nova de Gaia. Once a year they set sail in a good-humoured race to celebrate the feast day of Oporto's patron saint, São João.

Apart from making the region more accessible, the construction of the railway had a significant and lasting impact on settlement patterns in the Douro valley. Until its arrival in the late 1870s, nearly all the established towns and villages were located well above the river, away from disease-carrying insects and the stifling summer heat. But with railway stations at Régua and at the mouth of the Pinhão river, these places gradually became important service centres in their own right. Although the railway had not yet reached Pinhão when he visited, Henry Vizetelly provides the first detailed description of the place:

> The village of Pinhão comprises a cluster of small houses, and some half-a-dozen wine stores, grouped indiscriminately on the banks of the Douro. It boasts a straggling, undulating *praça*, planted with a few trees, on one of which there was usually hanging a newly slaughtered sheep, which the butcher would be cutting up, while women waited to secure the primer parts for their husbands at work on the railway in the course of construction on the opposite bank of the Douro*, and on the railway bridge that spans the River Pinhão. A *venda*, a barber's shop, and one or two general dealers' stores look on to the *praça*, and in the short winding streets of the village, children, pigs, dogs and poultry mingle indiscriminately before the cottage doors. Such are the main features of Pinhão, which, from its central position, is a place of some importance in the Alto Douro region.

Writing nearly twenty years later in his book *Viticultura e Vinicultura*, Villarinho de São Romão describes Pinhão (with some optimism) as 'an important place with a great commercial future'. A contemporary photograph of Pinhão in the same publication shows the terraces at Quinta da Foz destroyed by phylloxera.

Other villages in the Douro were clearly picturesque but insanitary. Vizetelly visited Celleirós (archaic spelling) where he notes

> the squalid houses, rudely built, are too frequently grimy on the outside and foul within. The roads are often filthy in the extreme, smells undefinable assail one's nostrils as much from the open doorways as from the refuse littered street . . . Turning from the houses the eye lights on dirty children, yelping curs, emaciated poultry and, above all, long legged pigs, basking at full length in the middle of the road, disdaining to move out of your horse's way . . .

---

*Vizetelly is somewhat confused here as the railway runs on the north bank of the River Douro, the same side as the village of Pinhão.

Over a century later, the pigs are no longer in evidence but the famous Douro dogs still bask in the middle of the road, moving grudgingly only when a car draws close.

NEW WEALTH

Such was the devastating impact of phylloxera on European vineyards that the French government offered a reward of 300,000 francs to anyone who came up with a remedy. The prize was never paid out for no remedy as such has ever been found. The solution came instead from the North American vines which had probably carried phylloxera to Europe in the first place. American species like *Vitis labrusca, berlandieri, riparia* and *rupestris* were able to resist phylloxera in a way that the European *Vitis vinifera* could not. By grafting native vines on to American rootstock, it was established that European varieties could survive and indeed flourish.

In Portugal the replanting of vineyards was a painfully slow and somewhat erratic process. For a time the government prohibited the importation of American vines believing them to be the cause of phylloxera rather than a cure. However, some clandestine replanting on American rootstock undoubtedly took place, for example at Offley Forrester's Quinta da Boa Vista where the Douro's first grafted vineyard was planted in 1880. Following pressure from both growers and shippers, the ban was lifted in 1883 and replanting began in earnest. But even as late as 1896 in a detailed manual on viticulture in the Douro, Villarinho de São Romão recommends flooding the vineyards as a means of asphyxiating the phylloxera aphid.

For a time, phylloxera had a positive effect on sales of Port and Portuguese wine in general. With France the first country to be affected, wine merchants in England looked to Iberia for supplies. During the 1880s when the damage was at its greatest, exports of Portuguese wines rose sharply. France, which had barely registered as a market for Portuguese wine in the 1860s, imported nearly a million hectolitres a year between 1885 and 1889 at a time when the country's total production struggled to reach four million hl. A large proportion of this wine was exported from Viana do Castelo, briefly reviving a trade that had died when the English transferred their allegiance to Oporto and the Douro two centuries earlier. In Oporto, a number of new firms were in a good position to capitalise on the crisis in production, among them Wiese & Krohn, Delaforce, Cálem and Ramos Pinto, all of which were established between 1859 and 1880. Brazil became an important market, importing as many as 20,000 pipes of wine a year until the country was hit by a severe financial crisis in the mid-1920s.

The increase in turnover put a number of important shippers in a strong position when it came to purchasing property in the Douro. Until this time, few shippers had owned land but with the local economy in ruins, *quintas* were changing hands at rock-bottom prices. One such entrepreneur was George Acheson Warre, who was then in charge of the winemaking at Silva & Cosens. Between 1887 and 1896 he purchased three prime *quintas* starting

Verandah, Quinta do Bomfim

with Quinta do Zimbro just upstream from Tua. Warre began replanting and monitored the results. He records 'the '88 planting to be infected with phylloxera – badly – must replant. Am.[erican] vines good, but Portuguese bad'. But by 1896 when grafting on to American rootstock had become accepted practice, Warre wrote 'this year's wines are I consider better than any since 1878 and will I hope and believe start a new era in the Port wine trade'. Warre's most astute purchase was undoubtedly Quinta do Bomfim close to Pinhão, which was developed with its own railway siding to transport the wine downstream to Gaia.

By the turn of the century, the Douro valley was a hive of activity once more. Vieira da Costa, writing in *Uma Illustração Portuguesa* in 1906, describes the Douro as 'engaged in an immense, indescribable, never before seen activity. Legions of workers, numbering in the thousands, busy as ants, dug deep into the sterile womb of barren land . . . life, in all its potency and creativity began to emerge and bear new fruit, a new wealth'.

OPORTO AT THE END OF THE NINETEENTH CENTURY

The new wealth in Oporto was much more conspicuous. The same British wine merchant who had compared the phylloxera crisis to the Irish potato famine visited Oporto in 1874 and wrote that arriving by sea is a 'positive danger, for the entrance [to the Douro] is at best no more than 150 yards wide, is very shallow and the tide tears in at a tremendous rate while the course is continually changing by shifting sand . . .' He goes on to describe the city of Oporto itself with its 'crooked, rugged narrow streets' adding 'how the horses got along and how the springs stood the jolting is a mystery. Up as well as down hill the hardy beasts galloped to the tune of a cowhide whip played in a manner that would flay the skin of horses at home: while wheels rattled over boulders planted where they were for generations . . .'

By the end of the century much of this had changed. Charles Sellers considers how 'Oporto has very much improved during the last forty years.' A new seaport was built on the coast eight kilometres to the north-east at Leixões and a system of tram lines extended around the city although 'the Rua dos Inglezes was one of the very few streets paved right through'. (In 1893 it was renamed the Rua Infante D. Henrique). The Ponte Dom Luíz, the impressive two-tier bridge linking Oporto with Vila Nova de Gaia, was opened in September 1886.

Life for the British community also continued to improve for, as Sellers recounts in his 'personal reminiscences', many of the shippers had built houses on the coast at Foz do Douro or Leça da Palmeira where they spent the summer months, taking their furniture with them. They frequented a beach at Foz which became known as the Praia dos Inglezes (English Beach – a name which survives today), although police regulations stipulated that all bathers in public places must be 'completely clad as if going for a walk'. Bathing gradually became fashionable among the Portuguese. In order to encourage the inhabitants of the city to wash more regularly, the Portuguese clergy declared that everyone should have taken at least thirty-three baths by 24 August, St Bartholomew's Day. Needless to say, many people assembled at the new seaside resorts to take all the prescribed baths on the same day!

Still keeping their distance from the Portuguese, the British maintained their national sporting traditions. Cricket had been played in Oporto for as long as anyone could remember and the shippers had their own cricket field and clubhouse near the Palácio das Carrancas where they assembled on Saturday afternoons. One of the most important social events at the time was the annual cricket match between the teams of Mr W. R. Teage and Mr H. Murat, both prominent Port shippers, which invariably ended with a dinner at the Factory House. At one stage in the late nineteenth century, the British also had their own pack of foot beagles to hunt hare which, according to one visitor, 'had turned out well, and was at the time maintained in good style'. Horse racing and fox hunting had been tried according to Sellers but 'the turf was a dead letter to them [the Portuguese] as was hunting'.*

Across the river in Gaia, a minor industrial revolution was underway. Although generally conservative in their approach to change, Port shippers built new lodges to house ever larger volumes of wine, equipping them with new labour-saving devices like steam pumps and tramways. Another important significant innovation

*A pack of fox hounds known as the *Equipagem de Santo Humberto* still survives in the Ribatejo province of central-southern Portugal. It is a legacy from Wellington's time.

was the steam cooperage. At the end of the nineteenth century, nearly all Port was shipped in pipe (mainly to Britain) where it was bottled by individual wine merchants. Prior to shipment, all but the finest Vintage Ports would be transferred from the vats or oak casks in which they were matured to cheaper chestnut shipping pipes, few of which were ever returned. The turnover in the cooperage, therefore, came to symbolise the success of a business and became an integral part of every Port-shipping firm. A novelty at the time of his visit in the 1870s, Henry Vizetelly describes a newfangled steam cooperage:

> In front of the lodge is a steam cooperage, where a sixteen horse engine sets in motion saws which divide the planks into three, reduce the staves to their proper length, give to the heads of the casks their circular form and neatly bevel their edges. There are also cutting machines, certain parts of which perform their 3,000 revolutions a minute, which after rough shaping the staves, finish them off and bevel their joints, and finally give them their convex and concave form. Here, too, the rough shaped staves are steamed in a tank to extract all colouring matter and flavour from the wood, the completed pipes being also slightly steamed in order to detect any imperfections in them. A crane is employed for letting down the casks to a long store, situated on a lower level, where they under go the requisite seasoning with wine.

But the industrial revolution in Gaia was not without its Luddites. When Silva & Cosens decided to merchandise casks in 1894, the other coopers – fearing for their jobs – hijacked the new boiler imported from England and rolled it into the river!*

It was against this backdrop of industriousness and enterprise that a certain Andrew James Symington arrived in Oporto from Glasgow in 1882 at the age of nineteen. He began working for the Graham family's textile concern but was immediately attracted to the Port trade. In 1894, twelve years after first setting foot in Portugal, Symington was asked by the Lisbon government to take part in the 'Great Burnay Port Sale' comprising 20,000 pipes which had been taken as surety from the Burnay family when their bank failed. Symington subsequently became a partner in the firm of

---

*Silva & Cosen's steam boiler was made at Dukinfield near Manchester, and the certificate issued with the boiler is signed by Stanley Pollitt, a distant relative of the author of this book.

Warre & Co. and nearly a century later, after some astute business deals along the way, his successors are collectively the largest Port shippers with six firms to their name (see Chapter 5).

PLAGUE AND POLITICS

The turn of the century was a particularly turbulent time for Portugal. An outstandingly good and well-received vintage in 1896 declared by the majority of shippers came to be viewed in retrospect as the calm before the storm. The first calamity hit in August 1899 when cholera broke out, there having been previous scares in 1892 and 1884. A 'sanitary cordon' was imposed on Oporto, restricting the movement of the city's inhabitants. As vintage approached, the Port shippers appealed through the British Consul for the right to visit their properties and growers in the Douro. The Minister for Foreign Affairs in Lisbon replied that 'he could not consider such a question' and that 'as no exceptions were allowed in the case of the native Portuguese, they could grant no favours to foreigners'. Writing in *Port Wine and Oporto* (published in 1949), Ernest Cockburn argues that the regulations were both 'unreasonable' and 'absurd' but with the Port shippers effectively imprisoned in Oporto, the vintage took place without them.

In the meantime, Portuguese politics were once more in ferment. Throughout the latter years of the nineteenth century, Republicanism had been gaining momentum encouraged by the overthrow of the Brazilian monarchy in 1889. In the Oporto military garrison feelings ran high enough for a republican revolution to be attempted two years later. It brought an end to over half a century of settled politics. In 1907 the beleaguered Portuguese king, Carlos I, reacted to the growing political upheaval by appointing João Franco as Prime Minister and effective dictator.

The same year saw the loss of the lucrative Russian market which favoured sweet White Ports. In an effort to boost sales of their own wines, the Russian authorities raised the duty on Port to the equivalent of £60 a pipe. Shipments had fallen sharply in the early 1900s as other wine-producing nations recovered from phylloxera and with stocks piling up in their lodges the shippers themselves were not eager to buy wines from growers in the Douro. Tobacco became an important crop in the Douro with 207 ha in cultivation by 1907, concentrated especially around the towns of Armamar and Santa Marta de Penaguião. There were also legitimate concerns about the amount of so-called 'Port' reaching the market from regions other than the Douro. Californian 'Port', Tarragona 'Port' and Australian 'Port', some bearing the Portuguese coat of arms, were also being sold alongside wines masquerading as Port from southern Portugal.

João Franco responded to the growing crisis in the Douro by enacting new protectionist legislation. In an attempt to control exports and stamp out fraud, the government stipulated that any wine with the right to the name 'Port' must be shipped either across the bar of the Douro river or from the new port of Leixões. But as a sop to the growers in southern Portugal who had the most to lose from this, the new regulations prohibited the distillation of wine from the Douro. In future nearly all the *aguardente* used to fortify Port wine would originate from outside the region. Franco also extended the Port demarcation as far as the border with Spain to include the entire municipalities of Valpaços and Alfândega da Fé, both of which are on the *planalto* and produced wine of inferior quality. A year later, after a barrage of complaints from shippers, the Port demarcation was reduced in size. It still reached the Spanish border and remains (with the exception of minor alterations in 1921) the same to this day.

Shortly after this legislation had been enacted, Carlos I was assassinated along with his eldest son and heir as they drove in a carriage through the streets of Lisbon. The throne fell upon his second son, Manuel ('the unfortunate'), who at eighteen years of age was in no position to quell the troubles. The unpopular and dictatorial João Franco resigned from office but it was too late to save the Portuguese throne. Two years later, in the face of a naval revolt, Manuel II abdicated and left quietly for England. On 5 October 1910 Portugal became a republic.

THE FIRST REPUBLIC AND THE FIRST WORLD WAR

The sixteen years of Portugal's so-called 'First Republic' were some of the most turbulent in the country's history. Between 1910 and 1926 there were no less than forty-nine different administrations with over sixty ministers of agriculture. Serious rioting broke out in Oporto in 1910 and, concerned for their safety, the British residents in Oporto requested naval protection from the government in London. A ship duly arrived but, to everyone's consternation, was too large to cross the bar of the Douro. Anticlericism quickly took hold in Lisbon alienating the deeply Catholic populace in the north of the country. At Pinhão one of the main characters in the area was Abel de Carvalho, an ardent monarchist and devout Catholic who managed Silva & Cosens's interests in the Douro. Seeing an anti-ecclesiastical protest in the village shortly after the proclamation of the Republic, he walked over to one of the demonstrators who was mocking a local saint and exclaimed 'the only thing missing here is blood' before rapping him smartly on the head with a walking stick and marching off!

Uprisings, protests and bankruptcies occurred with bewildering frequency both at a national level and in the Douro. Some shippers had to seek the protection of armed troops after the story surfaced that they had been buying in cheaper wines from the south to blend with Port. The regional commission created by João Franco to oversee viticulture in the Douro was powerless to intervene. Legislation introduced to help farmers, including the reorganisation of agricultural credit institutions to encourage the formation of co-operatives, was unenforceable in the unstable political climate.

The First World War provided the British community with an unwelcome diversion from their problems in Portugal. The able-bodied men in the Port trade left to fight in the trenches while the women remaining behind in Oporto spent their time knitting socks and scarves for the troops. But November 1914 was remembered by the Port shippers for the Anglo-Portuguese Commercial Treaty Act which established the first legal definition for Port wine. Quotas were introduced in the following year forcing an increase in the price of Port. The First World War also brought an end to a fifty-year-old practice of sending Portuguese eggs to Britain along with Port. According to Ernest Cockburn, whose book is full of anecdotes from the time, they were usually sent over in baskets containing about 100 eggs and despite having no more than a piece of canvas tied over the top, breakages were apparently rare. The eggs were kept fresh by sealing them with insinglass or milk (both fining agents) before shipment and were much appreciated in the United Kingdom. Cockburn adds that 'it was usually found for culinary purposes that two such Portuguese eggs would do the work of three English eggs'. Much the same could be said of subsequent Portuguese eggs until large battery farms were set up in the 1980s!

Fearing that the African colonies would become bargaining pawns among the combatants, Portugal entered the First World War on the side of the Allies in 1916. In August of the same year the second of commercial treaties was signed between Portugal and the United Kingdom which prohibited the importation of Port unless it was accompanied by a Certificate of Origin from the Portuguese authorities. This effectively closed the lucrative UK market to the multitude of 'lookalike' wines from other destinations. Although shipping became increasingly hazardous and insurance costs rose dramatically owing to the activities of enemy submarines, Port grew steadily in popularity. The tax on spirits was raised in Britain to the extent that many people gave up whisky or gin for a glass of Port. Port and lemon (a shot of inexpensive Ruby Port let out into a long drink by the addition of fizzy lemonade) became the everyday drink at thousands of 'Rover's Return' pubs throughout the land. This new-found business helped to revive business for both growers and shippers in the years immediately following the war. Despite the loss of the remaining Russian market in 1917, Port began to enjoy a minor boom. Shipments to the UK alone reached 70,000 pipes in 1918, and some growers near Mesão Frio were expressly permitted to bring in grapes from outside the demarcation in order to satisfy demand. So great was the demand for Port that wines were offered to the British trade on the basis of 'PRWS' – Price Ruling When Shipped.

In the meantime, the political instability which had dogged Portugal since the beginning of the century continued well into the 1920s. Inflation was rampant and the lodgemen and coopers frequently came out on strike for higher wages. A minor civil war was taking place around Vila Real and a monarchy was briefly proclaimed in Oporto, but came swiftly to an end after republican troops filled the centre of the city. The state of Portugal's economy, deeply damaged by the war, went from bad to worse. Senior officers in the Portuguese army became increasingly restless when the junior officers and sergeants received pay increases of up to 1,200 per cent compared to their own meagre rises of 144 to 306 per cent. On 26 May 1926 they rose in rebellion and the liberal First Republic collapsed. For a time, the economic and political instability continued. In February 1927 a revolt broke out against the military government of General Oscar Carmona. Fierce fighting took place in Oporto and the local correspondent for the London-based *Wine Trade Review* stated that the bombardment that took place across the River Douro from the heights of Arrábida (now the site of the Arrábida bridge) 'was as good as any I've heard on the Western Front'. A number of stray shells fell on Port lodges but apart from shattered nerves, the shippers themselves survived unscathed.

One unusually enduring item of legislation from these unsettled times was the creation of the *entreposto* or entrepôt in Vila Nova de Gaia. From the spring of 1927, all Port wine destined for export had to be shipped through a tightly delimited area where the lodges were situated effectively handing the established shippers complete control of the industry. Needless to say, it caused a good deal of dissatisfaction among growers, 750 of whom went to lobby the minister in Lisbon. In the spirit of the age, their views fell on deaf ears and the *entreposto* continued to hold a monopoly on exports to the detriment of single *quintas* until Portugal joined the European Union in 1986.

THE STRONG ARM OF THE STATE

Such was the desperation with the state of the Portuguese economy that almost no one took any notice when Prime Minister Colonel José Vicente de Freitas appointed the demure son of a Dão smallholder, Antonio de Oliveira Salazar, to the post of Finance Minister in April 1928. On being sworn in as a minister he uttered the ominous phrase which eventually became his epitaph: 'I know quite well what I want and where I am going.' Salazar was given complete control of the country's purse strings and by pruning expenditure and raising taxes, Salazar accomplished what had been previously thought to be impossible and balanced the nation's books. This put Salazar in an extremely strong position and in 1932 he became Prime Minister, a post which he held on to as virtual dictator for thirty-six years.

Due to Salazar's combined financial prowess and increasing isolationism, Portugal survived the world slump of 1929–1931 almost unscathed. The same, however, could not be said of the Port trade, which had been steadily losing out to the 1920s fashion for cocktails and sherry as well as facing competition from the so-called 'Brandy Wines' of the British Empire. Prices fell and a number of firms encountered serious financial difficulties although, as always, the growers were hit hardest. With the notable exception of Quinta do Noval, nearly all the major shippers passed over the outstanding 1931 vintage, which is almost certainly the finest year in the twentieth century never to be widely declared (see page 182).

Although by no means autocratic in temperament, Salazar behaved as a neo-Pombaline saviour of the Douro. In 1933 (the same year as the constitution of his *Estado Novo* or 'New State' came into force) Salazar created the three corporate organisations which survive more or less intact to this day. Based in Oporto, the Instituto do Vinho do Porto (IVP) was to be the senior body with responsibility for the general supervision and administration of the industry but maintaining a particular interest in the day-to-day business of the Gaia *entreposto*. The Casa do Douro was set up as a secondary authority to monitor and supervise the 30,000 growers within the Port demarcation. Housed in a gloomy building that looks remarkably like a 1930s cinema on the main street in Régua, the Casa do Douro continued to operate with impunity until it was severely compromised by a questionable business deal in 1990 (see page 54). In order to balance the equation, all Port shippers had to belong to the *Grêmio dos Exportadores do Vinho do Porto* or Exporters Guild to which the IVP granted the Certificates of Origin that accompanied shipments abroad. However, in order to be registered as a shipper (i.e. exporter), two onerous conditions had to be fulfilled. Firstly, the company had to maintain a stock of at least 150,000 litres (just under 275 pipes) and secondly, it had to be in possession of a lodge in the Gaia *entreposto* capable of holding an amount in excess of this quantity of wine. With the exception of one or two flagrant abuses in recent years, Salazar's tripartite arrangement, which eventually came up with the annual *benefício* system (explained in Chapter 2), has served the industry reasonably well for nearly seventy years. Back in the 1930s when over-production had become a serious problem, the Casa do Douro's power to buy up excess stocks of wine from growers certainly helped to bring supply back in line with demand. Prospects for the Port trade improved in the mid-1930s, helped by the lifting of Prohibition in the United States and a growing market for inexpensive Tawny in France; however, nearly 50 per cent of all Port still went to the United Kingdom. In the last of many anecdotal entries in his book *Port Wine and Oporto*, Ernest Cockburn records how at the end of May 1938, the Port lodges closed 'to enable their staffs to participate in the great festivities organised . . . in celebration of the new regime in Portugal which had now reached its twelfth year of success'.

THE SECOND WORLD WAR

When world war again broke out in September 1939, the Port trade effectively came to a standstill. Although Portugal technically remained neutral throughout the hostilities, all British families were advised to leave Oporto and a destroyer was sent to Leixões to oversee the evacuation. Many of the older members of the trade chose to remain behind and enjoyed a life of relative comfort and plenty at a time when the rest of Europe was on its knees. Compared to Lisbon, which was a hotbed of intrigue and espionage, Oporto remained a quiet backwater. In the Douro where food was in relatively short supply, Pinhão and the vicinity were kept from going hungry by an enterprising local family who ran a flourishing black market in essential supplies. Wolfram was mined in the Douro near Sabrosa and at Quinta do Vesúvio and exported directly to Germany. Perhaps sensing the outcome of the war, Salazar finally suspended Wolfram shipments in 1944. In the meantime the British had invoked the Treaty of Windsor and from June 1943 Salazar permitted the Allies to use Lajes on the Azores as an airbase.

Despite the fact that total shipments of Port fell to just 11,000 pipes in 1942 (the worst year ever recorded), most shippers continued to maintain a London sales office throughout the war. Many arrived at their offices to find they had been blitzed the previous night, and there were stories of streams of precious vintages from the 1920s and 1930s running down the streets near London Bridge. When one shipper visited his bombed-out office, he found builders pouring the remaining bottles of pre-war Vintage Port (probably *estufado* from the heat) into an old kettle and drinking it from tin mugs! Port shipments began to recover slightly after the *grêmio* negotiated a quota system with Minister of Food, Lord Woolton, in 1942. The quota system divided Port into two grades: grade one for inexpensive Ports and grade two for 'superior wines' like Vintage Port and aged Tawny. The quota remained in force until 1949, at which time the latter represented a mere 5 per cent of annual shipments.

THE OPORTO TIME WARP

In the immediate aftermath of the war, the Port trade fully expected a recovery similar to that which followed the First World War. It was sorely disappointed. Until as late as the 1970s, shipments remained well below pre-war levels. Even a duo of exceptional post-war vintages, 1945 and 1947, failed to stimulate interest. Most British wine merchants were not interested in using up their valuable import quotas with Vintage Port so the shippers bottled the 1945s themselves and held the wine until the good times returned. A disparaging story was put about by the English wine trade that the corks used for the Oporto bottlings were of poor quality. This story was without foundation as I found in 1998 when I had the opportunity to compare the London and Oporto bottlings of Dow's 1945 Vintage Port side-by-side. Due to the shortage of glass, much of the latter was bottled in brown sherry bottles.

At this time just 2 per cent of all Port was bottled in Oporto. The remainder continued to be shipped in cask and bottled at its destination, either accompanied by appropriate labels from the shipper or under the merchant's own name. The creative marketing and public relations that has done so much to promote Port brands in the 1980s and 1990s was almost non-existent. When Sandeman advertised their brand on London buses before the war Walter Berry, a partner in the famous firm of Berry Bros. & Rudd, described their wine disparagingly as 'omnibus Port'!

Unlike much of Europe, which underwent a social revolution in the wake of the Second World War, Portugal, under the firm, authoritarian grip of Salazar, seemed to go backwards in time. One Port shipper who returned to Oporto after war-service remembers a 'time warp' with an 'upstairs-downstairs world' of domestic service. William ('Bill') Warre, who first went to Oporto in 1948, recalls a feeling of comparative luxury along with 'Victorian service'. He reached Oporto by cargo steamer which crossed the bar of the Douro, and moored at the quayside at Vila Nova de Gaia, which was stacked high with pipes of Port. With trade remaining slack he spent much of his time shooting partridge either on the Aveiro marshes south of Oporto or in the Douro. Wyndham Fletcher of Cockburn's records: 'There was no new business ... we spent our time examining stock; in other words tasting through our old Vintage Ports!'

Up in the Douro valley, all the *quintas* continued to make their wines in time-honoured manner, trodden by foot in granite *lagares*, most of which had been built in the nineteenth century or even earlier. Cars were still something of a rarity and, until the late 1950s, many shippers preferred to visit outlying properties on foot or by mule rather than risk their vehicles on the appalling roads and tracks. Sarzedinho, a village in the Torto valley producing some outstanding wines, was only accessible by stepping stones. Despite the difficult times, a number of Port shippers clubbed together to build a bridge across the river in order to reach the vineyards.

The continuing depression throughout the late 1940s and 1950s meant that many shippers fell on hard times. The situation was not helped by the sudden imposition of the so-called Lei do Terço in September 1959, which required each shipper to maintain a three-to-one stock ratio. In other words, for every pipe of Port sold in a year, a shipper needed to have two in the cellar in order to comply with the law. Port producers fell over each other trying to acquire stocks before the law came into force in 1960, stretching themselves further just to stay in business. Some sold *quintas* in order to survive, others folded or merged. When Alistair Robertson moved to Portugal in 1966 to take charge of Taylor's from his recently widowed aunt, Beryl Yeatman, he readily admits that he had to be persuaded to 'give it a go', such was the depression in the trade at the time.

Of the eighty-three registered shippers in existence at the end of the war, there were around fifty remaining in 1970, many of which had either been taken over by multinationals (Croft, Delaforce, Cockburn and Sandeman) or amalgamated into private groups. By the early 1970s, the only British shippers remaining in private family hands were Taylor/Fonseca and the Symington-owned houses of Dow, Graham, Warre, Quarles Harris, Gould Campbell and Smith Woodhouse.

NOT SO SWINGING SIXTIES

Flower power, miniskirts, rock music and all the other cultural icons of the 1960s virtually by-passed Portugal which was still kept on a tight leash by the elderly and idiosyncratic Salazar. But however much he protected the country from the outside world, Portugal was eventually forced to change. In 1961 a guerrilla war began in Angola and rapidly spread to the other colonies in Africa. As the young and able-bodied left Portugal, either to fight in the wars or emigrating to escape military service, the country suffered an increasingly debilitating drain of its resources. Over a million people emigrated (mainly to France and Germany) between 1960 and 1970 with the rural districts of Vila Real, Viseu and Bragança (i.e. the Douro) registering the highest rates of depopulation. Thousands of small farms were abandoned and whole villages left virtually deserted with a few elderly crones in charge.

In these circumstances, the traditional *lagares*, which required between one and two people per pipe (a total of twenty to thirty men) in order to tread the grapes effectively, were no longer viable and it fell to the shippers to come up with alternatives. Some adopted the so-called *movimosto* (see p. 131), an ill-fated adaptation of the traditional *lagares*, whilst others built huge centralised wineries equipped with autovinification tanks adapted from the Ducellier system used in Algeria (see Chapter 3). Although electricity had arrived in Pinhão in the mid-1930s, supply remained erratic and many outlying properties were still without power. Conventional methods of extraction like *remontagem* (pumping over with electric pumps) were hardly a valid option.

In the Douro, as in other Portuguese wine regions, Salazar promoted the formation of centralised co-operative wineries. The first of these was established at Mesão Frio in 1950 and a total of twenty-two were built over the following sixteen years. The co-ops were set up to attract small farmers in the Baixo Corgo and on the higher margins of the region and by the early 1990s they registered nearly 13,000 members, just short of half the total number of growers in the Douro. The largest co-operative at Santa Marta de Penaguião has 2,000 members, 85 per cent of whom tend less than one hectare of vineyard.

FLOODING THE DOURO

The River Douro had long been an unpredictable torrent, prone to serious floods or *cheias* in the winter months. One of the most devastating floods occurred in December 1909. Ernest Cockburn records how the lodges close to the river in Vila Nova da Gaia were completely flooded and steamers broke from their moorings such was the force of the current. One much-loved steamer, the S.S. Douro, was swept out to sea and wrecked on rocks near Leixões. When the *cheia* was at its height, it nearly covered the lower deck of the two-tier bridge linking Oporto and Vila Nova de Gaia and at one stage it was feared the entire structure might collapse. Conditions were no better in the Douro where pipes of Port were washed downstream and out to sea, being found, sometimes still full of wine, as far up the coast as Viana do Castelo. An entry in the visitors' book at Quinta do Bomfim records that the flood 'carried away lodges, olive trees and vineyards . . . the river rose with extraordinary rapidity, on the 23rd it reached the lodge here and the iron work of the Pinhão bridge'.

In the 1950s and 1960s plans were drawn up to harness the force of the river with a series of monumental dams equipped with hydro-electric stations. The last working *barco rabelo* descended the Douro in 1964 and the first dam was completed at Carrapatelo upstream from Oporto in 1971. Other dams at Bagauste (Régua), Cachão de Valeira, Pocinho and Crestuma followed in quick succession, transforming the Douro into a series of placid finger lakes. Apart from the obvious loss of land (although it was mostly poor quality vineyard on alluvial soils) and the inconvenience of re-routing part of the railway and the Régua–Pinhão road, the main concern among the Douro growers and Port shippers was the possible increase in humidity and the effect it might have on the vines. In the event few noticed much difference apart from the incidence of cold winter fogs which become trapped in the narrow valley during stable atmospheric conditions.

However, the building of a dam in the Côa valley, a wild and remote tributary in the Douro Superior, proved to be much more controversial. First mooted by Salazar, the scheme only began to take shape in the 1980s when EDP (the Portuguese electricity company) decided to create a reservoir which would cover over

1,700 hectares of land including Quinta da Ervamoira, an important vineyard belonging to Ramos Pinto. Apart from the ecological implications, the dam would undoubtedly have transformed the climate in this part of the Douro where summer temperatures sometimes reach 50°C. Initial protests fell on deaf ears with the government of Anibal Cavaco Silva seemingly determined to go ahead with the plan. Then, in 1995, archaeologists discovered palaeolithic engravings on the schistous rocks by the side of the Côa. Hundreds of pictures of wild animals were found etched into the rock recording human habitation in the area as far back as 26,000 BC. For a time the authorities refused to give in to demands to halt the dam, which was by now under construction, suggesting that some of the engravings could be either copied or moved. A leading article in *The Times* accused the Portuguese government of living in the Third World. In October 1995 the Côa dam became an election issue, the Socialists promising to put a stop to the project if elected. Following their victory, construction was halted and the entire Côa valley opened to visitors as a *parque archeologico* (see page 123). In 1998 the Côa was designated as a World Heritage site. At the time of writing there is speculation that EDP are looking to build their dam elsewhere, possibly in the Tua valley downstream.

REVOLUTION

When the tanks rolled into the streets of Lisbon on the morning of Thursday 25 April 1974, the establishment was taken completely by surprise. Salazar himself had died four years earlier and in the early 1970s his successor, Marcelo Caetano, had begun to liberalise the regime. Caetano's limited reforms were insufficient to satisfy the younger officers in the Portuguese armed forces, who believed increasingly in a negotiated political rather than military solution to the long-running colonial wars. There was little resistance and much jubilation in the streets when the Armed Forces Movement (MFA) brought an abrupt end to fifty years of totalitarian rule. The *coup d'état* itself was a good-natured affair with little bloodletting and, in the immediate aftermath, life continued much as it had before. Oporto was calm on the day of the coup and the British played their customary game of cricket on the Saturday after the military had seized power.

Port sales were showing sure signs of recovery by the mid-1970s. The outstanding 1963 vintage had been well received by the trade. According to Michael Symington 'we began to realise that things were picking up when we sold more 1963 Vintage Port than the 1896, making it the most successful declaration for over sixty years'. Declarations in 1966 and 1970 were similarly well received and during the late 1960s shipments gradually began to increase. Most Vintage Port was now being bottled in Gaia and in 1973 a law was passed making it obligatory for all future declarations to be bottled at source.

At first it seemed as though the new military 'Junta' would do no more than tinker with the existing institutions. All Salazar's *grêmios* were abolished, the *Grêmio dos Exportadores do Vinho do Porto* being replaced by a voluntary Port Wine Exporters Association (AEVP) whose first chairman was Burmester's Armando Silva. A commission of Douro elders was established to liquidate the Casa do Douro but apart from a few new faces in key positions as a result of the post-revolutionary *saneamento* (purge), business continued unabated in the months following the coup.

However, the 1974 vintage took place amid political chaos when President António Spinola, who had only taken office five months before, resigned, warning the Portuguese people of a 'new slavery'. Throughout the winter of 1974 and 1975 left-wingers in the armed forces, many of whom had garnered their politics from the African liberation movements, made a concerted bid for power. It culminated in the so-called *verão quente* (hot summer) of July and August 1975 when the ostensibly democratic revolution ran completely out of control.

Throughout this volatile period, Portuguese firms were more vulnerable than foreign companies, most of which kept a low profile. Much of the economy fell into state ownership when the banks were nationalised in March 1975 but only two Port shippers were seized. Borges & Irmão was nationalised along with the bank of the same name and Royal Oporto was taken over by its own workforce. Employees of another large wine producer in Vila Nova de Gaia set the fire hoses on the approaching revolutionary mob to prevent them from taking control. When in August 1975 Otelo Saraiva de Carvalho (one of the members of the ruling military triumvirate) returned from Cuba and declared that there may be a need to round up all Portugal's counter-revolutionaries and extinguish them in the Lisbon bull-ring, many leading Portuguese families decided it was time to pack up and leave. Fully expecting to have to abandon the country in a hurry, one leading Port shipper decided to send all his family photograph albums to England just to retain a record of life in Oporto and the Douro. Stories abounded that the entire Port trade was on the point of being nationalised in August 1975 but the dismissal of the cranky, pro-Communist Prime Minister, General Vasco Gonçalves, prevented the papers from being signed. Others say that the British Prime Minister, James Callaghan, intervened. There can be little doubt that but for the strong British presence in Oporto, the entire Port trade would have been nationalised.

In the midst of all this revolutionary fervour, a scandal broke which would have been deeply damaging to the Port trade had the world not been more concerned about the Portuguese political climate at the time. German authorities carrying out routine carbon-dating tests found that the three previous vintages (1972, 1973 and 1974) had been fortified with industrial alcohol instead of *aguardente* distilled from wine. At the time the Portuguese government exercised a monopoly in the distribution of fortifying spirit through the Casa do Douro. Eventually the fraud was traced back to an agent in France but with the Portuguese regime in turmoil, there was little that the shippers could do to claim recompense. Though it was completely harmless, the Casa do Douro intervened and bought up large quantities of spurious Port wine. For the following vintage, the Casa do Douro doubled the price of *aguardente* from 11,000 escudos to 22,000 escudos a pipe.

During the autumn of 1975, a violent backlash took place in northern Portugal which nearly paralysed the country. For a few weeks it seemed as though civil war might erupt but after another bid for power by the left-wing of the armed forces on 25 November when guns were mounted on the Arrábida bridge between Oporto and Gaia, Portugal's political mainstream returned to power. The African colonies were now gone and on 25 April 1976, the revolution ended peacefully with the first genuinely free elections for over fifty years. Portugal emerged with a democratically elected moderate Socialist government under Prime Minister Dr Mario Soares. In 1977, seeking both political and economic stability, his government took the first important step to becoming an enthusi-

astic member of the European Union. The revolution is now a
fading memory for most people, recorded only in countless street
names, 'Rua 25 de Abril' having substituted 'Rua Dr António
Oliveira Salazar'. As President of Portugal, in 1988 Mario Soares
dined with the Port shippers at the Factory House, the first head
of state to do so since Manuel II visited Oporto in 1908.

MODERN TIMES

In the last two decades of the twentieth century, the Douro landscape has changed more rapidly than at any time since the
phylloxera era of the 1870s. Reflecting the Portuguese love of
acronyms, the first major development was the PDRITM (Projecto
de Desenvolvimento Rural Integrado de Trás-os-Montes) supported by the World Bank. Commonly known in English as the
'World Bank Scheme', this ambitious project was initiated in 1983
offering low interest loans to farmers in one of Europe's poorest
agricultural regions. The scheme was seized upon by Douro
growers (relatively wealthy Port shippers included), who were permitted to plant or replant between 3 and 10 hectares of vineyard
provided that the land was officially classified as being of A or B
grade and that only five prescribed grape varieties were used (see
page 79). A year earlier ten leading Port shippers had joined forces
to create ADVID (Associação para o Desenvolvimento da Viticultura Duriense). Supported by the new University of Trás-os-Montes
and Alto Douro (UTAD) in Vila Real, this became the first properly
funded vineyard research programme in the Douro since the
replanting that had followed the phylloxera epidemic nearly a
century earlier. The World Bank Scheme allowed the members of
ADVID to put many of their ideas into practice and whole hillsides
of traditional stone-walled terraces (many never replanted after
phylloxera) were excavated and replaced by modern *patamares* or
vertical *vinha ao alto* (see Chapter 2). The PDRTIM was fully
subscribed and by the end of the decade 2,500 hectares (ha) of
new, high-quality vineyard had been planted and a further 300ha
replanted.

Portugal's accession to the European Community (now European
Union) in 1986 served to accelerate the pace of change. A law
came into force in June of the same year which permitted indepen-

dent growers to export their wines directly from the Douro without having to pass through the *entreposto* at Vila Nova de Gaia. For the first time for nearly sixty years single *quintas* were now permitted to sell Port abroad. The impact of this change was not, at first, as dramatic as might be expected. For a start individual properties had to abide by the three-to-one stock ratio and few had the wherewithal to compete on the open market against the established brands. However, two pioneering estates, Quinta do Infantado and Quinta do Côtto, founded the Associação dos Produtores Engarafadores do Vinho do Porto (the Association of Port Wine Producer-Bottlers). Helped greatly by the availability of European Union funds, a number of other properties have begun to export directly from the Douro. By the mid-1990s there were about thirty producer-bottlers in the Douro (including nine co-operatives) but their share of Port sales remained at less than 1 per cent. However, taking advantage of the legislation in reverse, one prominent shipper, Quinta do Noval, has relinquished its lodges in Gaia and moved lock, stock and barrel to new purpose-built *armazéns* in the Douro.

Another consequence of Portugal's membership of the European Union was the liberalisation of the distribution of *aguardente* used to fortify Port, which continued to be a state monopoly until 1990. Although quantities are still strictly controlled by the Port Wine Institute as a means of regulating the production of Port, shippers are now free to purchase *aguardente* on the open market with the result that the overall quality of spirit has improved markedly over recent years. In 1996 a number of major shippers came together and formed Gruporto in order to increase their purchasing power for *aguardente* (see page 138).

In 1990 there began a drama which attained the status of a soap opera through the early years of the decade. One of the largest shippers of the time, the Real Companhia Velha (better known as Royal Oporto) had lurched from one financial crisis to another ever since the company had been returned to private hands in 1978. In 1990 a substantial share of the company changed hands twice. Forty per cent of Royal Oporto was initially sold to Cofipsa, a firm belonging to the Italian financier Carlo di Benedetti. But shortly after the deal had been signed, the share was sold by Cofipsa to the Casa do Douro. However, the other Port shippers felt that the acquisition of shares in Royal Oporto by an organisation that purported to represent the growers in the Douro region amounted to a major conflict of interest. Faced with a wave of protest, the government none the less consented to the deal. Only after continued lobbying were some of the Casa do Douro's powers finally removed in 1995 and a new interprofessional body was created. The Comissão Interprofissional do Região Demarcada do Douro (CIRDD) has now assumed control of the annual *benefício* or authorisation while the Casa do Douro maintains the all-important *cadastro* or register of individual vineyards (see Chapter 2). However, at the time of writing, this long-running saga is by no means over as the Casa do Douro has nearly been bankrupted by its purchase of Royal Oporto.

Since Portugal joined the European Union in 1986, huge amounts of capital have been invested in the country's ailing rural infrastructure with impressive new mountain-breaching roads penetrating inland from the towns and cities on the coast. A new motorway opened in 1995, cutting the journey time from Pinhão to Oporto from three-and-a-half to a mere two hours, beating the time taken by the train. With an end to the Douro's intrinsic

'Bombs house', São João de Pesqueira

55

isolation, the region's commercial prospects have diversified and improved. As people return to villages they deserted in the 1960s, the rural landscape has been transformed (mostly for the worse) by the construction of anomalous little houses whose architectural styles derive from France and Germany where many of their occupants spent the intervening years. On the outskirts of São João de Pesqueira one such house is famously decorated with bombs, its owner presumably having been inspired by the colonial wars!

PORT UP TO DATE

At the end of the 1990s, a total of just over 33,000 growers were farming 38,000 hectares of vineyard in the Douro, mostly in the Baixo Corgo sub-region, nearly a third of which is under vine (see Chapter 2). In common with most of northern Portugal, the region is fragmented into tiny holdings numbering nearly 140,000. Over 80 per cent of these are less than 0.5ha in size, and a mere 0.01 per cent have an area greater than 30ha. Detailed statistics on the subdivision of the Douro's vineyards may be found in Appendix II.

Production of Port has averaged around 800,000 hectolitres (145,000 pipes) in the mid-1990s with unfortified Douro wines (demarcated in their own right since 1979) averaging 1.3 million hectolitres. These figures, however, disguise the huge variation in production between different vintages (see Chapter 2). Douro wines are covered separately in Chapter 6.

Between 1985 and 1997, world-wide Port shipments increased by a healthy 26 per cent, stabilising in the late 1990s at around 10 million cases (163,000 pipes). This exceeds all previous records and bucks the trend among other fortified wines like Sherry and Madeira, both of which have experienced a steady decline. Bulk shipments of Port, stable through the 1990s representing around 20 per cent of all exports, were temporarily suspended in 1996 and are unlikely to be reinstated. In the late 1990s, shippers' own brands accounted for over 70 per cent of all business. The 'special categories' of Port (i.e. Vintage Character, LBV, Crusted, *Colheita*, aged Tawnies and Vintage) make up 11 per cent of all sales (see Chapter 4).

France has been the principal market for Port for over thirty years, taking over from the United Kingdom in 1963. It is followed in the late 1990s by the Netherlands and Portugal in second and third place respectively. The United Kingdom, so intimately linked to the evolution of Port, is the fifth largest market in terms of volume but first when it comes to value with the special categories making up over 40 per cent of sales. The fastest-growing market in the 1990s has been the USA which, since the 1991 declaration, has become the largest market for Vintage Port. Here the special categories register around 50 per cent of sales. (See Appendix V for more detailed information on the world-wide market for Port.)

With a history dating back nearly five centuries, the future prospects for Port and the Douro are considered in a postscript at the end of the book.

2

Vines, Vineyards and Quintas

ROCK AND A HARD PLACE

Emotions run deep in the Douro, and occasionally conflict. Gazing up at his pyramid of terraced vineyards, a grower proudly explained that it was the 'eighth wonder of the world'. To the Port shipper who alludes to the Douro as 'our river', the region is primarily a place to do business. At certain times of the year when speedboats and skis ply through the water, others treat the river as something of a playground. But for the majority of the 33,000 growers who tend the region's tiny plots of vineyard, daily life in the Douro is plain hard graft.

It is difficult to imagine a more challenging place in which to grow grapes and, at first sight, hard to conceive how the banks of the Douro ever came to be planted with vineyards. An explanation can be found in the underlying geology. The bedrock beneath the greater part of northern Portugal is the grey Hercynian granite that can be seen in the gaunt civic buildings of central Oporto. Rarely very far from the surface, this hard rock frequently penetrates through the poor, thin quartzite soils making much of the land virtually unworkable. Vines, which need to root deeply in order to flourish, are frequently impeded once they reach the impregnable layer of granite. On the high plateaux or *planaltos* to the north and south of the River Douro, growers do little more than scratch a living from their plots of land.

The geology of the upper part of the Douro valley is different from the remainder of northern Portugal. Most of the bedrock belongs to a formation known as the Pre-Ordovician Schist-Grey-wacke Complex or merely 'schist' for short. Unlike the surrounding granite, this foliated, slate-like rock can be worked into a coarse soil. Lumps of schist on the surface shine almost like polished steel in strong sunlight, absorbing heat and reducing erosion during heavy winter downpours. Over time the schist weathers into a fine silt-like dust, clouds of which billow up from trails and tracks, covering cars during the dry summer months. The Douro's soils are naturally rich in potassium and magnesium but tend to lack calcium and boron, causing a condition known locally as *moromba* (curling and drying of the leaves during the growing season). This was originally thought to be a virus, but is now successfully treated by applying borax to the soil. The proportion of organic material in the Douro's schistous soils is low and regular application of both organic and inorganic fertilisers is necessary to correct the imbalance of nutrients. Below the topsoil the schist tends to fracture vertically facilitating the infiltration of water and the penetration of roots to depths that would be impossible on the granite. It is not surprising that to those farming the Douro, schist is almost a religion and it is not uncommon to come across an outlying chapel dedicated to Santo Xisto ('Saint Schist'). Here and there huge outcrops of rugged granite pierce the schist, notably from Carrazeda de Ansiães to the Douro at Cachão de Valeira, which marks the natural boundary of two of the Douro's three sub-regions (see below). Few have ever attempted to cultivate these intractable soils.

The boundary of the demarcated Port region has been modified a number of times since it was first established in the mid-eighteenth century but tends to follow the outline of the schist. It begins at Barqueiros 75 km inland from Oporto and stretches eastwards to Barca d'Alva on the frontier with Spain, 160 km as the crow flies from the coast. The region encompasses a total of 250,000 hectares of which nearly 40,000 are planted with vines. Forming a deep cleft in the rock, the River Douro runs from east to west and is therefore the natural axis for the region. The river itself, dammed to form a series of placid finger lakes, flows at an altitude of between 60 and 140 metres above sea level. The terrain either side of the Douro is irregular in the extreme with deeply incised tributaries draining the mountains, which rise in places to over 1,000 metres on the edge of the region. With half the region's vineyards planted on slopes with a gradient in excess of 30 per cent, there are few wine regions that are so arduous and costly to cultivate as the Douro. Further detailed information on the subdivision and gradients of the Douro's vineyards may be found in Appendix II.

CLIMATE: MACRO, MESO, MICRO

'Shut your eyes and think of England' might be an appropriate maxim for the weather in north-west Portugal. Rain-bearing westerlies surge in from the Atlantic causing frequent downpours on the hills and mountains that rise from the narrow littoral. Oporto, by no means the wettest place in northern Portugal, receives an average of 1,200 mm of rain a year. By way of a comparison, the annual rainfall in Manchester, north-west England (the butt of many a 'wet' joke), amounts to 800 mm. It is therefore no coincidence that the coast north of Oporto is known to all as the Costa Verde (Green Coast) and the local wine is the distinctly cool climate high acid/low alcohol Vinho Verde.

Although the Vinho Verde region abuts the Port wine demarcation, no two wines could possibly be more different. Surrounded on three sides by high mountains, the upper reaches of the Douro are largely protected from the Atlantic onslaught earning it the provincial name of Trás-os-Montes ('Behind the Mountains'). To the north the Serras de Alvão, Padrela and Bornes shield the region from cold northerlies whereas directly to the west the granite massif of the Serra do Marão, rising to 1,400 metres, casts a rain shadow over the entire region. Along the entire length of the Douro Valley there is a steady but dramatic transition from the temperate, humid Atlantic conditions that prevail on the coast towards the much more extreme continental/Mediterranean climate of the central Iberian *meseta*. It is not uncommon to leave Oporto shrouded in grey mist, traverse the Marão in a downpour and emerge on the other side in bright sunshine.

At a meso-climatic level the transition is evident within the 90 km extent of the Port wine region itself. This is most clearly illustrated by the annual rainfall figures along the course of the River Douro. Lying immediately to the east of the Serra do Marão at an altitude of 430 metres, Vila Real (the regional capital of Trás-os-Montes) receives an average of 1,130 mm (see Map 1). Down by the river at an altitude of roughly 100 metres, the annual average rainfall at Régua is around 950 mm, falling to 650 mm at

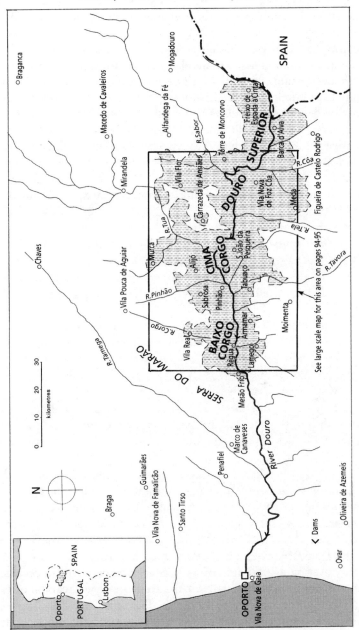

Map 1. The north of Portugal and the Douro.

Pinhão in the heart of the Port wine region 20 km upstream. But by the time you reach Pocinho, now the eastern terminus for the railway line that runs alongside the river, the rainfall total is as little as 400 mm a year. Rainfall in the Douro is highly seasonal with heavy rains in the winter and spring giving way to long periods of unrelenting drought during the summer months broken only by occasional localised thunderstorms. Rainfall is also somewhat unpredictable and vineyard yields are easily diminished by relatively cool, wet Atlantic weather at the time of flowering in late May or early June. A westerly air stream prevails for most of the year but the wind occasionally veers round from the east bringing scalding weather conditions from central Spain during the summer months and dry, biting winds in the winter. This gives rise to the rhyme readily trotted out by locals that *'nem bom vento, nem bom casamento vem de Espanha'* – neither a good wind nor a good marriage comes from Spain!

As rainfall declines inland, so temperatures increase. The annual average daytime temperature in Oporto is 14.4°C rising to 15.5°C at Régua, 16.2°C at Pinhão and 16.5°C at Pocinho. But these figures obscure the extremes which increase markedly towards the Spanish border. During the winter months the thermometer frequently falls below freezing on the easterly *planalto*, sometimes rising to an unbearable 50°C in the summer months. Since the river was dammed in the 1970s (see page 49) a blanket of freezing fog often hangs over the Douro when atmospheric conditions are stable during the winter. Late spring frosts are not uncommon at higher altitudes damaging young shoots in the vineyard and slashing yields.

The Douro breaks down into three sub-regions, each of which has its own distinct meso-climate and therefore tends to produce a very different style of Port. The smallest of the three sub-regions in overall area is the Baixo Corgo or Lower Corgo. This is the most westerly and therefore most accessible part of the Douro centred on Régua where the Port trade first took hold (see page 17). Covering a total area of 45,000 hectares, it is still much the most intensively planted part of the Douro valley with a total of 13,500 hectares under vine. In the shadow of the Serra do Marão, the Baixo Corgo is much the coolest, wettest and most fertile of the three zones and therefore tends to produce large volumes of lighter wines for the standard Ruby and Tawny blends that are the bread and butter for the majority of Port shippers.

Curiously the River Corgo itself, which joins the Douro just upstream from Régua, does not quite mark the official boundary between the Baixo Corgo and the second sub-region, the Cima Corgo (Upper Corgo). This is to be found about 8 km upstream at Covelinhas. Embracing a total area of 95,000 hectares, vineyards amounting to 17,000 hectares tend to be somewhat larger than in the Baixo Corgo with the main properties concentrated on the banks of the River Douro and its tributaries; the Tedo, Tavora, Torto, Pinhão and Tua. Representing the zone where the Atlantic influence gives way to the continental Mediterranean, the climate is considerably warmer, drier and more reliable than it is downstream. All the major shippers own vineyards in the Cima Corgo, and wines from the area form the basis for premium styles of Port, especially aged Tawnies, LBV and Vintage.

The most easterly sub-region, the Douro Superior is a relative newcomer to Port having been hampered for centuries by poor access and isolation (see page 18). It is the largest of the three covering 110,000 hectares of land of which just 8,000 are planted with vines. With a climate marked by continental extremes, this is much the most arid part of the Douro and with drought a recurring problem a number of growers are now resorting to irrigation in order to make up for the natural deficit. The Douro Superior is capable of producing some fine, powerful wines, most of which are used for premium blends including Vintage.

Given the contortions of the terrain there is also considerable variation in the micro-climate, not merely within a single property but right down to the vine canopy itself. Apart from one or two empirical studies, little research has been carried out on the potentially significant micro-climatic ramifications of differing methods of cultivation, vine-spacing and trellising. However, most growers have come to know the climatic variations within their own properties, some of which embrace a number of different aspects and span an altitude of up to 300 metres. At Quinta de la Rosa, for example, which ranges from 90 metres to 260 metres above sea level, there is a 3–4°C difference in temperature between the top and bottom of the vineyard. In the Cima Corgo it is generally accepted that the best wines originate from the *meia encosta*: halfway up the slope.

The climate of northern Portugal also has a bearing on the maturation of Port and this is considered in Chapter 4.

VINEYARD CLASSIFICATION

No matter how hard you try, it is impossible to find a word either in Portuguese or English with the same meaning as that quintessential French expression *terroir*. It combines soil, aspect, macro-, meso- and micro-climate and is used to justify, sometimes in rather nebulous terms, the difference in the character of a wine produced in one place from another. For want of a better word, *terroir* forms the basis of a detailed classification of Douro vineyards on which the Port of production is based. Devised by Alvaro Moreira da Fonseca in the 1940s when most of the world was at war, the system has served the region well with only minor revisions since.

Each and every vineyard plot within the Douro (and in the mid-1990s there were nearly 140,000 separate holdings) is graded according to a system of points. Twelve different physical variables are incorporated into the classification in order of importance as follows:

Altitude: on the basis that altitude has a marked effect on climate, scores vary between 240 positive points for vineyards situated up to 150 metres above sea level to 900 minus points for those above 650 metres. Combined with the locality element below, this effectively rules out Port production from vineyards on the highest and therefore coolest margins of the region.

Locality: reflecting the meso-climatic differences within the demarcated region, the Douro is divided into five sections, each of which contain a number of different sub-sectors as follows:

Section 1: the higher parishes of the Baixo Corgo north of Régua with the coolest Atlantic climate: o–plus 60 points
Section 2: from Barqueiros to the River Corgo on the north side of the Douro (including Régua) and from Barro to the River Vilar (Fontelas) on the south side (i.e. most of the Baixo Corgo): minus 50–plus 250 points (27 sub-sectors)
Section 3: from the mouth of the Corgo to the River Ceira (near

64

Gouvinhas) on the north side of the Douro and from the Vilar to the Tedo rivers on the south side: minus 50–plus 460 points (18 sub-sectors)

Section 4: the heart of the Cima Corgo and some of the Douro Superior extending all the way from the Ceira and Tedo rivers in the west as far east as the Saião valley (near Pocinho). It takes in all the main tributaries including the Tavora, Torto, Caedo, Pinhão and Tua rivers: minus 50–plus 600 points (38 sub-sectors)

Section 5: from the Saião to Barca d'Alva on the Spanish border (most of the Douro Superior): plus 140–plus 450 points (15 sub-sectors)

Productivity (yield): based on the principle that more productive vineyards produce poorer wines, a maximum score of 120 points has traditionally been awarded to vineyards producing 600 litres per thousand vines to a minimum of minus 900 points above 1,800 litres per thousand vines. However, in the light of the increasing mechanisation of Douro vineyards and consequent lower planting densities (see the section on Planting below), the regulation now asserts a global maximum of 55 hectolitres per hectare. At the time of writing a new productivity scale is under consideration.

Soil Type: a maximum of 100 points is awarded to schistous soils, minus 100 for soils described as 'transitional', minus 250 for granite and minus 400 for alluvium. The latter are virtually non-existent since the valley floor was flooded in the 1970s.

Vine Training: given that vines trained closer to ground level yield riper fruit, vines grown up to a height of 0.8 m are awarded 100 points (although an exception is made nowadays for widely spaced vines). Vines growing on pergolas (aka Vinho Verde) are completely excluded from Port production.

Grape Varieties: these are covered in much more detail below but the numerous varieties planted in the Douro were originally classified by Moreira da Fonseca into five groups ranging from 150 points for grapes described as 'very good', 75 points ('good'), 0 points ('regular'), minus 150 points ('mediocre') and minus 300 points ('bad'). Nowadays the system has been simplified into varieties which are either 'recommended' or simply 'authorised'. Many of the poorer quality varieties have been eliminated since wholesale replanting began in the late 1970s.

Angle of Inclination (slope): *Bacchus amat colles* (Vines love hills) wrote Virgil and it is certainly true that the best vineyards are usually to be found on well-drained slopes. No points are awarded to vines grown on a flat site; up to 101 points for slopes in excess of 35 degrees.

Aspect and Exposure: the angle at which the sun's rays strike the soil and the duration of insolation are particularly important during the maturation period. In the cooler westerly sub-sections of the Douro, a southerly exposure is favoured over a north-facing slope whereas in a hot year south-facing vineyards in the Douro Superior may suffer from excess heat. For this reason points vary from minus 40 for a north-facing property in sub-section 1 (above) to plus 100 for a slope facing south in sub-section 4.

Stoniness (soil texture): stonier soils allow rainwater to penetrate and the schist both reflects sunlight and acts as heat reserve thereby modifying the micro-climate below the vine canopy. Stony soils are therefore awarded 80 points with no score being given to soils lacking in stone.

Age of the Vines: older vineyards generally yield less but produce more concentrated wines. For this reason vines less than four years old are excluded altogether from Port production (with implications for the methods of grafting outlined below). Those between four and twenty-five years of age receive 30 points and those more than twenty-five years old are given 60 points.

Shelter: the narrow tributaries of the Douro are more sheltered and therefore hotter than the exposed *planaltos* north and south of the river. Consequently, the most sheltered sites are awarded a score of 60 points as opposed to the most exposed which receive zero.

Vine Density: higher densities generally reduce the vigour of each vine, the theory being that as every plant yields less it produces grapes of better quality. It is curious that in the Douro densities above 5,700 vines/ha are penalised whereas densities between 4,000/ha and 5,700/ha are awarded 50 points.

66

After taking each of the variables into account, the maximum number of points that can be awarded to any one vineyard is 1,661 with the minimum being a potential (but virtually impossible) minus score of 2,440. After a great deal of number-crunching, each holding is classified according to the total number of points as follows:

Class A: 1,200 points
Class B: 1,001–1,200 points
Class C: 801–1,000 points
Class D: 601–800 points
Class E: 401–600 points
Class F: 201–400 points

The 'A grade' vineyards are almost all located deep in the Douro valley and its tributaries upstream from Covelinhas with properties rated 'B' to be found at slightly higher altitudes. Many of the 'C grade' vineyards are situated around Régua or on the high ground north and south of the river. Vineyards categorised as D, E and F are either in the westernmost part of the region downstream from Régua or on the *planalto* around Vila Real, Murça, Meda and Lamego.

THE *BENEFÍCIO*

The vineyard classification is the basis for the *benefício* or authorisation which regulates the amount of Port that may be produced in any one year. Taking into account the previous year's sales and stocks of Port held by the shippers, the Oporto-based Instituto do Vinho do Porto (Port Wine Institute or IVP) determines the total amount of grape must that may be fortified to make Port. The amount of *benefício* (measured in pipes of 550 litres) during the 1990s is shown in Appendix III. In 1998, the maximum amount of grape must or juice that could be fortified to produce Port was 742,500 hectolitres, making a total production of around 900,000 hectolitres or 163,000 pipes of Port.

In the past the responsibility for apportioning the *benefício* among each of the 38,000 growers was undertaken by the Casa do Douro in Régua who held the *cadastro* or register of individual properties. On the basis of the vineyard classification a licence would be issued permitting the grower to produce a certain amount of Port per thousand vines. Any excess grapes would have to be fermented dry into unfortified Douro wine or sent for distillation. In 1991 this was altered to take account of the newer, mechanised vineyards planted at lower densities and the *benefício* is now allocated per hectare. Six years later in 1997 the Casa do Douro was forced to surrender most of its powers to the new interprofessional committee representing both growers and shippers. The Régua-based Commissão Interprofessional do Região Demarcada do Douro (or CIRDD pronounced rather like 'Sid' for short) has now assumed overall responsibility for regulating the *benefício* via the *communicado da vindima* or vintage communiqué, which is issued to growers in early August before each harvest. Further information on the plethora of official bodies that regulate and promote Port can be found on page 44 and in Appendix I.

VINEYARD LAYOUT

Planting a vineyard in the Douro is rather like planning a new town. Access, gradients and density all have to be considered in detail if the property is to function efficiently over a commercial life of fifty or more years. Over the past four centuries the slopes of the Douro have been sculptured into various shapes and forms according to economic circumstances. The feature that all these methods of cultivation have in common is the initial deep ploughing or ripping of the earth to create a coarse top soil roughly 1–1.3 metres in depth.

The first vineyards were planted on narrow, step-like terraces supported by retaining dry-stone walls built to a height of between 1 and 2 metres (see figure 1a). On the steepest slopes these traditional terraces or *socalcos* support no more than a single row of vines planted at a density of around 3,500 per hectare. Some of the oldest *socalcos* dating from the seventeenth century still display *pilheiros* or *boeiros*; the regularly spaced square holes in the vertical walls from which vines sprouted thereby leaving the horizontal surface free for the cultivation of cereals. When phylloxera swept through the region in the 1870s many were abandoned leaving whole hillsides of *mortórios* (mortuaries), the patterns of which are still discernible under the blanket of scrub that has taken over

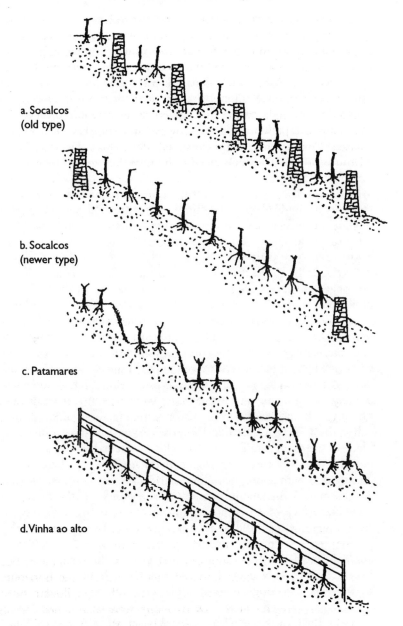

a. Socalcos
(old type)

b. Socalcos
(newer type)

c. Patamares

d. Vinha ao alto

Fig. 1. Different systems of cultivation in Douro vineyards.

in the intervening years. Although *pilheiros* have long been abandoned, many of these early step-like terraces were replanted after
phylloxera and a few examples are still in use, notably at Quinta
da Boa Vista and Quinta do Bom Retiro.

The terraces that were rebuilt following phylloxera tend to be
broader and inclined, supporting ten or more rows of vines at a
density of 5,000–6,000 per hectare (figure 1b). Photographs from
the 1900s clearly illustrate the extent of the reconstruction with as
many as twenty men armed with crowbars hacking away at the
schistous bedrock. Much of the rock was used to construct
retaining walls up to 5 metres high, some of which are unnecess-
arily thick reflecting the amount of stone that had to be removed
from the ground. The finest example of contrasting pre- and post-
phylloxera terraces can be seen on the Pinhão–São João de Pesqueira road at Quinta do Bom Retiro and Quinta da Côrte in the
Torto valley (see plate 5)

By the early 1960s these traditional methods of terracing were
no longer viable. Yields from vineyards replanted in the wake of
phylloxera were falling to uneconomic levels and with sales of Port
in the doldrums many growers either sold or abandoned their
quintas. Labour was also in chronically short supply (see page 48)
and mechanisation was the only option for the Port trade to
survive. The first bulldozers arrived in the Douro in the mid-1960s
and began carving out new contour-hugging terraces known as
patamares (figure 1c) The first of these were built at Ramos Pinto's
Quinta do Bom Retiro in conjunction with a research organisation
called the CEVD (Centro de Estudos Vitivinicolas do Douro). In
place of the high retaining walls, which impeded access and had
become so costly to construct and maintain, the *patamares* were
constructed with a steeply inclined earth ramp known as a *talude*.
Tracks angled diagonally across the slope link up the terraces,
allowing vehicles into Douro vineyards that had previously been
the preserve of man and mule. The early *patamares* were densely
planted, each terrace supporting up to three rows of vines which
could be tended by specially adapted tractors known as *enjambeurs*. This quickly proved to be completely impractical as the
enjambeurs are designed to straddle a row of vines and consequently have a high centre of gravity causing them to topple over
and roll down the slope with predictably catastrophic results. Subsequent *patamares* have therefore been planted with up to 2.2

metres between each row of vines compared to a spacing of 1.3 metres on the traditional terraces. This allows small caterpillar tractors (many of which are made by Lamborghini) to circulate between the rows of vines. Speaking rather like a professor who has just solved a particularly knotty mathematical problem, Ramos Pinto's João Nicolau de Almeida illustrates the saving in time and costs: one man can now carry out the same amount of work in ten hours that used to take fifteen men a total of fifteen hours!

The Douro's ambitious mechanisation programme gathered pace in the 1980s under the PDRITM. Offering low interest loans financed by the World Bank, growers were authorised to plant or replant up to 10 hectares of A or B grade land (mainly in the Cima Corgo) provided the vines were set out on *patamares*. For nearly a decade the Douro echoed to the sound of earth movers and explosives as whole hillsides, many abandoned in the wake of phylloxera, were carved up and replanted. Occasionally controversial and by no means as graceful as the traditional terraces with their dry-stone walls, *patamares* have been a qualified success. Some of the early *patamares* suffered from problems of erosion but this has been largely resolved by a minor modification so that the horizontal soil surface inclines gently into the hillside thereby aiding water accumulation and preventing run-off.

The main drawback of the *patamar* system is the lower planting density of around 3,500 vines per hectare. This induces greater vigour in the individual plants making the vineyard more difficult to manage as well as producing excessive shade with the consequent effects on fruit quality. In the late 1970s and early 1980s, Port shippers Ferreira and Ramos Pinto, who own adjoining *quintas* in the Torto valley, came up with a radical alternative: *vinha ao alto* (see figure 1d). By ignoring the contours and planting vines in vertical rows up and down the slope, densities of 5,000 vines per hectare can be easily attained. At Ferreira's Quinta do Seixo, tracks cross the slope at right angles to the rows of vines giving access to tractors equipped with winches to hoist a plough or the giant cannons used for spraying the vines against fungal diseases. Although *vinha ao alto* is more challenging to cultivate than the *patamar* system, João Nicolau de Almeida maintains that it produces better quality wine.

Since the PDRITM scheme was wound up in the early 1990s, a number of other prominent producers have become passionate advocates of *vinha ao alto*. Chief among them is Alistair Robertson of Taylor's, who have replanted a considerable area of Quinta de Vargellas and Quinta da Terra Feita. At the latter property, deep in the Pinhão valley, vertical planting has been successfully carried out on a slope with an angle of up to 45 per cent. In order to speed up vineyard treatments, Taylor's have dispensed with the Lamborghini tractors and replaced them by ATVs (All Terrain Vehicles), which resemble four-wheel drive motorbikes.

Much of the Douro has been transformed but over 70 per cent of the region's vineyards are still planted on traditional *socalcos*. As one grower remarked, 'the only machine in the Douro which will go up steps is a mule'. But there is one final twist in this thirty-year quest for mechanisation. Not wanting to destroy their particularly fine post-phylloxera terraces, Quinta do Noval have replanted much of their vineyard on miniature *patamares* within the old terrace walls. These provide a flat surface for a narrow, lightweight caterpillar tractor known as a 'Multijyp'. Developed in Switzerland where small, steeply inclined vineyards are the norm, this agile little vehicle can climb a couple of parallel planks to move from one terrace to the next. Still undergoing trials in 1999, this might just help to save the remaining stone terraces in the Douro which, like the buildings of a historic town, merit preservation on aesthetic grounds alone.

GRAFTING, TRAINING AND PRUNING

Ever since phylloxera ravaged European vineyards towards the end of the nineteenth century, nearly all *Vitis Vinifera* varieties have been grafted on to phylloxera-resistant American roots (see page 34). The choice of rootstock is important, to ensure compatibility between the scion and the root as well as the soil and environment. In the Douro a rootstock known locally as *Montícola* (Rupestris du Lot) proved to be the most popular because of its ability to adapt to the poor, schistous soils. This has subsequently been found to promote too much vigour in the plants, aggravating the recurring problem of excessive vegetative growth combined with poor fruit set. Since the 1950s a number of *Rupestris* x *Riparia* hybrids (R99) have been used, the best of which seem to be the R110 and 1130P, both of which are resistant to drought and help to limit the natural vigour inherent in certain Douro varieties. However, in common with so much of Portuguese viticulture, there is still a lack of scientific research into rootstock/scion compatibility.

Until the 1990s, American rootstocks were planted directly into the newly prepared soil where the vine would be allowed to establish itself before being cut back and grafted with a *Vinifera* variety. Given the fairly arid conditions in the Douro this method (known as field grafting) resulted in an unacceptable level of failures (up to 20 per cent in some places). As vines are only permitted to produce grapes for Port in the fourth year after grafting, field grafting delays the first commercial crop of grapes by a year. Nowadays most Douro vineyards are planted with pre-grafted vines, often bench-grafted in France. These are considerably more costly and require a higher initial investment but reduce the number of failures, and bench-grafting (i.e. grafting prior to planting) eventually saves time as well as money. It also makes for a stronger, more regularly shaped vine that adapts more readily to mechanisation.

When the ground has been excavated, ploughed and tilled, planting takes place at the end of the winter or early spring when soil water reserves are fully replenished. Slim posts hewn from local slate were traditionally driven in to the ground to support the row of vines but the brittle nature of the slate coupled with increasing mechanisation has led to treated wood or steel being used as a replacement. A new vineyard will normally undergo training and trellising in its second year. Unlike Australia and New Zealand, precious little research has been undertaken into the implications of vineyard canopy management; however, there is a general view that a higher vertical training leads to better photosynthesis. Two methods of training are commonly used. The first is an imperfect form of double *guyot* in which the vine is pruned back to leave two shoots with around ten buds per plant. More recently this has been superseded by a spur-pruned permanent cordon with roughly eight buds per metre. Although this is more difficult to maintain and yields less than *guyot* it has a number of advantages, chief among which is the ability to adapt to mechanised pre-pruning. Nowadays vertically planted, *vinha ao alto* vineyards tend to be pruned to a single cordon whereas vines at lower densities on *patamares* are on a bilateral cordon. The vine canopy is generally supported on three wires. Depending on the method of training, the canes or spurs are normally tied to a first wire approximately 60 cm from the ground, followed by a single or double movable wire 30–35 cm above to support the year's growth. A final wire roughly 1.6 metres from the ground helps to strengthen the trellis and provides further support for wayward tendrils. At first sight many of the Douro's vineyards appear unruly compared to the neatly trimmed hedges of vines seen in Bordeaux and Burgundy. In an attempt to achieve greater sunlight penetration within the canopy, a number of quality conscious growers now practise summer pruning which helps to ripen fruit more evenly.

Octagenarian vine

PESTS AND DISEASES

Vine diseases are rife in the Douro. Among the most insidious are oidium and mildew, both of which reached the region in the nineteenth century and are controlled respectively by sulphur dusting ('*enxofre*') and systemic sprays. The number of treatments varies according to the year and the location of the vineyard. In the Douro Superior two or three treatments will normally suffice whereas growers in the Baixo Corgo may have to spray their vineyards as many as eight times in a damp spring and still find themselves fighting a losing battle. Most of the old, densely planted vineyards have to be sprayed by hand although in 1998 (a particularly difficult year due to the unsettled, wet spring and early summer) a number of properties near Pinhão used a helicopter to treat the vines against oidium and mildew. Bunch rot (*Botritys cinerea*) is endemic throughout much of the region, especially in old, mixed vineyards with a high proportion of Tinta Amarela, which is particularly susceptible. It is controlled by spraying with *calda bordelesa* (copper sulphate known as 'Bordeaux mixture'). But rot is most damaging when induced by rain late in the growing season by which time it is often too late to spray as chemical residues might find their way into the wine. The harvest in 1993 was notorious for producing poor, pale wines, frequently tainted by rot.

The grape-moth (Cochylis and Eudemis) can cause severe damage in the vineyard, destroying buds or boring its way into ripe grapes, bringing on bunch rot. In the Douro Superior a leaf hopper known as *Cicadela* has begun to be a serious problem at some vineyards, damaging the leaves of the vine and reducing levels of photosynthesis. Tinta Roriz and Tinto Cão seem to be particularly susceptible. Leaf hoppers are also the vectors for bacterial diseases, among them Pierce's Disease and *Flavescence Dorée*, neither of which have thankfully been identified so far in the Douro.

Viral diseases introduced from the rootstock are a continuing problem, frequently reducing yields and delaying the ripening of fruit. *Enrolamento* or leafroll virus seems to be most acute in dry years. The deep autumnal colours that are frequently admired by visitors to the Douro at the end of the growing season are a manifestation of the problem. A co-ordinated programme to elim-inate viral diseases from the Douro's vine stock is sorely needed.

At the opposite end of the scale from these microscopic pests and diseases are the marauding wild boar that frequently venture into the vineyards eating grapes or tearing at young vines. In a region where so much of the wildlife has been shot, poached or pilfered, hunting wild boar is a sport which continues with understandable impunity.

FERTILISERS AND HERBICIDES

Fertilisers are applied to correct the soil balance before planting, with the emphasis on phosphorous, nitrogen, calcium, boron and organic material. Thereafter most growers practise a three/four year rotation applying both organic and inorganic fertilisers. Agro-chemical salesmen have been working hard in the Douro. Perhaps viewing fertilisers as a panacea for low yields some growers (including one or two major shippers) undoubtedly over-fertilised their vineyards in the 1980s, thereby upsetting the vegetation balance to the detriment of their wines.

The use of herbicides has increased dramatically with the con-struction of *patamares* in the 1970s and 1980s. Although weeds have to be hand-picked for the first two years, Mediterranean arbutus shrubs quickly take root on the *taludes* and need to be controlled. The need to apply systemic sprays and herbicides makes organic cultivation almost impossible on all but the highest, well-ventilated *vinha ao alto* slopes. Both Quinta do Infantado and Casal dos Jordões produce organic Port and Fonseca Guimaraens maintains two hectares of organic vineyard at the top of Quinta do Panascal. They restrict their treatments to *enxofre* (sulphur) and *calda bordelesa* and use pheromones to trap insects. With the absence of chemical fertilisers, Fonseca's organic plot is noticeably less vigorous than the surrounding vineyards. Weeds which die back naturally in the dry summer months are picked by hand although the tough arbutus shrubs which survive the whole year present a particular problem.

IRRIGATION

Technically forbidden throughout the European Union, some form of irrigation is none the less essential in order to establish a vineyard in the Douro. Young vines are often watered by hand. Hampered in the early 1990s by recurring drought, some growers in the Douro Superior have installed drip irrigation on an experimental basis. At the time of writing, all the white varieties planted at Cockburn's Vilariça vineyard are irrigated.

GRAPE VARIETIES

Ask a Douro farmer how much of this or that grape variety he has growing in his vineyard and he will probably shrug his shoulders and utter the immortal words *não sei* – I don't know! He is not being coy or secretive; in most instances he really won't know. The reason for this is that most Portuguese vineyards have traditionally been set out in a haphazard fashion with a bewildering number of grape varieties interplanted amongst each another. In the Douro where as many as ninety different varieties have been sanctioned at any one time, this means that there are sometimes twenty or more different grapes growing cheek-by-jowl on the same small vineyard plot.

This viticultural anarchy has continually hampered research. Although a local authority named Ruy Fernandes described the best grapes growing in the Lamego region in the sixteenth century, by 1853 Baron Forrester complained that 'an infinite number of different wines could be produced in the Douro if only there could be a separation of the grape varieties'. The situation was further compounded by the arrival of phylloxera. Disease-resistant American vines intended for use as rootstock were also interplanted by small growers seeking an increase in yield, and at the same time a handful of the more troublesome European *Vinifera* varieties were probably rendered extinct. Writing in 1876 when the phylloxera outbreak was at its height, the Visconde de Villa Maior lists a total of twenty-eight different grapes commonly planted in the Douro at the time. It includes some intriguing names, among them two red grapes Pé-agudo ('pointed foot') and Entreverde ('green between', so-called because it suffered from uneven ripening) that have long since left the local lexicon. Other varieties described in detail by Villa Maior include Alvarelhão, Mourisco, Mureto (*sic*) and Tinta Castelloa (probably Periquita/Castelão Frances), all of which are high-yielding varieties and have generally fallen from favour today. But as Ruy Fernandes had already observed as far back as 1531, 'if some varieties fail to yield well in a particular year the others would compensate'. The interplanting of numerous different types of grapes was therefore the insurance method used by farmers to counteract the Douro's variable and notoriously unpredictable climate.

The post-phylloxera predicament was complicated by the huge number of synonyms applied to native varieties. Villa Maior remarks that 'it must be born in mind that the same kinds [of vine] are grown in different places by different names; and what still more thwarts the study of ampelography is that the same name is often used in different places to denote very dissimilar kinds'. The extent of this confusion was quantified by Pedro Bravo and Duarte de Oliveira forty years later. Travelling around the country they found a total of around 900 different names for grapes growing in Portugal at the time. In a manual entitled *Viticultura Moderna* published in 1916 Bravo and Oliveira readily admit that many of these are in fact the same varieties with a number of different synonyms and complain about the lack of research to date.

The first recorded attempt at any serious varietal research in the Douro was undertaken in the 1920s by Dick Yeatman (of Taylor, Fladgate & Yeatman) at Quinta de Vargellas. Working in isolation he planted a number of varieties in separate rows and was able to conduct varietal vinifications a decade later, the results of which were never divulged. John Smithes, a close friend of Dick Yeatman, began block-planting separate grape varieties at Cockburn's Quinta do Tua in the 1930s and this subsequently provided the material for the Vilariça project in the late 1970s. An edict was issued banning the use of poor quality American vine species for Port in 1935 but no further attempt was made to co-ordinate research into Douro grape varieties for another thirty years. At the same time as mechanisation began to be an issue in the late 1960s, the CEVD (Centro de Estudos Vitivinicolas do Douro) planted a number of experimental plots strategically placed in the three different sub-regions of the Douro. Based on empirical information gathered from some of the leading Port tasters and blenders of the day, ten different red grape varieties were selected for study. After five years of intensive investigation led by José Rosas and João Nicolau de Almeida of Ramos Pinto, five red varieties were selected in 1981. Touriga Naçional, Touriga Francesa, Tinta Barroca, Tinta Roriz and Tinto Cão became known as the *top cinco* (top five). Under the PDRITM or World Bank Scheme of the 1980s, 2,500 hectares of the five varieties (mainly Touriga Francesa and Tinta Roriz) were subsequently batch planted in single varietal plots. It is perhaps not a coincidence that these were among the grapes that had been selected by Dick Yeatman sixty years earlier.

Since the varietal breakthrough in the early 1980s, viticultural research in the Douro has been advanced by a privately funded association known as ADVID (Associação para o Desenvolvimento da Viticultura Duriense). Established by a number of leading Port shippers in 1982, ADVID's principal objective is the modernisation of viticulture in the Douro leading to an improvement in the overall quality of wine. At the time of writing there are ninety-six members including most of the leading single estates. ADVID's brief is wide-ranging and covers research into mechanisation, methods of cultivation, soil erosion, disease, rootstocks, grape varieties and yield. In the case of the latter, ADVID has a number of climatic stations in the Douro (one of which is on top of the giant Sandeman don on the opposite side of the river from Régua) where pollen is monitored during the flowering in an attempt to predict yields. The results are announced at the beginning of August shortly before the annual *benefício* is issued in the *communicado da vindima* (communiqué issued by the IVP before the start of the harvest).

There are currently nearly ninety different red and white grape varieties sanctioned for planting in the Douro, twenty-nine of which are 'recommended' as opposed to the remainder which are merely 'authorised'. Some strange names are still to be found on the 'authorised' list, among them a white grape called Branco Sem Nome ('white without name') and another entitled Medock (*sic*). There are nearly as many white varieties as red although most of the attention in recent years has been focused on the 'famous five' to the exclusion of other potentially interesting grapes (see below). A programme of clonal selection was instigated at Cockburn's Vilariça vineyard and Ferreira's Quinta do Seixo in the early 1980s and this has subsequently been taken up by the University of

Trás-os-Montes and Alto Douro (UTAD) at Vila Real. Although a dozen varieties are being studied, the main emphasis has been on the capricious Touriga Naçional with the object of balancing commercial yields with acceptably high sugar levels. The selection of ten Touriga Naçional clones to date has brought about an increase in yield of over 30 per cent. It remains to be seen whether Portugal in the new millennium makes the same mistake as France in the 1960s and 1970s when clones were frequently selected on the basis of quantity, often at the expense of quality.

The painstaking viticultural research that has been undertaken since the 1970s has by-passed the majority of growers in the Douro who continue to tend their tiny plots in much the same way as they did in Grandfather's day. An estimated 70 per cent of all the vineyards in the Douro are still planted with the time-honoured pick and mix – hence the shrug of the shoulders when you ask a question that would be fairly straightforward elsewhere. But the importance of many of these old, gnarled interplanted vineyards should not be underestimated. Although different grape varieties continue to be harvested at varying (uneven) degrees of ripeness, old vines still provide the core for the finest, most concentrated Vintage Ports just as they did in earlier outstanding years like 1927, 1945, 1963 and 1966. However, with mechanisation unfeasible and yields steadily declining, many older, mixed vineyards are increasingly less economic. In order to justify its continued existence at Quinta de Vargellas, Taylor has started to bottle Vinha Velha (Old Vineyard) as a separate lot (see page 238).

Apart from the *top cinco*, most Douro varieties are still something of an unknown. White grapes, in particular, have been largely ignored and still tend to be found in older vineyards interplanted among red varieties. For this reason many of the profiles below are necessarily based on empirical observation rather than on co-ordinated scientific research.

The following grape varieties are listed in order of their relative importance in the vineyard. A full list of both 'recommended' and 'authorised' varieties may be found in Appendix IV.

Touriga Francesa
Although by no means the most talked about, Touriga Francesa is much the most widely planted grape variety in the Douro accounting for around 20 per cent of the total vineyard area. Of the famous five, it is the least well researched. Touriga Francesa flourishes on warmer south-facing slopes and is favoured by growers for its relatively consistent yields (roughly 2.5 kg per vine). Like many Douro varieties, it suffers from excess vigour and produces grapes with low sugar levels if yields are too high or the local climatic conditions are less than ideal. At high altitudes sugar levels struggle to reach 11 degrees baumé. When it reaches the winery, Touriga Francesa requires plenty of work to extract both colour and tannin from the relatively thick skins. It is highly prized for its aromatic qualities, lending a floral (some say 'violety') character to the blend. Touriga Francesa rarely packs the same punch as Touriga Naçional but none the less it is valued by both growers and shippers as a good all-round grape lending both structure, up-front fruit and elegance to Port. Despite its name, there is no ampelographic evidence that Touriga Francesa has any connection with France.

Tinta Roriz
One of the few varieties with a pedigree outside Portugal, Tinta Roriz has gathered a bewildering number of names on its travels round the Iberian Peninsula. Known in Spain as Tempranillo, it probably reached the Douro via the Alentejo in central-southern Portugal where it continues to acknowledge its Spanish heritage under the title Aragonez. Although Roriz has been in the Douro since the early nineteenth century (presumably having been planted at Quinta do Roriz), it is not listed by Villa Maior as an important pre-phylloxera variety. It now stands in second position behind Touriga Francesa taking up about 10 per cent of the total vineyard area. Tinta Roriz is particularly favoured by growers in the Cima Corgo and Douro Superior where it vies with Touriga Francesa as the most popular variety. Relatively easy to grow (it sprouts vertically), Roriz has a tendency to over-produce and quality can vary alarmingly. It performs best in those years when yields are inherently low, producing wines that combine tight, firm fruit with

finesse and length. However, in a high-yielding year like 1996 Roriz-based wines tend to be rather pale, thin and weedy.

Tinta Barroca

Just behind Roriz in the popularity stakes, Tinta Barroca tends to be planted at higher altitudes or on cooler north-facing slopes in the Cima Corgo where it generally yields well (2.5 kg per vine). Of the five main varieties it is generally the first to ripen, but with a thin skin Barroca is very susceptible to extreme heat and berries raisinise easily on the vine. As a result it tends to produce must that is very rich in sugar attaining a baumé reading of 15 or 16 degrees when planted on a south-facing slope. Planted in the right situation, Barroca produces deep-coloured, supple, well-structured wines which frequently have a distinctly rustic, earthy character. It is a variety much favoured by the Symington family, who have planted substantial quantities at Quinta do Bomfim and on the higher reaches of Quinta da Cavadinha in the Pinhão valley. Formerly known as Boca da Mina ('mouth of the spring'), Tinta Grossa and Tinta Gorda ('fat red'), it is one of the few Port grapes that is planted in any quantity outside Portugal having made a successful foray into South Africa.

Tinta Amarela

Excluded from the famous five, Tinta Amarela is nevertheless very highly regarded in the Douro where it represents around 8 per cent of the total vine stock. But Amarela is a notoriously tetchy grape, very susceptible to apical growth and disease. Due to its tightly packed bunches, Tinta Amarela is particularly prone to rot in damp weather and choice of location is therefore crucial to its success. A canopy management programme would surely help. It is surprising that so much Tinta Amarela has been planted in the Baixo Corgo where it forms the major part of many old mixed vineyards. On well-exposed, arid soils in the Cima Corgo and Douro Superior Tinta Amarela produces extremely fine, fragrant wines with great balance and poise. Tinta Amarela has fared more successfully in the Alentejo where, under the name Trincadeira, it has quickly become established as one of Portugal's leading red wine grapes.

Mourisco

Wine-makers tend to have a love-hate relationship with Mourisco. It is mostly hate because the fat, pale-coloured Mourisco resembles a table grape rather than a wine variety. It is very difficult to pollinate and is therefore subject to poor fruit set and low yields unless interplanted with other varieties. As a result there are few instances where Mourisco is planted on its own but it crops up frequently among plots of old vines and therefore makes up around 5 per cent of the total vineyard area. Cockburn are one of the few fans of Mourisco and have planted a significant amount at their Vilariça vineyard in the Douro Superior. Although it produces relatively pale-coloured wine, it is rich in sugar and provides a good, aromatic base for old Tawnies. Villa Maior was also a fan, describing Mourisco 'as one of the finest and most precious kinds cultivated in the Douro'.

Malvasia Preta
The name 'malvasia' has been attached to so many Portuguese grapes that it is difficult to separate fact from fiction. No one in the Douro ever mentions Malvasia Preta ('Black Malvasia') but it is clearly a significant variety in old, mixed vineyards as it still represents around 4 per cent of the total vine stock.

Tinta Carvalha
Just behind Malvasia Preta in the popularity stakes, Tinta Carvalha is favoured by small growers for its high yields and therefore makes up a significant proportion of older, mixed vineyards in the Baixo Corgo. Although it apparently has some aromatic qualities, on its own Tinta Carvalha generally produces pale, washed out wine.

Touriga Naçional
Of all the grapes planted in the Douro, Touriga Naçional has the most noble pedigree and is certainly the variety most talked about by shippers. It therefore comes as something of a shock to find that it only accounts for a meagre 2 per cent of the region's vine stock. Often confused in the past with other Tourigas (Villa Maior mentions three), Touriga Naçional's praises have been sung by wine-makers since the eighteenth century. Its problem is that it is so utterly disliked by growers. Such was its unpopularity that in the 1970s Touriga Naçional would have barely registered among Port wine grapes. It is only since the PDRITM project of the 1980s that Touriga Naçional has made a welcome come-back, especially in the Cima Corgo and Douro Superior. The reasons for its unpopu-

larity are multiple but chief among them are poor fruit set and low yield. In the late 1970s when varietal planting began to take place Touriga Naçional commonly produced a measly 0.5–0.8 kg per vine but with a programme of clonal selection yields have increased to 1–1.5 kg (compared with 2.5 kg/vine for Touriga Francesa). Touriga Naçional continues to suffer from excess vigour and is very susceptible to poor weather at the time of flowering. Yields are consequently extremely variable. For example, a 5-hectare plot of Touriga Naçional at Quinta do Crasto produced forty pipes of wine in 1996 (220 hectolitres), twenty-five pipes in 1997 (138 hl), but just six pipes in 1998 (33 hl). Provided the grapes are picked at the correct moment (Touriga Naçional easily over-ripens), its small thick-skinned berries produce the darkest and most concentrated of Ports: deep, dense and focused with cast-iron backbone. At prominent *quintas* in the Cima Corgo and Douro Superior, Touriga Naçional now makes up between 20 and 30 per cent of the vineyard. Miguel Corte Real, the director at Cockburn with responsibility for vineyards, sums up Touriga Naçional succinctly as 'an oenologist's' rather than viticulturalist's grape'.

Touriga Naçional is the most thoroughly researched of all Portuguese grape varieties and significant quantities have been planted in Dão, Bairrada, Estremadura and the Alentejo. At the time of writing, the University of Trás-os-Montes and Alto Douro (UTAD) is conducting a comprehensive study into the effects of different *terroirs* on Touriga Naçional. Some Touriga Naçional has also been planted abroad; however, nearly all the so-called 'Touriga' used for fortified wines in California and Australia is Touriga Francesa.

Rufete

This is a productive early-ripening variety that still makes up a significant proportion of old, mixed vineyards in the Douro, representing around one per cent of the total vine stock. It produces wines with little colour, lacking in structure and volume. Rufete is the same as Tinta Pinheira in the Dão region.

Tinto Cão

Despite being one of the oldest established of all Port grapes, the Douro's 'red dog' was almost driven to extinction in the post-phylloxera era. Tinto Cão is even more challenging to grow than Touriga Naçional and, until it joined the ranks of the famous five, it was frequently overlooked by growers who became frustrated by the small size of the bunches and continually low yields. Tinto Cão is thankfully making a modest come-back (although it barely registers in percentage terms), mainly due to larger shippers who are intrigued by its capacity to produce long-lasting wines. It ripens late but needs to be picked at exactly the right time to achieve the delicate balance of alcohol and acidity for which Tinto Cão has become renowned. Neither the deepest in colour or the most showy of the major Port varieties, at properties like Taylor's Quinta da Terra Feita and Cockburn's Vilariça it now makes up around 4 per cent of the vineyard.

Souzão
'Colour, acid and more acid' is the way in which one grower described this red-fleshed grape, which forms a major part of Quinta do Noval's legendary Naçional vineyard. It is unquestionably the same variety as Vinhão, which is grown in the adjoining Minho province of Portugal for rasping, inky-red Vinho Verde. Souzão is also grown in South Africa and California. In the Douro it is mostly planted in old, interplanted vineyards and few growers have much idea of its attributes apart from being a useful variety to bolster colour, perhaps making up for Mourisco!

Alvarelhão
Formerly much planted in the *altos* (high lands) around Vila Real, Alvarelhão produces light, pale red wines, which represent something of a transition between Vinho Verde and the Douro. No doubt Mateus Rosé (much of which was originally sourced from this area) used to include a high percentage of Alvarelhão. The grape has now fallen from favour although it still exists in old, mixed vineyards north of the Douro. There are also pockets of Alvarelhão in California where it is more highly regarded.

Bastardo
Vigorous, early-ripening variety favoured by growers prior to phylloxera. Villa Maior notes that it often became ripe at the beginning of July! Small amounts of Bastardo remain in old, mixed vineyards although its only attributes today seem to be low acidity and high sugar levels. It is also susceptible to rot in damp weather.

Cornifesto
A productive variety grown in old vineyards throughout Trás-os-Montes producing light, inconsequential wines.

Tinta de Barca
An unfashionable grape occasionally found in the hot country towards the Spanish border where it produces a distinctive, concentrated style of wine. Interestingly, it forms around 25 per cent of the blend for Quinta de Vargellas's Vinha Velha.

Tinta Francisca
Not to be confused with Touriga Francesa, Tinta Francisca is thought to be true to its name having originated in Burgundy as Pinot Noir. There are two stories as to its genesis, neither of which can be proved. One asserts that it was brought to Portugal by Henry of Burgundy in the eleventh century, the other that it was sent from Burgundy for Robert Archibald, the founder of Quinta do Roriz (although it seems more likely that this is the Tinta Roriz – see above). More ampelographic evidence is clearly required.

WHITE GRAPES

Most white varieties in the Douro are interplanted with red grapes. Consequently, much less is known about their individual characteristics.

Codega
Formerly known as Malvasia Grossa ('fat Malvasia'), Codega is the most planted white grape in the Douro accounting for around 30 per cent of all the white varieties in the region. Large quantities were traditionally planted in the Douro Superior. It yields well (2–3 kg per vine) and produces a soft, flat, low acid wine that forms the basis for White Port. Codega is thought to be the same as Siria in Beira Alta immediately to the south of the Douro and Roupeiro in the Alentejo where its reputation is somewhat higher.

Malvasia Fina
There are many so-called 'Malvasias' in Portugal, some of which are undoubtedly descended from the distinguished Mediterranean grape of the same name and others are entirely false. Malvasia

Fina ('fine' Malvasia), the second most planted white grape in the Douro, is the same as Assario in Dão. It is a particularly unstable variety which readily mutates and the wine varies greatly from one clone to another. It is also very susceptible to oidium and poor fruit set in spring making yields extremely variable. Villa Maior records that 'in certain places its fruit becomes unfit for wine making'. With a soft, fat, vaguely honeyed character, the wine is better than that from the Codega but could hardly be described as 'fine'. It used to be known as Malvasia de Passa because of its tendency to raisinise on the vine.

Malvasia Rei
By no means 'King' of the Malvasias, Malvasia Rei accounts for around 14 per cent of the white varieties in the Douro and produces huge quantities of bland wine. It is no longer 'recommended' but merely 'authorised'.

Rabigato
Named after the elongated shape of its bunches, Rabigato ('cat's tail') is one of the better white grapes in the Douro making up about 12 per cent of the white varieties. It yields well (up to 3 kg per vine) and tends to be planted at higher altitudes where it is favoured by wine-makers for the fresh acidity that it contributes to White Port. In southern Portugal it is known as Rabo de Ovelha ('ewe's tail').

Gouveio
None other than Madeira's Verdelho, Gouveio is one of the best and most established white varieties in the Douro. It yields less than the others (hence its relegation to fifth position in the popularity stakes) but produces balanced wines with good levels of natural acidity. Gouveio is increasingly favoured for dry white Douro wines.

Moscatel
A number of different types of Moscatel (Muscat) are planted in the Douro, principally on the higher land around the towns of Favaios and Alijó. Villa Maior names a variety of Muscats: Moscatel Branco, Moscatel de Jesus, Moscatel Roxo and Moscatel Preto (the latter two being pink and black respectively). Although

these may still remain, the officially recognised form of Muscat is 'Moscatel Galego'. In all probability, this is the Muscat of Alexandria that is planted widely throughout the Mediterranean and tends to produce a coarser style of wine than the Muscat à Petits Grains. Muscat continues to be an important component in White Port or may be bottled as a varietal fortified wine known as Moscatel de Favaios.

Viosinho
Little is known about this low-yielding variety that is capable of producing some high quality wines. According to João Nicolau de Almeida, who has planted Viosinho at Quinta dos Bons Ares, its only real drawback is a lack of acidity and it therefore performs better at high altitudes. Viosinho is one of the few white varieties that is currently undergoing an extensive programme of clonal selection.

Arinto
Known in the neighbouring Vinho Verde region as Paderná, Arinto is not nearly as highly regarded in the Douro as it is in the south of Portugal. However, given its ability to hang on to natural acidity whatever the weather, Arinto is a potentially interesting variety for planting in warmer parts of the region.

Fernão Pires
One of Portugal's most adaptable varieties, Fernão Pires grows in the Ribatejo and Bairrada (as Maria Gomes) where it forms the basis for sparkling white wines. Planted on the *altos* around Lamego, it is used in the Douro for both sparkling wines and White Port.

OTHER WHITE GRAPES IN THE DOURO

Esgana Cão ('dog strangler')
Folgosão
Boal
Cercial
Donzelinho Branco
Samarrinho

THE CONCEPT OF THE *QUINTA*

The building block of the Douro is the *quinta*. Applied to everything from a modest farm to a large country estate, it is a word
that almost defies translation and is probably best thought of
merely as an area of agricultural land. It is impossible to quantify
the number of *quintas* in the Douro but suffice to say that in the
late 1990s there were 33,000 growers in the Douro farming nearly
140,000 holdings. Over 90 per cent of these are less than one
hectare in area.

The extreme fragmentation of land holdings in the Douro is the
logical consequence of Portugal's Napoleonic laws of inheritance
whereby all offspring are entitled to inherit a share of the family
estate. In the relatively densely populated Baixo Corgo, there has
been a greater tendency to split vineyard holdings among families
than in the more remote Cima Corgo or the Douro Superior. As a
result some of the larger properties in the Cima Corgo may have
as many as fifty or sixty absentee shareholders, most of whom take
absolutely no part in the day-to-day running of the *quinta* but
cause considerable problems when it comes to taking strategic
management decisions. This helps to explain the unkempt look of
so many family-owned houses in the Douro.

It is fair to say that the popular image of a Douro *quinta* has
come about because of trade and press visits to some of the more
grandiose properties belonging to the major Port shippers. These
estates, usually between 30 and 150 hectares in extent, make up a
minute 0.01 per cent of the total number of holdings in the Douro
and their overall importance has therefore been exaggerated. Most
quintas are much more modest affairs with the *adega* (winery),
armazém (storage) and rustic dwelling all combined within a single
structure. The building would invariably be built into the slope
with the *adega* on the upper level feeding the *armazém* below by
gravity. The living accommodation is typically above the *armazém*,
providing simple accommodation for the *caseiro* (foreman) and his
wife, who are employed to run the *quinta*. Many of the smaller
properties have neither house nor winery and the owner and his
or her family will tend the vines from a nearby village. The heady,
but often rank smell of fermenting grapes and young Port used to
be all-pervading in Douro villages at harvest time, but most of

these small growers now sell their grapes directly to a Port shipper or the local co-operative.

Many of the larger and more remote *quintas* are almost self-sustaining communities, farming their own pigs and poultry, growing vegetables and supporting as many as three or four families all the year round. Most have their own chapel located either alongside the house (as at Quinta do Porto, Quinta do Seixo) or out in the vineyard (Quinta da Roêda). Two outlying properties, Quinta de Vargellas and Quinta do Vesúvio, even have their own railway station.

Harvester's kitchen, Quinta do Bomfim

Depending on the time of year, Port *quintas* provide employment for an army of labourers rising to thirty or forty people during the harvest. Like most armies, the Douro marches on its stomach and the kitchen is the focus of the *quinta*. Usually the largest room in the house, the cavernous Douro kitchen still has medieval appeal. Food in the form of a hearty 'all-in-one' soup or stew is cooked in a huge black pot, which is sometimes hoisted by means of a pulley or crane on to an open wood fire. There is a hole in the roof for the smoke to escape. Children scream and squawk on the floor, especially during the winter months when the kitchen is the only warm place to be. One of the few modern concessions is the television, which has the capacity to bring this industrious scene to a virtual standstill when the latest episode of a melodramatic Brazilian *telenovela* (soap opera) starts.

In spite of the political changes that have taken place in Portugal since the revolution of 1974–5, the larger Douro *quintas* are still resolutely hierarchical. The *patrão* or owner will eat in his own comparatively comfortable quarters, usually well away from the hubbub of the kitchen. The *artistas* or skilled workers have another dining room, simply furnished with a long wooden table and bench seats. The remaining *pessoal* (staff) either eat outside at a huge stone table or in a spartan *refectório* (refectory). Most major *quintas* have also built *cardenhos* (dormitories) to accommodate the *roga* or gang of pickers for the duration of the harvest. The *cardenhos*, densely packed with bunk beds, are frequently the scene of many a melodrama in their own right. With the sexes separated from each other by a flimsy wall or a wooden screen, it is not unusual for affairs of the heart to come to a head in the middle of vintage. Although generally good-humoured, with a few glasses of *aguardente* passions are occasionally inflamed. At one *quinta* the police had to be called out to intervene in a violent domestic dispute in which a man was stabbed for making eyes at another's girlfriend.

Quintas enjoyed more independence in the nineteenth century than they have for most of the twentieth. Properties like Quinta da Boa Vista, Roncão, Romaneira, Roriz and Zimbro were much better known in the 1870s than they are today. Henry Vizetelly remarked at the time that the house of Feuerheerd maintained 'certain of its vintage wines from particular *quintas* intact.' Following the devastation wreaked on the region by phylloxera, vineyard yields fell to such low levels that shippers were compelled to blend wines from a number of properties. Many prominent *quintas* were therefore absorbed into declared Vintage blends and lost their independent status as a result. Legislation followed in 1927 which also discriminated against the individual *quinta* (see page 43).

Although there were notable exceptions like Quinta do Noval which retained its independence throughout, the Douro *quinta* only began to recapture lost ground in the early 1960s. Taylor's launched 1958 Quinta de Vargellas as a single-*quinta* Vintage Port and other shippers followed suit, using the *quinta* designation to distinguish between fully declared (blended) vintages and good intervening years. Independent *quintas* were given a fillip following Portugal's accession to the European Union in 1986 when the monopolistic legislation introduced in 1927 was finally revoked. For the first time in nearly sixty years, individual *quintas* were given direct access to overseas markets thereby allowing them to circumvent the major shippers. At the time of writing the single *quinta* is still on the ascendant with properties like Quinta do Crasto and Quinta de la Rosa becoming leading shippers of both Port and Douro wine under their own steam.

Granite chapel, São Salvador do Mundo

PROMINENT *QUINTAS*

Listed in geographical order from the Baixo Corgo in the west through the Cima Corgo to the Douro Superior in the east, the following prominent *quintas* are the keystones of the Douro. Where possible I have attempted to indicate the quality and style of the wine produced by the *quinta* with reference to the variations in the local *terroir* discussed earlier in the chapter. Wines from *quintas* that have become important exporters in their own right are covered in more detail in Chapters 5 and 6.

In order to encourage tourism in the Douro, a number of official entities came together in the 1990s to promote the Port Wine Route. Modelled on the French idea of the *route du vin* (although operated without any of the Gallic flair and efficiency) a number of *quintas* are now open to visitors. Apart from Fonseca's Quinta do Panascal, which is open every day of the week except Saturday and Sunday, most properties require an appointment. Telephone numbers have a habit of changing but the *quintas* that form part of the Port Wine Route are indicated (*) and addresses are given below. The grading system of Douro vineyards is explained in detail on pages 64–7.

BAIXO CORGO

Quinta do Côtto* Cidadelhe, 5040 Mesão Frio   Grade C
One of the most impressive estates in the Baixo Corgo, Quinta do Côtto was among the first properties to export their own Port taking advantage of the change in legislation from 1986 onwards. The fine eighteenth-century house is now the headquarters for shippers Montez Champalimaud and is being restored to receive paying guests as a *turismo d'habitacão* (see pages 199 and 257).

Quinta de Santa Julia*, Loureiro, 5050 Peso da Régua   C/D
With a view over Régua, the Douro and the valley of the Rodo, this immaculate rated property belongs to Eduardo da Costa Seixas, an ardent monarchist who doubles up as chief taster and blender at Sandeman. In spite of its rather lowly rating, I can vouch for the fact that the estate is capable of producing some impressive wines having tasted a Port from Santa Julia dating from the nineteenth century. Nowadays the Port is sold to Sandeman and in good years may form part of a vintage *lote* (blend). The remainder of the production is made into red and white Douro wine bottled under the name of the *quinta*. A small house has been built in the grounds to receive paying guests.

Quinta das Quartas*, Lugar das Quartas, Fontelas 5050 Peso da Régua
Owned by the Poças family since 1923, Quinta das Quartas has subsequently been developed as the wine-making and storage

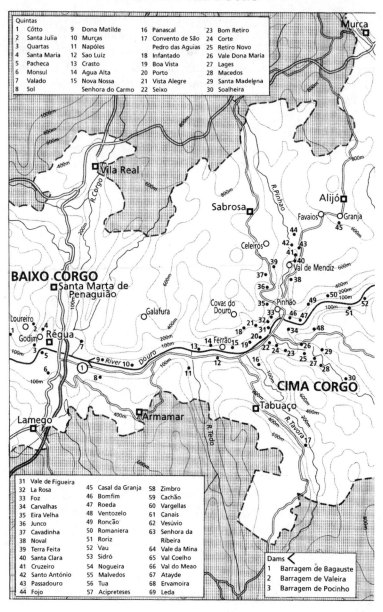

Quintas

1	Côtto	9	Dona Matilde	16	Panascal	23	Bom Retiro
2	Santa Julia	10	Murças	17	Convento de São	24	Corte
3	Quartas	11	Napóles		Pedro das Aguias	25	Retiro Novo
4	Santa Maria	12	Sao Luíz	18	Infantado	26	Vale Dona Maria
5	Pacheca	13	Crasto	19	Boa Vista	27	Lages
6	Monsul	14	Agua Alta	20	Porto	28	Macedos
7	Valado	15	Nova Nossa	21	Vista Alegre	29	Santa Madelena
8	Sol		Senhora do Carmo	22	Seixo	30	Soalheira

31	Vale de Figueira	45	Casal da Granja	58	Zimbro
32	La Rosa	46	Bomfim	59	Cachão
33	Foz	47	Roeda	60	Vargellas
34	Carvalhas	48	Ventozelo	61	Canais
35	Eira Velha	49	Roncão	62	Vesúvio
36	Junco	50	Romaniera	63	Senhora da
37	Cavadinha	51	Roriz		Ribeira
38	Noval	52	Vau	64	Vale da Mina
39	Terra Feita	53	Sidró	65	Val Coelho
40	Santa Clara	54	Nogueira	66	Val do Meao
41	Cruzeiro	55	Malvedos	67	Atayde
42	Santo António	56	Tua	68	Ervamoira
43	Passadouro	57	Acipreteses	69	Leda
44	Fojo				

Dams
1 Barragem de Bagauste
2 Barragem de Valeira
3 Barragem de Pocinho

Map 2. The Douro, showing prominent *quintas*.

94

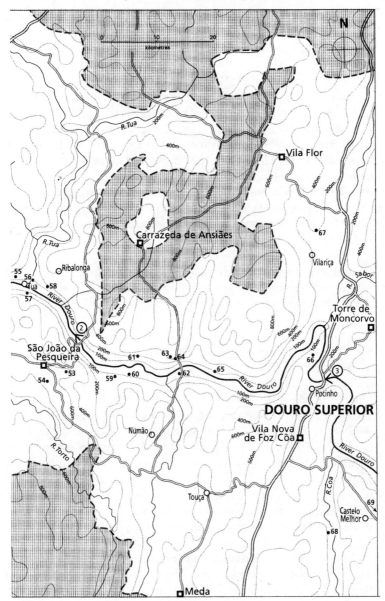

centre for the family firm of Poças Junior. The company also owns Quinta de Santa Barbera at Valdigem facing the mouth of the River Corgo on the opposite side of the Douro.

Quinta de Santa Maria*, Godim, 5050 Peso da Régua   C

Although nearly consumed by Régua's dreary urban sprawl, Quinta de Santa Maria still retains a vestige of its rural past. The property was acquired by Cockburn in 1973, not for its vineyards which are of relatively minor importance, but as a strategic site for storing large volumes of wine. The huge temperature-controlled *armazém* behind the house has been furnished with wooden vats or *balseiros*, originally from Guinness in Dublin but latterly belonging to English cider-makers Showerings. These are now used for ageing the large volumes of wine that make up Cockburn's Special Reserve and Ruby Ports.

Quinta da Pacheca*, Cambres, 5100 Lamego   C/D

A huge Sandeman don marks Quinta da Pacheca on the opposite side of the river from the centre of Régua. This largely flat property belongs to the Serpa Pimentel family, which produces Port for Cockburn and bottles its own Douro wine under the *quinta* label. Sandeman also maintains a huge storage facility on another part of the estate.

Quinta do Monsul, Cambres   C

This extensive property on the south side of the river has one of the longest documented histories of any in the Douro, dating back to the time of Portugal's first king, Afonso Henriques, who owned it until 1163. It also boasts the first 'Rua 25 de Abril' in Portugal, named not after the military coup of 1974, but after the marriage of one of its owners in 1881. The vineyard is mainly planted with white grapes. Production is either sold to Taylor or Sogrape, or made into Douro wine at Quinta do Valado (below).

Quinta do Valado*, Vilarinho dos Freires, 5050 Peso da Régua C

This estate, which straddles the River Corgo just upstream from Régua, was the first property in Dona Antónia Ferreira's Douro empire. It was bought by her father, António Bernardo Ferreira in 1818 and has remained with the family ever since. The production from Valado's 64 hectares of vineyard is split almost equally between Port (for Ferreira) and an impressive Douro wine which is bottled under the *quinta*'s own label. With its distinctive yellow-ochre buildings, the property is easy to identify from the Régua–Valarinho dos Freires road.

Quinta do Sol, near Bagauste   No *Cadastro* grade

This landfill site from the dam at Bagauste can hardly be called a conventional '*quinta*' as it does not have a single vine. But since the Symington family bought Sol in the mid-eighties, it has become one of the most strategically significant locations in the Douro. Well placed to serve growers in both the Baixo and Cima Corgo, the huge stainless-steel winery built in 1996 is now the main vinification centre for Dow, Graham, Warre, Smith Woodhouse, Quarles Harris and Gould Campbell. Together they are the largest single shippers of Port. With the capacity to process 72 tons of grapes (the equivalent of 100 pipes) per hour during the height of vintage, Sol has relieved pressure on the Symington's Quinta do Bomfim winery (below). The so-called 'Bomfim queue' of tractors and trailers, which in the early 1990s frequently stretched back through the centre of Pinhão, is now happily a thing of the past.

Quinta Dona Matilde, Bagauste   B

With a fine view of Quinta do Sol and the Bagauste dam, Dona Matilde is also occasionally known by its old, much less pronounceable, title of Enxodreiro. The property was renamed after it was purchased by the Barros family in 1927, who rebuilt the house and used the *quinta* as a family retreat. The predominantly south-facing vineyards were substantially replanted in the 1990s. The wine is made at Barros Almeida's Quinta de São Luíz *adega* (see below), although a small amount of Tawny has been released under the Dona Matilde label and Barros has given its white Douro wine the name of 'Enxodreiro'.

Quinta das Murças, Covelinhas   B

Once under the same ownership as Dona Matilde, this huge property claims the very first vertical plantings in the Douro undertaken in the 1940s. Most of the *quinta* is now planted this way and can be viewed easily from the Régua–Pinhão road on the south side of the river.

CIMA CORGO

Quinta de Napoles, Vila Seca   A

Until they purchased Napoles in 1988, the family-owned shipping firm of Niepoort had no presence in the Douro preferring instead to buy-in and blend wines from growers. Niepoort found Napoles (along with its smaller sibling Quinta do Carril) in a complete state of abandonment but quickly replanted the vineyard on *patamares*, which they now endeavour to cultivate using organic methods. Situated on a meander in the lower reaches of the narrow Tedo valley, Napoles produces powerful, concentrated wines that are useful components for Niepoort's fine Vintage and LBV Ports.

Quinta de São Luíz*, Adorigo, 5120 Tabuaço   A

One of the most prominent *quintas* on the south side of the Douro, if only for its impressive white painted terraces and the large black letters on the wall of one of the buildings that proclaims 'founded in 1638'. This refers to the firm of Kopke, which was acquired by Barros Almeida along with Quinta de São Luíz in 1952. Although an eighteenth-century house and chapel are at the core of the *quinta*, it is now used by Barros as their main vinification centre and, internally, the property has lost much of its innate charm as a result. The wines from São Luíz form the basis of some impressive and often unfairly overlooked Vintage Ports bottled under the Barros and Kopke labels.

Quinta do Crasto*, Gouvinhas, Ferrão, 5060 Sabrosa   A

Illustrated on one of the famous panels of decorative *azulejos* (tiles) at Pinhão station, Quinta do Crasto covers a hogs-back on the north side of the Douro and can be viewed from the Régua–Pinhão road. The name is believed to derive from the Portuguese word '*castro*' (Latin *castrum*), which signifies a Roman fort. Crasto formed a part of Pombal's first demarcation, and a sturdy granite pillar marking the geographical boundary of the *feitoria* can be seen on the estate. For much of the twentieth century Quinta do Crasto has been the property of Constantino de Almeida, formerly of Port shippers Constantino (now part of Ferreira). Crasto is currently one of the leading independent *quintas* in the Douro, owned and run by Constantino de Almeida's granddaughter Leonor

('Tita') and her husband Jorge Roquette. A number of other smaller historic properties, notably Quinta da Sobreira or Pasteleira, have been integrated into Crasto (see also pages 200 and 259).

Quinta da Agua Alta, Ferrão   A

Agua Alta (meaning 'high water') is one of a number of estates belonging to the Borges de Sousa family. Although much of the vineyard has been replanted on *patamares*, the buildings on the *quinta* are traditional and largely unrestored. A huge wooden beam press remains in the *adega*. Sheltered by a fold in the hillside, the local climatic conditions here are hot and Quinta da Agua Alta produces a rich, sometimes rather burnt style of Port. The wine is bought by Churchill and forms a major part of their declared Vintage blend. In good, interim years it is released as a single-*quinta* Vintage.

Quinta Nova Nossa Senhora do Carmo, Ferrão   A

Named after a small chapel built on the site in 1795, Quinta Nova (as it is known for short) was purchased by Port shippers Burmester from Royal Oporto in a run-down condition in 1991. The *quinta* has now been extensively restored and serves as the main vinification centre for the company. Since 1992 Quinta Nova has become a separate label within Burmester for a range of well-made Ports spanning from Ruby to Vintage.

Quinta do Panascal*, Valença do Douro, 5120 Tabuaço   A

Facing south-west in the lower reaches of the Tavora valley, Panascal is one of a famous trio of *quintas* belonging to Fonseca Guimaraens (the others are Cruzeiro and Santo António in the Pinhão valley). The *quinta* was only acquired by the company in 1978 but had long been an important component in Fonseca's vintage blend. Wines from the Tavora valley are prized for their solid backbone and concentration (perhaps sacrificing elegance), a characteristic that can be seen in the single-*quinta* Vintage Port and Fonseca's Bin no. 27, the majority of which is produced from Panascal. Grapes are foot-trodden on the property in five temperature-controlled *lagares*, one of which was built as recently as the late 1980s making them among the newest in the Douro. The vineyard was extensively replanted on *patamares* during the 1980s but a small area of vertical planting was carried out towards the top of the property. This is now cultivated organically without recourse to systemic pesticides or herbicides. Quinta do Panascal is one of the few properties in the Douro that is equipped to welcome passing visitors. It is well signposted from the main Pinhão–Régua road.

Quinta do Convento de São Pedro das Aguias, Tavora   B/C

Just within the southern boundary of the demarcated region, this former monastic estate is a relic of the age when most of the significant Douro vineyards were controlled by religious orders. It fell into secular hands after the civil war of the early 1830s, and since 1986 the property has been owned by Vranken, who bottle a range of Ports under the São Pedro das Aguias label, mainly for the French market.

Quinta do Infantado, Covas do Douro   A

Without a house to its name, Infantado comprises numerous different parcels of land centred on the untidy little village of Covas do Douro. The Roseira family, who own Infantado, were among the first to make and market their own single-*quinta* Ports on the domestic market in the late 1970s. The family was therefore in a good position to take advantage of the change in legislation in 1986 that permitted exports from the Douro thereby circumventing the shippers in Vila Nova de Gaia (see also page 213).

Quinta da Boa Vista, Chanceleiros   A

This dramatic *quinta* below the hamlet of Chanceleiros undoubtedly has some of the finest traditional terraces in the Douro. Since it was used by Joseph James Forrester in the mid-nineteenth century, the property has had a somewhat chequered history falling into a number of different hands until it was bought back by the firm of Forrester & Co. in 1979. Situated on either side of a deep ravine, Boa Vista has a particularly warm meso-climate with temperatures often four or five degrees higher than in neighbouring *quintas*. As a result, it is usually one of the first *quintas* to harvest in the Cima Corgo, at least a week in advance of other properties. Forrester (now owned by Sogrape) are intent on conserving this historic *quinta* and plan to establish a 'vineyard museum' representing every different type of cultivation in the Douro. Another point of interest is the old track leading from the *adega* to the river along which bullock carts once hauled pipes of Port for shipment down to Gaia. Some of the vertical stones used as a primitive braking system for the carts still remain.

Quinta do Porto, Chanceleiros   A

One of Dona Antónia Ferreira's many properties in the Douro, Quinta do Porto is still under the control of her successors running the Port house Ferreira. The simple whitewashed house and adjoining chapel at Quinta do Porto have been restored and maintained as a showpiece for trade guests. Grapes from the south-facing terraces and *patamares* are vinified at Ferreira's Quinta do Seixo on the opposite side of the river although the wine is sold under the *quinta* label as a ten-year-old Tawny.

Quinta da Vista Alegre, near Pinhão   A

Vista Alegre means 'happy view' but in this case it is something of a misnomer. The view of this property facing Quinta do Seixo is marred by an ugly modern winery. This is the vinification centre for a sizeable Douro-based operation called Sociedade Agricola Barros, who sell their wines under the 'Vista Alegre' brand name (see page 240).

Quinta do Seixo*, Valença do Douro, 5120 Tabuaço   A

Touring the Douro in the 1870s, Henry Vizetelly describes Quinta do Seixo as 'commodious and well arranged' with 'an air of pretention about it'. Sadly, the well-proportioned nineteenth-century house and adjoining chapel are now virtually obscured by an over-bearing concrete and stainless-steel edifice built as a central winery for Ferreira in the early 1980s. Seixo occupies a prominent position overlooking the confluence of the River Torto with the Douro. Under the aegis of the late Jorge Maria Cabral Ferreira, the vineyards were substantially restructured with vertical planting *(vinha ao alto)* favoured on all but the very steepest slopes. Wine from Seixo (the name means 'pebble') now forms part of Ferreira's vintage blend and has on occasion been bottled as a single-*quinta* Vintage Port.

Quinta do Bom Retiro, Valença do Douro   A

Bom Retiro is divided in two. The greater part of the property belongs to Ramos Pinto, who developed the *quinta* in the early twentieth century on profits generated by the sale of Port to Brazil.

As a result it boasts the earliest swimming pool in the Douro (disguised as an ornamental pond) and a long, level promenade shaded by palm trees designed for a gentle saunter after lunch or dinner. José Rosas and João Nicolau de Almeida were the true pioneers of both *patamares* and *vinha ao alto* in the Douro and the first practical examples of these planting systems can be seen at Bom Retiro. Wine from the *quinta* is an important component in Ramos Pinto's Vintage Port but is also sold as a twenty-year-old Tawny and a premium Ruby, the latter known as Quinta da Urtiga, which now makes-up part of the property. Bom Retiro is one of the two *quintas* that makes up Duas Quintas Douro wine.

The smaller part of the property, known as Bom Retiro Pequeno, belongs to the Serôdio family, who supply Warre.

Quinta da Corte, Valença do Douro   A
Closely associated with Delaforce, who make and market the wine, Quinta da Corte is in fact leased from independent owners Pacheco & Irmãos Lda. Seen from the road on the opposite side of the Torto valley, Corte is one of the most singularly impressive properties in the Douro with its impeccably maintained inclined stone terraces. In the spring after the harvest most of the wine from Corte is transferred to the Delaforce lodges in Vila Nova da Gaia; however, small quantities are retained in pipe at the *quinta* where they make up an unusually comprehensive reference library of reserve wines/*Colheitas* for blending into old Tawnies. Apart from a single-*quinta* Vintage Port bottled by Delaforce, Quinta da Corte makes a major contribution towards His Eminence's Choice Ten-Year-Old Tawny and declared Delaforce vintages. It is hard to envisage how they could possibly do without Corte when the present contract expires in 2002.

Quinta do Retiro Novo, Sarzedinho   A
Located deep in the Torto valley adjacent to the river, Retiro Novo belongs to the Portuguese firm of Wiese & Krohn, who purchased the property in 1989. It now serves as a vinification centre for the company's range of Ports.

Quinta Vale Dona Maria, Casais do Douro   A
For many years this 10-hectare property in the Torto valley was contracted by the Symingtons to make wine for Smith Woodhouse

and provided the backbone for some of its excellent but under-valued vintages. Now back in the hands of the Lemos family it is run by Cristiano van Zeller (ex-Quinta do Noval), who is gradually replanting the vineyard and restoring the *lagares* (which are unusually on the same level as the *armazém* – see page 131). He is producing both Vintage and Crusted Ports from the property as well as a red Douro wine under the *quinta*'s own label.

Quinta das Lages, Sarzedinho   A
By no means a showpiece *quinta*, Lages is a large rustic estate extending upwards from the banks of the Rio Torto close to the village of Sarzedinho. Wines from the property have been bought by Graham's for the best part of a century and Lages has become crucially important to the style and overall balance of their wines. The fruit and finesse that characterises Port from the Torto seems to complement the big, intense wines from Graham's Quinta dos Malvedos further up the Douro.

Quinta de Macedos, near Sarzedinho   A
This modest property perched on a knoll above the Torto has been bought by Englishman Paul Reynolds. With help from his brother Raymond (who used to be a wine-maker for Taylor's) they intend to produce a single-*quinta* Vintage Port from the property's seven hectares of old vines.

Quinta da Madelena, Casais do Douro   A
This unsung property in the Torto valley is the basis for some of the exceptional Vintage Ports produced by the Symington-owned firm of Smith Woodhouse. In 1995 it was made as a single-*quinta* wine. The adjoining Quinta da Santa Madelena also supplies Smith Woodhouse.

Quinta da Soalheira (between São João de Pesqueira and
Castanheiro do Sul)   A
Approaching the town of São João de Pesqueira on the *altos* above the Douro, a sign on the right reads Quinta da Soalheira 5.5 km. The dust-choked cart track then plunges back down into the Torto valley. The property belonged to Borges & Irmão until the company was broken up in 1998 and the name appeared on their ten-year-old Tawny. Now back in private hands, at the time of writing the future of the *quinta* is unclear.

Quinta da Val da Figueira, near Pinhão   A

A fig tree in the Douro usually indicates a water course and Val da Figueira means 'valley of the fig tree'. Although it was mentioned in Pombal's day, the property came to prominence in 1878 when the first trials with American vines were conducted there in the wake of the destruction wrought by phylloxera. A plaque in the *adega* records the event. Since the 1930s Val da Figueira has been owned by the Hoelzer family, who sold their wines to Port shippers Cálem. Following the acquisition of Cálem by Manuel António Saraiva and Rogerio Silva in 1998, the wines are now purchased by the Symingtons. A small amount of wine is retained and bottled under the *quinta*'s own label.

Quinta de la Rosa*, 5085 Pinhão   A

There can be no finer christening present than Quinta de la Rosa which was given to Claire Feuerheerd by her English grandmother in 1906. It was originally named Quinta das Bateiras after the hamlet on the opposite side of the river but was renamed 'La Rosa' by the Feuerheerds after a brand of Sherry. The property still belongs to the same family although the Port-shipping firm of Feuerheerd became separated from the *quinta* when it was taken over by Barros Almeida in the 1930s. In the interim La Rosa sold its wine to a number of shippers, latterly to Sandeman, who built up the *lagares* and installed the *movimosto* system to make Port both with grapes from the *quinta* and nearby properties. Disappointed by the quality of the wine being made at La Rosa, Tim Bergqvist, Claire Feuerheerd's son and current owner of La Rosa, decided it was time to strike out on his own and in the late 1980s the family began producing its own Ports and Douro wines. Built into the terraces just above the railway line, the rather topsy-turvy house at La Rosa is one of the most appealing in the Douro. The Bergqvists have built a number of rooms to receive paying guests (Turismo Rural). A stay at La Rosa is the best way to experience the life of a working *quinta* (see also page 228).

Quinta da Foz*, 5085 Pinhão   A

Overlooking the mouth of the River Pinhão (from where the property earns its name), Quinta da Foz marked the easternmost limit of Pombal's initial demarcation. The estate was bought by the Cálem family in 1885 having been devastated by phylloxera a decade earlier. A contemporary photograph in Vilarinho de São Romão's book *Viticultura e Vinicultura* illustrates the abandoned terraces. The railway line which was built at the same time comes so perilously close to the house that it feels as if the early morning train is coming through your bedroom! Foz remains in the hands of the Cálem family and for many years it formed the backbone of their Vintage Ports along with wines from the neighbouring Quinta da Segrado and Quinta da Val da Figueira. However, following the sale of the family shipping firm in 1998 the wines were purchased by Noval.

Quinta das Carvalhas, opposite Pinhão   A

The entire hill opposite Pinhão belongs to the Silva Reis family, majority shareholders in Real Companhia Velha (Royal Oporto) and among the largest landowners in the Douro. Carvalhas itself extends to some 600 hectares. The property has looked somewhat out of sorts throughout the 1990s but new planting has taken place on the other side of the *quinta* which curves round into the Torto valley. The summit of the hill is crowned by the modern Casa Redonda (Round House), known to some locally as the 'Holiday Inn'! It commands one of the best views in the Douro although Quinta do Seixo on the opposite side of the Torto must feel slightly threatened by the two cannons that point in their direction.

Quinta da Eira Velha, near Pinhão   A

At an altitude of nearly 200 metres, Eira Velha looks straight down on the railway station and main street of Pinhão and boasts one of the finest views in the Douro. The *quinta* has a long recorded history having been owned by the See of the Archbishop of Braga in the sixteenth century. In 1893 it was bought by the firm of Hunt Roope and thence passed into the hands of the Newmans, an old established trading family from Devon, England, who were among those to exchange Portuguese wine for *bacalhau* in the seventeenth century. Eira Velha is famous for its panels of blue and white tiles or *azulejos* surrounding the *lagares*, one of which illustrates the Newmans' shipping interests. The house at Eira Velha is something of a time warp, seemingly unchanged since the early years of the century. Since the late 1970s the property has been managed by

Cockburn's, which makes and markets an exceptional single-*quinta* wine under the Martinez label.

Quinta do Junco, São Cristovão do Douro   A

So precipitous are the slopes of the Pinhão valley at Quinta do Junco that it is difficult to see the property from the Pinhão–Sabrosa road which runs underneath. Owned by Borges & Irmão for most of the twentieth century, in 1988 it was sold to Taylor's in a somewhat rundown condition along with nearby Quinta da Casa Nova.

Quinta da Cavadinha, near Provezende   A

Wine from the Rio Torto has customarily been at the heart of Warre's Ports but in 1980 the Symington family took the decision to buy Cavadinha high above the Pinhão valley. With a north-easterly aspect and an altitude ranging between 120 and 450 metres, this is the last of the Symington family's many properties to be harvested, usually in early October. Although much of the upper part of the *quinta* is planted with Tinta Barroca, the enormous height variation ensures a balanced wine. The entire production is made in modern stainless-steel autovinifiers on the property. In the years when Warre's declare a vintage, Cavadinha forms a substantial part of the blend together with wine from the Serôdio-owned Quinta do Bom Retiro Pequeno. A single-*quinta* wine is produced in good intervening years. Quinta da Cavadinha was the setting for Miguel Torga's story *A Vindima*, a fact that is now recorded on a panel of tiles on a wall at the *quinta*.

Quinta do Noval, near Vale de Mendiz   A

Noval is perhaps the best example of the aphorism that you have to visit another *quinta* to appreciate your own. Seen from Warre's Quinta da Cavadinha on the opposite side of the Pinhão valley, the view of Noval is certainly among the finest in the Douro. In spite of its rather chequered history, Noval's vineyards have always been immaculately maintained and the whitewashed steps connecting one walled terrace to another are visible for miles around. Since it was bought by the French insurance company AXA in 1993, nearly half the vineyard has been replanted but the traditional terraces have fortunately been retained. The famous ungrafted 'Nacional' vineyard extends to just two hectares and occupies three terraces above and one terrace below the main drive up to the house which bisects the estate. Although 'Noval' is a brand that appears on wines that come from outside the *quinta*, the name 'Quinta do Noval' is reserved for LBVs, *Colheitas* and Vintage Ports, all of which originate from the property itself. For more information on the history and wines of this remarkable *quinta*, see page 218.

Quinta da Terra Feita, near Celeirós A

Taylor and Fonseca own an enviable amalgam of *quintas* deep in the Pinhão valley, which together count as one of the finest vineyard holdings in the Douro. With 48 hectares of vineyard, Quinta da Terra Feita is Taylor's largest property. It covers a low spur on the right bank of the river and is easy to recognise because of the small flat vineyard on the summit that was made by blasting away nineteen metres of rock from the top of the knoll. The richly perfumed wines from Terra Feita are a major component in Taylor's Vintage Ports bolstered by those from Quinta de Vargellas upstream in the Douro Superior. Small quantities of single-*quinta* Vintage Port from Terra Feita are released in good interim years.

Casa de Santa Clara – Museu dos Lagares*, Vale de Mendiz, 5070 Alijó No *Cadastro* grade

Sandeman has restored this unusual property in the centre of Vale de Mendiz and installed a museum charting the history and traditions of Port wine. The centrepeice of the museum is the duo of shallow, round *lagares*, which were built by the eccentric António Pinto Gouveio at the end of the nineteenth century. He apparently believed that the treaders could hurt their feet in the corners of the conventional rectangular *lagares*. These are the only known round *lagares* in the Douro region.

Quinta de Cruzeiro, Vale de Mendiz A

An imposing crenellated gateway marks the entrance to this seemingly modest property on the edge of the village of Vale de Mendiz. Facing Terra Feita on the opposite side of the River Pinhão, Cruzeiro has been at the heart of Fonseca's Vintage Port for most of the twentieth century. It was purchased by the company in 1973 in a rundown condition and most of the vineyard has subsequently been replanted on *patamares*. Touriga Francesa and Tinta Barroca together now account for over 60 per cent of the vines on the property producing beautifully balanced, fragrant Ports, complemented by the bigger, rather more robust wines from Panascal. The wines from Cruzeiro are foot trodden on the *quinta* in *lagares*.

Quinta de Santo António, near Vale de Mendiz   A

Slightly further up the Pinhão valley, Santo António is the smallest of the Fonseca properties with just ten hectares of vines. The grapes are vinified in *lagares* at Cruzeiro and form part of Fonseca's vintage blend.

Quinta do Passadouro*, Vale de Mendiz, 5085 Pinhão   A

Hidden and almost forgotten for many years, Quinta do Passadouro has enjoyed a renaissance since it was bought by Belgian sand and gravel magnate Dieter Bohrmann in 1992. The wines are made in *lagares* on the property under the aegis of Dirk Niepoort, who markets Passadouro's single-*quinta* Vintage Ports. The simple dwelling at Passadouro has been refurbished to receive paying guests, rabbit in chocolate sauce being the house speciality! (See also page 217.)

Quinta do Fojo, near Vale de Mendiz   A

Few properties in the Douro are more peaceful than Quinta do Fojo where all that can be heard is the rush of water from the River Pinhão. It is owned (along with the adjoining Quinta da Manuela) by the Serôdio Borges family, who supply wines to Churchill, Morgan and Niepoort. Fojo is also the source of an admirable single estate Douro wine (see page 262).

Quinta Casal da Granja, Granja   C, D, E and F

This large property on the plateau or *planalto* near Alijó is the vinification centre for Real Vinicola. At an altitude of 520–640 metres, the surrounding vineyards are largely used for the production of White Ports and Douro wines.

Quinta do Bomfim, Pinhão   A

Approached from the chaotic main street in Pinhão, Bomfim is something of an oasis and certainly one of the most civilised of all *quintas* in the Douro. It occupies an enviable site, facing southwest, and (with the exception of the upper part of the property) is not nearly as steep as many vineyards in the Cima Corgo. The location was known originally as Vale Bem Feito ('well-made valley') but the Quinta do Bomfim ('good end') does not seem to have had much of a history until it was bought for Silva & Cosens (Dow's) by George Acheson Warre in 1896. He clearly had foresight because Bomfim has subsequently become the centre of Dow's operations in the Douro. Warre built a modest but comfortable residence at Bomfim, inspired by the tea-planters' houses in Ceylon (Sri Lanka), and his shady veranda with its view over the river continues to be one of my favourite places to enjoy a glass of cool twenty-year-old Tawny. Port was made in *lagares* at Bomfim until the early 1960s when they were phased out and replaced by autovinifiers. Wine from the property continues to form the backbone of Dow's solid Vintage Ports and is also produced as a single-*quinta* wine in intervening years.

Quinta da Roêda, near Pinhão   A
The vineyard at Roêda interlocks with Bomfim and enjoys a similar aspect and exposure. The property belonged to the Fladgates (of Taylor, Fladgate & Yeatman fame) until it was acquired by Croft in 1875. A colonial-style house similar in style to that at Bomfim was built in the 1920s but with pictures of other United Distillers brands on the wall, Roêda lacks the family feel of its neighbour. The 1970s winery overlooking the river serves as Croft's principal vinification centre. Originally equipped with autovinifiers it has been modified to take specially adapted *remontadores*. Roêda is capable of producing some outstanding wines, the best of which form the basis for Croft's Vintage Ports with single-*quinta* vintages being released in other good years.

Quinta do Ventozelo*, Ervadosa do Douro, 5130 São João de Pesqueira   A
Facing Roêda on the opposite side of the Douro, Ventozelo is a substantial estate occupying a natural amphitheatre in the hillside. Wines are made in *lagares* on the property and sold on the domestic market under the *quinta*'s own label. Approached from the Pinhão–São João de Pesqueira road, Ventozelo is open to visitors and boasts a fine house for guest accommodation close to the river. In 1999 Ventozelo was sold to a Spanish fishing company for the astonishing price of 1.6 million contos (£5.3 million).

Quinta do Roncão, Vilarinho de Cotas   A

The deeply incised Roncão valley has a particularly hot, dry meso-climate that differs markedly from its surroundings. Facing south-east and sheltered on all sides it produces wines which are prized for their richness, intensity and concentration.

Quinta da Romaneira, Cotas/Castedo   A

One of the largest and most imposing *quintas* in the Douro, Rom-aneira is also among the most isolated, and can only be seen to full advantage from the river. It has belonged since the 1960s to the Vinagre family (former owners of Borges & Irmão), who were among the first to make and market single-*quinta* Ports. A full range (from Ruby to Vintage) is now bottled on the estate.

Quinta do Roriz, near Ervadosa do Douro   A

One of the earliest-recorded vineyards in the Cima Corgo, Roriz was already well established by the end of the seventeenth century. The estate was purchased from a religious order by the Kopke family and thereby passed through marriage to a branch of the van Zellers, who still own Roriz today. It lays claim to be one of the first single-*quinta* Ports and continued to be bottled as such by Gonzalez Byass through the early years of the twentieth century. The name was lost in the post-war period but Roriz has recently been revived as a single-*quinta* Vintage Port by Noval. Lesser wines from the property are blended into Ports sold under the Noval label.

Quinta do Vau, near Soutelo do Douro   A

'Vau' is the Portuguese word meaning 'ford' and this *quinta* on the south bank of the river must have marked a shallow crossing point in the Douro prior to the construction of the dams in the 1970s. Since the property was purchased by Sandeman as part of its general improvement plans in the late 1980s, Vau has largely been replanted and a new pump-over winery built on the site. So far single-*quinta* Vintage Ports from the property have been on the light side but once the new vineyards are fully established, Vau will undoubtedly be an important component in Sandeman vintage blends.

Quinta do Sidró, São João de Pesqueira   **D, E and F**

This undulating estate on the outskirts of São João de Pesqueira was bought by Real Companhia Velha (Royal Oporto) in 1970 having previously belonged to the family of the Marquês de Soveral. The ostentatious white-painted *pálacio* appears somewhat stark amidst 136 hectares of vertically planted vineyards. Situated at an altitude of between 450 and 600 metres, this property is considered too high for premium quality Port and most of the production is used for Real Vinicola's red and white Douro wines, bottled under the names of Marquês de Soveral and Quinta do Sidró. Traditional varieties are planted alongside substantial quantities of Cabernet Sauvignon and Chardonnay.

Quinta da Nogueira, São João de Pesqueira   No Cadastro grade

Formerly known as Quinta da Cismeira, Quinta da Nogueira is a rather grand name for the practical but somewhat utilitarian vinification centre serving Taylor, Fonseca and Romariz. The name of the latter appears at the entrance to the property, which stands on the main road from São João de Pesqueira to Vila Nova de Fozcoa.

Quinta dos Malvedos, near São Mamede da Riba Tua   A

Malvedos is synonymous with W. & J. Graham, having been a component in their renowned Vintage Ports for over a century. The *quinta* briefly parted company from Graham in the lean years of the early 1970s but was repurchased in poor condition by the Symington family in 1982, who have subsequently spent substantial sums restoring the property. A winery equipped with robotic stainless-steel *lagares* is likely to be the next development. Predominantly south-facing and rising up to 400 metres, Malvedos produces big but balanced, lasting wines that stand up on their own as single-*quinta* Vintage Ports. The simple nineteenth-century farmhouse at Malvedos has been extensively revamped and for two summers in the mid-1990s provided peaceful holiday accommodation for British Prime Minister John Major. A brass plaque on the café at Senhora da Ribeira upstream records the event.

Quinta do Tua, Tua   A

Overlooking the confluence of the River Tua with the Douro, Quinta do Tua belonged to Dona Antónia Ferreira until it was

AQUI ALMOÇOU O
JOHN MAJOR
EM 30 - 08 - 1993

Senhora da Ribeira. 'John Major had lunch here'

bought by Cockburn at the end of the nineteenth century. The simple but well-proportioned mansion or *solar* has been joined by a rather more utilitarian winery and a line-up of concrete *balões* for bulk storage. This serves as a vinification centre both for Tua and Cockburn's neighbouring Quinta da Chousa as well as for grapes from other outlying properties. Depending on the year

Quinta do Tua and Quinta da Chousa are bottled as single-*quinta* Vintage Ports or may form part of Cockburn's Vintage blend. Quinta do Tua was the site of some of the first varietal plantings in the Douro, carried out by John Smithes in the 1930s.

Quinta dos Acipreteses, near Soutelo do Douro   A

For a decade or more, visitors to the café by Tua railway station have watched in awe as the hillside opposite was excavated and a huge new vertically planted vineyard emerged. Now covering ninety hectares, grapes from this *quinta* belonging to the Silva Reis family of Royal Oporto are mostly being used to produce Real Vinicola's red Douro wines.

Quinta do Zimbro, near Tua   A

Formerly owned by Silva & Cosens, Zimbro (meaning Juniper) continues to form an important part of Dow's Vintage blend. Grapes grown on the predominantly south-facing terraces above the river are vinified downstream at Quinta do Bomfim. The house and chapel at Zimbro along with the huge juniper tree face on to the railway line and can be seen shortly after leaving Tua station on the train heading for Pocinho.

DOURO SUPERIOR

Quinta do Cachão, Ferradosa   A

Named after the former rapids nearby, Quinta do Cachão and neighbouring Quinta do Rei belong to the Port shipper Messias, who maintain their own *adega* on the site. Wines from the property form the basis for their Vintage Ports.

Quinta de Vargellas, near Val da Figueira   A

With its own railway station, Vargellas is almost a self-contained community high in the Douro Superior. In the nineteenth century a significant part of the property belonged to the Ferreira family until three *quintas* bearing the name of Vargellas were merged into one by Taylor Fladgate & Yeatman in 1893. Curving with the river, Vargellas forms an extremely impressive property and (although not the largest of their vineyards) is treated by Taylor as their flagship estate. Vargellas produces strong, dark wines with a scented character which Alistair Robertson, Chairman and Managing Director of Taylor's, describes as 'violety'. Taylor's were the first of the current generation to release a single-*quinta* Vintage Port with the launch of Quinta de Vargellas 1958. In order to justify the extra costs, wine from the old unmechanised vineyards on the property is now being bottled separately under the name Vinha Velha. In declared years Port from Vargellas forms a major part of Taylor's vintage blend along with powerful wines from the company's other estates in the Pinhão valley. The so-called 'chalet' at Vargellas has been progressively transformed by Gillyanne Robertson into a dwelling modelled on an English country house. It no doubt inspired the late Willie Rushton's cartoon, which depicts the railway station at Vargellas with bowler-hatted commuters as the 'last outpost of the British Empire'!

Quinta dos Canais, near Beira Grande   A
Much to the chagrin of some of the neighbours, the once wild hillside opposite Vargellas has been completely reworked on *patamares* since Quinta dos Canais was bought by Cockburn in 1989. But with the huge waterfalls that streak the rugged granite backdrop in winter and spring, Canais is still an undeniably imposing sight. The property is named after the series of channels that divert the water from the foot of the falls to irrigate the *quinta*'s olive trees. Many of these have been uprooted to make way for vines but Cockburn's has since planted thousands of trees and plants throughout the *quinta* that will eventually soften the visual impact of the new terracing. The predominantly south-facing vineyard now extends to 100 hectares that will eventually produce 500 pipes of top quality Port. A new winery has been built on the property, modelled on that at Château Latour but partly equipped with so-called 'techno-*lagares*'. Jim Reader, Production Director at Cockburn's, intends that Quinta dos Canais should be the 'Château Latour of the Douro'. It certainly has the potential.

Quinta do Vesúvio, near Numão   A
This legendary *quinta* is undeniably among the most impressive in the Douro. It boasts the largest house, some of the biggest *lagares* and rather like Lisbon, Rome and San Francisco, it covers seven hills. The estate was largely created in the early nineteenth century by António Bernardo Ferreira (father-in-law of Dona Antónia) and

remained with the Ferreira family until it was acquired by the Symingtons in 1989. It was in a poor state of repair at the time and some of the best vineyards had been lost to the flooding of the river in the 1970s. Predominantly north-facing, the entire property covers an area of 408 hectares of which less than a quarter are under vine. Much has been done to revive the property since the Symington family decided to produce a single-*quinta* Vintage Port from Vesúvio independently of their other brands. Bottled in all but the most dismal years (1993 is the exception to date), Quinta do Vesúvio has quickly risen to join the premier league of Vintage Ports.

Quinta da Senhora da Ribeira, Senhora da Ribeira   A

Facing Vesúvio across the Douro, Senhora da Ribeira was one of three *quintas* to be bought for Silva & Cosens at the end of the nineteenth century by George Acheson Warre (the others are Bomfim and Zimbro). The property remained with Silva & Cosens until it had to be sold by the Symington family in the mid-1950s just to make ends meet. An entry in Dow's Quinta do Bomfim visitors' book dated 21 May 1954 records: 'Went to Senhora da Ribeira to conclude sale ... It's been a most sad occasion but we leave the happiest memories and many good faithful friends here.' The wine continued to be an important component in Dow's Vintage Ports, being foot-trodden at the *quinta* in traditional stone *lagares*. In 1998, just as Dow's celebrated their two hundredth anniversary, Quinta da Senhora da Ribeira was bought back by the Symingtons and is once more part of the family fold.

Quinta Vale da Mina, Senhora da Ribeira   A

This tiny property above Senhora da Ribeira belongs to Cristiano van Zeller (ex-Quinta do Noval), who began making a Vintage Port from the *quinta* in 1995.

Quinta do Vale Coelho, near Vilarinho da Castanheira/Lousa   A

On the north bank of the Douro, Quinta de Vale Coelho ('Rabbit Valley') and neighbouring Telhada are some of the most peaceful and unassuming of all properties in the Douro. Vale Coelho, the first of Cockburn's many *quintas*, was bought by the firm in the 1880s. Apart from electricity which arrived in 1965 and still seems something of an imposition, the house is little changed since.

Like all of Cockburn's properties, it is impeccably maintained and the money has been lavished on the vineyards that were mostly replanted in the 1980s. Depending on their quality, the grapes from Vale Coelho and Telhada are vinified in central wineries at Quinta da Tua or Vila Nova da Foz Côa.

Quinta do Vale do Meão, near Pocinho   A/B

Vale do Meão is the easternmost of all the historic Douro *quintas* and one of the most fascinating. It must have been a huge challenge for Dona Antónia Ferreira, who completed the imposing house and chapel shortly before her death at the age of 85 in 1896. Now in the possession of her great-great-grandson Francisco Olazabal, the interior of the house remains in much the same way as she left it and the attic is full of *fin de siècle* memorabilia. Since 1952 Vale do Meão has been the home of the best-known Douro wine, Ferreira's Barca Velha. Initially it was produced in the *quinta*'s impressive thirty-pipe *lagares* but these have now been decommissioned in favour of temperature-controlled stainless steel. The Barca Velha story is recounted in Chapter 6.

Quinta do Atayde, Vilariça   A

Better known merely as 'Vilariça', this was virtually virgin territory until Cockburn made a foray into the area in 1979. The acquisition of Atayde and a number of neighbouring properties marked the beginning of a new generation of vineyards in the Douro with greater emphasis on research and development aimed at improving yields and reducing costs. The principal advantage of planting a new vineyard in this isolated corner of the Douro is the terrain. Apart from a few *patamares* on the edge of the 300-hectare property, Vilariça is almost level and despite the schistous nature of the soil relatively easy to mechanise. Even mechanical harvesting, still unthinkable elsewhere in the Douro, would be feasible here at some stage in the not too distant future. The only drawback is the unforgiving climate with irregular rainfall and high summer temperatures sometimes in excess 50°C. Vilariça was acquired with the specific intention of building up a base for Cockburn's Special Reserve Port and, although the property still lacks a winery, it seems to be serving its purpose admirably. In 1991 wine from Vilariça also entered Cockburn's vintage blend but I am yet to be convinced that the Ports reach the grade.

Quinta da Ervamoira, near Muxagata A

Formerly known as Quinta de Santa Maria, Ervamoira was the result of a painstaking search by the late José Rosas, one-time President of Ramos Pinto. He found his promised land in the early 1970s and began planting vines at this relatively flat but remote site in the Côa valley in 1976 with the intention of mechanising production. No sooner had the 100 ha vineyard established itself than the entire valley was threatened by flooding to generate hydro-electric power. In the event the estate was saved by the chance discovery of palaeolithic engravings on the schistous crags beside the River Côa and the whole area has subsequently been designated as a *parque archeologico*. Ramos Pinto claim that Ervamoira is the first vineyard in the Douro to be block planted with individual grape varieties. To João Nicolau de Almeida, who looks after the production at Ramos Pinto, Ervamoira represents 'the future of the Douro'. A small museum has been set up at the property to record the past.

Quinta da Leda, Almendra B

Ferreira's easterly outpost was planted in 1979 when Cockburn and Ramos Pinto were setting up similar labour-saving operations in the Douro Superior. The 'house' at this isolated property consists of nothing more than a couple of air-conditioned huts. Vineyards cover 40 hectares of gently undulating but extremely rocky, schistous terrain. The wines from Leda tend to have a typically hot, ripe, foursquare character and are destined to form part of Ferreira's vintage or traditional LBV blends. An increasing portion of fruit from the property is used in Barca Velha with single-*quinta* Douro wines bottled under the names Callabria and Quinta da Leda.

DIRECTIONS IN THE DOURO

Until as recently as the 1980s, the Douro was a place for travellers rather than tourists. Hardy souls would return from the region bristling with tales of privation and discomfort. Hotel accommodation was lacking and a visitor to the Douro would easily recognise Henry Vizetelly's description from a century earlier:

... owing to the absence of any kind of accommodation, the traveller is entirely dependent on the courtesy of owners or occupiers of *quintas* along his lines of route. When an invitation is given to you to take up your quarters in one of these *quintas*, it is invariably accompanied by the intimation that you must be prepared to 'rough it'. But it usually happens that the only roughing of it you have to undergo is over the villainous roads which lead to your destination. There is no lack of hospitality, and you are feasted on fowls, turkeys, and hams, and on beef and mutton – which, by the way, have to be sent for a distance of ten miles ... the finest grapes are of course in abundance. The choicest of Tawny Port, which has lost all its fruitiness during a quarter of a century in cask, is at your service ...

Access to the Douro has improved greatly during the 1990s. Whereas it used to take a good three hours to reach the region by car, some Port shippers can almost now commute to Oporto from their *quintas* in the Cima Corgo. But a visitor with rather more time to spare would be well advised to leave the car behind. It's not for the intoxication of 'the choice Tawny Port' (although happily there is still an abundant supply) but because most of the region's corkscrew roads traverse the valley and afford few good views of the river and vineyards.

Second only to the cruise boats, which occasionally ply the river in the summer months, much the best way to appreciate the grandeur of the Douro landscape is to board the train. The journey upriver begins at Oporto's São Bento railway station from where trains leave for Pocinho, now the end of the line, at three-hour intervals. São Bento station itself is worth a visit. Built on the site of an old convent, its sepulchral concourse is covered from floor to ceiling with blue and white tiles *(azulejos)* depicting some of the glorious moments from Portuguese history.

The journey to Pocinho lasts nearly five hours but it is worth taking the train at least as far as Pinhão, the small town in the heart of the wine region. Allowing for an early start, the return journey can be undertaken in a day but be sure to buy a first-class ticket. Second-class carriages are grimy and uncomfortable and it can be difficult to find a seat. On leaving the tall suburbs of Oporto, frequently swathed in morning mist, the train emerges into Vinho Verde county. Pergola-trained vines, often strung with washing, brush alongside the windows of the carriage but there are no views of the River Douro until after the train has stopped at Marco de Canaveses when about an hour of the journey has elapsed. (The train blasts its horn before each and every crossing so it is difficult to fall asleep!) From here until the end of the line, the train snakes alongside the river through country that is so rugged in places that neither mule nor motor vehicle could gain access. When the weather is hot the doors of the carriages are left open so the brave (or foolhardy – and that includes me) sit on the steps of the carriage drinking cans of cold Super Bock (the local beer). In places the train runs so close to the edge of the river that your feet almost dangle into the Douro.

It is quite easy to see where the Vinho Verde region ends and the Port vineyards begin. As the river curves north at Barqueiros, hard granite gives way to flaky schist and terraced vineyards, like hanging gardens, take over from the unruly pergolas. The first major stop inside the Douro region is the 'city' of Peso da Régua and this is the terminus for some trains known as *inter-cidade* (inter-city). Apart from its setting, Régua itself has never been a very attractive town and over recent years its modicum of charm has been further eroded by indiscriminate modern construction. The only building worthy of note is the headquarters of Pombal's old Companhia around which the town grew in the mid-eighteenth century. Régua is also the railway junction for a slow, narrow gauge train, which used to ascend the Corgo valley travelling as far as Chaves, but the line has now been pruned back to Vila Real.

Soon after leaving Régua, the railway passes under the monolithic concrete bridge that carries the new highway across the Douro. Shortly after passing over the River Corgo and the village of Covelinhas, a string of famous *quintas* come into view. Quinta do Crasto can just be seen to the left of the train with Barros Almeida's Quinta de São Luíz on the opposite side of the river. Burmester's Quinta Nova, Fonseca's Quinta do Panascal, Offley's Quinta da Boa Vista and Ferreira's Quinta do Porto, Quinta do Seixo and Quinta de la Rosa all follow in fairly quick succession before the train arrives at Pinhão.

Pinhão owes its existence to the railway and the station, with its remarkable panels of *azulejos*, is the only building of note. It is also a passing place on the single track railway where the 'up' train meets the 'down' train. At vintage time the station platform

Pinhão station

frequently resembles a cocktail party as wine-trade visitors and Port shippers forcibly meet and exchange vineyard gossip. Pinhão's position is spectacular and there are many famous Port *quintas* just a short distance from the cobbled main street. The town itself is something of a disappointment. Once described by a Port shipper as a 'one horse town where the horse left', Pinhão has nevertheless improved immeasurably in recent years with a number of local *quintas* offering accommodation and a hotel (see below). Rather like Vizetelly, who described nineteenth-century Pinhão in some detail, first-time visitors still gaze in amazement at the antics of local dogs, which have a remarkable propensity to stand on one leg and scratch themselves with the other three!

Upstream from Pinhão, the train passes a succession of the most famous vineyards. Royal Oporto's Quinta das Carvalhas faces the town itself and Dow's Quinta do Bomfim, Croft's Quinta da Roêda, Sandeman's Quinta do Vau, Graham's Malvedos and Cockburn's Tua can all be seen clearly from the train. The hamlet of Tua is the next important stop and the station is always a scene of consternation as railway passengers alight to buy bread from the little motorised cart that sits on the platform before returning hurriedly to the train. Tua serves as a junction for the narrow gauge train that used to crawl up the Tua valley as far as Bragança but now takes two hours to reach the town of Mirandela high on the *planalto*. For anyone with time to spend exploring the Douro, this branch line is worth taking for the scenery alone. The Tua valley is a deep gorge and the railway track follows a narrow ledge hewn out from the rock above the river. Passengers frequently flag-down the train for an unscheduled stop and, until as recently as the 1980s, the only means of reaching one of the stations along the line was in an aerial basket that was hoisted from one side of the valley to the other. The need for this daunting exercise has been removed by the construction of a bridge.

Returning to the Douro, the train passes an abandoned halt called Alegria ('happiness'), presumably so-named because of the relief felt by the boatmen having descended the rapids of Valeira immediately upstream. The train now proceeds beneath the 1970s dam and emerges from the tunnel in the forbidding chasm where Baron Forrester drowned in 1861. The water no longer smashes over the rocks but Cachão de Valeira is still a sinister place with lofty grey mountains reflected in the jet black waters of the river.

Storks, herons and the occasional bird of prey can be seen hovering above the crags. Cachão de Valeira marks the boundary between the Cima Corgo and Douro Superior. At Ferradosa, just above the former rapids, the railway crosses to the south bank of the river and some of the most stately of all *quintas* come into view. Taylor's Quinta de Vargellas and the Symington family's Quinta do Vesúvio both have their own railway stations. On the opposite side of the river, Cockburn's Quinta dos Canais, the Symingtons' Senhora da Ribeira and Cockburn's Vale Coelho can all be seen from the window of the train. As the train reaches Pocinho the valley opens out and apart from Quinta do Vale do Meão, there are more olive trees to be seen than vines. Pocinho itself is no more than a collection of down-at-heel buildings and a few rusting steam engines. It feels more like the end of the world than the end of the line!

For anyone with a car, there are a number of good vantage points from which to appreciate the sheer scale and extent of the Douro region. The belvedere or *miradouro* at São Leonardo da Galafura is one of the best. Approached from the main road that runs between Régua to Vila Real (via Vila Seca), on a clear day it provides a vista of much of the Cima Corgo, with the Baixo Corgo and the outline of the Serra do Marão in the distance. On the border between the Cima Corgo and the Douro Superior, the view from the five chapels of São Salvador do Mundo (Saint Saviour of the World) is even more dramatic. It is reached from the São João de Pesqueira–Ferradosa road and allows you to peer down from amongst the cactus plants and crags on to the river more than 400 metres below.

Away from the river, a number of the older towns and villages are of both historical and architectural interest. On the south side of the Douro, the rural city of Lamego is dominated by the sanctuary of Nossa Senhora dos Remédios, the steps from which cascade into the main avenue that bisects the town. Just outside Vila Real on the northern margin of the region, the baroque Palace

of Mateus, which lent its name to the world-famous rosé, is open to passing visitors. Overlooking the Pinhão valley in the Cima Corgo, the manorial community of Provezende (near Sabrosa) is one of the few villages to have survived the constructional onslaught of recent years and the eighteenth-century houses built from profits generated by Pombal's *companhia* have largely escaped alteration. There are ruins of defensive castles north and south of the river at Lavandeira and Numão, both of which afford fine views of the surrounding countryside. The remote town of Vila Nova da Foz Côa in the Douro Superior boasts a fine, richly decorated parish church.

Foz Côa has also become the centre for visiting the extraordinary Côa Valley archaeological park. Between 1992 and 1995, a whole series of palaeolithic engravings were discovered, etched into the rock along a 20 km stretch of the River Côa. A number of engravings in the lower reaches of the Côa valley undoubtedly disappeared under the waters of the Douro when it was dammed in the 1970s, and for a time in the early 1990s it seemed as though the remainder might disappear under a new dam to be built near Vila Nova da Foz Côa. Fortunately the dam was shelved and a number of archaeological sites in the Côa valley have been opened up to visitors. The whole area has been declared a World Heritage site. A museum is being built on the site of the half-completed dam and the engravings, mostly depicting wild animals, can be visited by four-wheel drive vehicles from visitor centres at Castelo Melhor and Muxagata. The existence of the engravings had been common knowledge among local shepherds long before the archaeologists 'discovered' the site. At one place on the Côa a local wit has added to the pre-historic graffiti, etching a charming picture of the old Douro *paciência* (steam train) into the schist!

Accommodation in the Douro is much better than it was in Vizetelly's day although visitors may still have to 'rough it' on

occasion. In the Baixo Corgo, the Solar da Rede near Mesão Frio is a grand eighteenth-century mansion with views over the river, now converted into a luxurious hotel with the atmosphere of a private country house. Upstream, Régua boasts a large modern hotel but it does not have much in the way of local character. The little town of Pinhão provides much the most convenient base for visiting the Douro. Port shippers Taylor's have recently converted one of their *armazéns* into a stylish four star hotel (The Vintage House) with an enviable location by the river. There is more modest accommodation in the town but the best way to soak up the atmosphere of the Douro is to stay on a Port *quinta*. Quinta de la Rosa (see page 104) offers bed and breakfast accommodation and has two houses to rent on the estate. Nearby at Chanceleiros, a German family have converted an old manor house (Casa Visconde de Chanceleiros) into holiday accommodation with both a swimming pool and a squash court. In a quiet setting away from the river at Vale de Mendiz, Quinta do Passadouro (page 108) also offers bed, breakfast and evening meal. For more luxurious accommodation, it is worth climbing to Casal de Loivos above Pinhão where the Sampaio family have converted a seventeenth-century house (Casa de Casal de Loivos). Don't be put off by the scruffy approach through the village. At the front of the house, the terrace and swimming pool afford an uninterrupted view of the Douro.

Food in the Douro tends to be homespun and limited in availability. Soups are hearty and eggs are plentiful but after a few days in the region it is easy to see why there are 365 ways of cooking *bacalhau* (salt cod)! The best restaurants tend to be in the most unexpected places: the petrol station in Sabrosa, on the roundabout in Régua, near the quayside in Pinhão. All Douro restaurants have their ups and downs so don't be afraid to ask a local for recommendations.

One of the world's great train journeys

3
Making Port: Tradition and Technology

THE START OF VINTAGE

Even the most minor sound has a strange resonance in the Douro. At no time is this more apparent than at the start of vintage when the babble of an excitable conversation can suddenly be heard from the opposite side of the valley. As expectations rise, great gangs (*rogas*) of high-spirited pickers descend on Douro *quintas* from outlying villages. The *cardenhos* (dormitories), silent for most of the year, fill to the sound of cheerful voices and the aromas of sardines and *bacalhau* begin to rise as fires are stoked in huge kitchens. The same families often come to work at the same property year after year and, despite the political and social changes of the late twentieth century, a strong bond of loyalty is maintained between the *roga* and the *patrão* or owner of the *quinta*. For all concerned there is an intense feeling of personal involvement as the year's work in the vineyard reaches its culmination.

The exact timing of vintage depends upon location and the weather conditions during the growing season. In the Douro Superior the harvest can begin as early as mid-August whereas downstream in the cooler Baixo Corgo some growers may hang on until early October to coax the maximum amount of sweetness from their grapes. However in Pinhão, in the heart of the Douro region, the harvest is usually well underway by 20 September and depending on the size of the crop will last to mid-October.

In the weeks immediately prior to the harvest, most wine-makers tour the region, visiting farmers and taking samples of grapes from different plots to monitor development. Baumé (a measure of the concentration of grape sugars), pH and total acidity are crucial readings but tasting grapes or juice is increasingly gaining ground as a method of determining optimum ripeness. All grapes destined for the production of Port must legally be above 11 degrees baumé although in all but the weakest of years, potential alcohol levels in the Cima Corgo and Douro Superior usually register between 12 and 14 per cent by volume and possibly higher. For the few crucial days before picking begins, farmers gather together exchanging ideas and comparing levels of baumé. In excessively hot years, the shrivelling or raisining of grapes as they hang on the vine can be a problem, especially with heat-sensitive varieties like Tinta Barroca. This was a feature in 1995, for example, where some growers like Ramos Pinto with holdings in the Douro Superior brought the date of the harvest forward to mid-August in order to prevent damage to the crop. In these conditions, levels of natural acidity are usually low when compared to light (i.e. unfortified) wines although an excessively hot, dry summer can cause the vines to close down and produce unbalanced wines with a 'green' under-ripe character. Total acidity (principally tartaric and malic) may be as low as 5g/l and pH levels are frequently as high as 4.0. This will warrant correction once the grapes have reached the winery.

Cestos, old and new

It almost goes without saying that picking in the Douro is carried out entirely by hand. Mechanical harvesting is only possible in some of the larger, flatter vineyards of the Douro Superior but, to date, only one producer has carried out trials. Grapes were traditionally cut into large, coarse woven baskets (*cestos da vindima*) with a capacity of up to 75 kg at a time. These would then be carried to the *adega* by a regimented line of pickers, egged-on by a small band of musicians. Although *cestos* are still used by some smaller growers, nowadays they are loaded on to trailers and towed to the *adega* by tractor. Following on from the centralisation of Port production in the 1960s, the majority of grapes are now transported to the winery or *adega* in 1,000 kg steel bins known as *dornas*. Usually emblazoned with the name of the owner, these are lent out to independent growers during vintage. As the grapes are crushed under their own weight, *dornas* frequently encourage the onset of fermentation, particularly if conditions are warm and there is a delay in reaching the winery. Worse still are the black plastic bags occasionally used by small growers into which grapes are compressed and then left out on the roadside in the sun awaiting collection. A number of leading quality-conscious producers have therefore begun to use small plastic crates with a capacity of no more than about 25 kg each. In this way the grapes tend to arrive at the *adega* intact and undamaged.

TRADITION

The key to the production of a quality red Port is in the vigorous extraction of colour and flavour compounds (anthocyanins and phenolics) found in the skins of the grapes. The deep hue, firm tannin structure and ripe flavours that characterise a young, premium quality Port have to be extracted before the fermentation is prematurely arrested by the addition of grape spirit known as *aguardente*. Compared to a dry red wine, the extraction process is a race against time. Whereas a classed-growth Bordeaux may be allowed the luxury of a ten-day fermentation/maceration on the skins, the skin contact for Port may be no longer than forty-eight hours.

The time-honoured method used to extract colour and flavour from Port grapes is the *lagar*. This is a square stone tank made from granite or cement, usually no more than a metre in depth with a capacity varying between 15 and 25 pipes (8,000–14,000 litres).

Over the course of a day's picking, the *lagar* is filled to within 15 to 20 centimetres of the brim – the width of an outstretched hand is the crude measurement. Before the advent of electricity, baskets of grapes arriving from the vineyard would be emptied directly into the *lagar* or into a hand-turned roller-crusher. Nowadays, electric roller-crushers and pumps are commonly used and, depending on the overall maturity of the grapes, a proportion of the stalks may be removed. Sulphur dioxide will also be added at this stage and the acidity of the must may be adjusted with the addition of tartaric acid.

Towards the end of the day as the sun begins to set the pickers return to the *adega*, and after a hearty supper they each don a pair of shorts and step thigh-deep into the mass of crimson-coloured grapes. Although vintage is an excuse for a great deal of mirth and merriment, treading grapes in a *lagar* is both arduous and monotonous, especially after a long, hot day in the vineyard. For the first two to three hours, the treaders link arms and march slowly back and forth; the soles of their feet crushing the grapes gently against the stone floor of the *lagar*. This regimented treading, known as the *corte* or cut, is usually accompanied by the rhythmic chant of *um-dois* (one-two) or *esquerda-direita* (left-right) from the *rogador*, a senior member of the *roga* who acts as a drill sergeant for the vintage. At the end of this period (usually around 10 p.m.) *liberdade* (freedom) is declared. Cups of *aguardente* and (sometimes) cigarettes are doled out and the treading continues informally until midnight to the accompaniment of a local accordionist or, more prosaically, to the sound of a booming cassette player. Ideally, there should be two treaders per pipe in a *lagar* in order to extract sufficient colour and flavour for a high quality, potentially Vintage, Port. By the end of the evening with forty well-oiled souls dancing around in a 20-pipe *lagar*, there is often quite a party. Needless to say when foreign wine-trade visitors arrive in the *adega* (usually after a good dinner), the party sometimes runs out of control and people emerge from the *lagar* dripping with grape must.

In spite of late twentieth-century technological advances, the scene at many a *quinta* during vintage has remained virtually unaltered for over a hundred years. Visiting the Douro in the 1870s, Henry Vizetelly found 'a score of men in a clammy purple bath . . . treading the grapes to the sound of fife and drum', adding that 'they half march, half dance round the large *lagar*'. The only difference seems to be a minor matter of hygiene. When Vizetelly was offered the opportunity to taste the must, one of the treaders lifted his brawny leg and a large white saucer was 'held beneath his dripping foot to receive the *mosto* [juice] as it trickled down'!

Lagares are a repository of seemingly arcane myths and rituals, a number of which are based on practical reasoning at some time in the dim and distant past. For example, a few *quintas* still continue to forbid women from treading a *lagar* with the claim that 'they spoil the wine'. This seemingly sexist ruling relates back to hygiene. Putting it delicately, the Portuguese are generally fairly small and women are somewhat shorter than men so that the level of the must in the *lagar* reaches parts higher up the body! Nowadays, people tend to be taller and with labour in relatively short supply most properties can hardly afford to pick and choose. When no ladies were present, it was not uncommon for the treaders to improvise their own rather coarse songs during the period of *liberdade*. In recent years a number of *quintas* have returned to employing local musicians who play Portuguese folk songs or tub-thumping *musica pimba*. Traditional music demands that the treaders lift their legs higher and therefore crush the grapes more effectively than they would to a disco shuffle coming from a cassette player!

Depending on the temperature at which the grapes reach the winery, fermentation will begin quite soon after treading, possibly during the night. The action of human legs and feet helps to warm the must. A few fermentations are inoculated with a selected strain of dried yeast but nearly all *lagares* rely on wild ambient yeasts from the grapes and the *adega*. When the fermentation is underway and the cap (*manta*) of stalks and skins has risen, a couple of planks are placed over the top of the *lagar* and, at periodic intervals, men with long spiked paddles known as *macacos* (monkeys) will stand above the must, plunging down the floating cap. This further aids extraction and prevents the cap from drying out and developing acetic off-flavours.

Ideally the grapes will arrive at the *adega* registering temperatures of around 20°C, rising to 28–30°C at the height of fermentation. Musts fermented at these temperatures will generally show a greater extraction of anthocyannins thereby producing darker wines. Cool ambient temperatures at the time of harvest

Macacos: 'monkey sticks'

will delay the start of fermentation causing a serious log jam of grapes at the winery in a year when production is large. However, a short period of skin maceration before the onset of fermentation helps to aid extraction and in cooler vintages *lagares* will take more work (i.e. treading and plunging) than in a warmer year before they are run off and fortified. But hot ambient temperatures may have more serious implications and it is not uncommon for a perfectly healthy crop to be spoiled if the temperature in a *lagar* runs out of control. In the past, *lagar* fermentations were in the lap of the gods but most producers now rely on heat exchangers to cool the must as necessary.

Once a sufficient amount of colour and flavour has been extracted and sugar levels have fallen to around 7 or 8 baumé, the partially fermented must is run off the skins and mixed with the fortifying *aguardente*. Blended in a proportion of roughly 20 per cent *aguardente* to 80 per cent grape must, the alcohol is raised to a level where the fermentation yeasts are unable to survive. The result is a deep, dark, naturally rich wine with between 80 and 120 g/l residual sugar and an alcoholic strength of 19–20 per cent by volume: embryonic Port.

In the Douro, where there are few flat sites, most traditional *adegas* are built on two levels. The *lagares* on the upper level correspond in size to wooden vats or *toneis* situated in the *armazém* on the floor below. Before electric pumps became the norm, the partially fermented must was simply run off from the *lagar* by gravity leaving behind the mass of grape solids. The remaining stalks and skins then have to be manhandled into a basket press to extract the last of the fermenting must. This in itself is a time-consuming process taking two or three hours. It is 'sod's law' that most *lagares* seem to reach the point at which they have to be run off at two or three o'clock in the morning! However, a number of technical innovations have taken place in the 1990s aimed both at reducing labour costs associated with traditional *lagar* fermentation and easing the entire wine-making process.

TECHNOLOGY

The mass emigration that afflicted rural Portugal in the early 1960s nearly made *lagares* into a thing of the past. With labour in short supply, it fell to the larger shippers to devise alternative methods for making Port and the quest for sufficient extraction has been under consideration ever since. By building up the sides of a traditional *lagar* and installing a pump to spray the cap, Cockburn and Sandeman initially adopted a hybrid system that generally became known as the *movimosto*. This was a reasonably successful method for the production of relatively lightweight Rubies and Tawnies but provided inadequate extraction for high quality Vintage Port. The *movimosto* system had generally been discarded by the end of the 1980s.

Autovinification has proved to be much more enduring. Adapted from an Algerian design known as the Ducellier system, some of the first autovinifiers were built at Royal Oporto's Quinta das Carvalhas and Dow's Quinta do Bomfim in 1963–64 and are still in use. Autovinification is a much more vigorous process than the *movimosto* and has the singular advantage that it is self-sustaining being powered by a natural build-up of carbon dioxide in the system. The early autovinifiers therefore required no external power source and were widely adopted in the Douro during the 1960s when electricity was either unavailable or, at best, unreliable.

The mechanics of the autovinification system are described in detail below.

Nowadays, large wineries are fully automated from start to finish. As soon as a consignment of grapes arrives at the winery, a core sample is taken from each of the *dornas* or bins and the must weight or baumé is recorded by refractometer to determine the amount of fermentable sugar. This may be used to determine a bonus over the basic grape price to the grower, who will be paid when the harvest is over. Some shippers will also pay a further premium for selected grape varieties. After the *dorna* has been weighed it is tipped into a reception hopper from where a large Archimedes screw (known locally as a *sem fim* – 'without end') conveys the grapes to a crusher-destemmer, which removes at least a proportion of the stalks from both red and white grapes. Although stalks were included in the past (mainly because equipment for their removal was not generally available) in modern wineries their inclusion in the ferment can produce harsh, bitter characters in the wine especially if the stems are green and under-ripe. Before the crushed grapes reach the fermentation tank or autovinifier, the must is dosed with sulphur dioxide at levels of between 40 and 150 mg per kg depending on the condition of the grapes. Larger amounts are sometimes used to delay the onset of fermentation and thereby aid extraction. Most wine-makers will adjust the acidity of the must at this stage to around pH 3.6–3.7 by adding the appropriate amount of tartaric acid. A few producers inoculate with selected dried yeasts but most rely on sulphur dioxide to delay fermentation thereby culling undesirable strains of wild yeast. Specific cultured yeasts only tend to be used when a fermentation is reluctant to start as there is a very real risk of ethyl acetate forming if the fermentation fails to commence fairly promptly after crushing.

Where an autovinifier is being used, the vat illustrated in figure 2 is filled to within a metre or so of full capacity. The autovinifier is then closed by lowering the central unit (A) into place. As the fermentation begins carbon dioxide is given off and the pressure builds up inside the tank. This forces the fermenting must up an escape valve (B), which spills out into an open holding tank on top of the vat. Once a certain pressure has built up inside the autovinifier, the carbon dioxide escapes through a calibrated hydraulic valve (C). No longer supported by the pressure inside

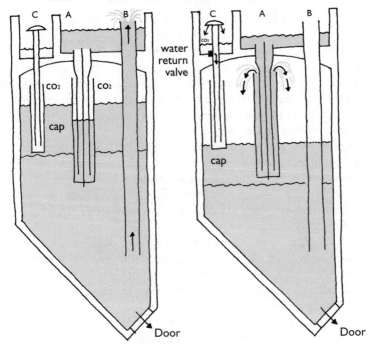

Fig. 2. Autovinification

the vat, the fermenting must falls back down the central autovin-ification unit by force of gravity, spraying the cap or *manta* below. At the same time the hydraulic valve resets itself ready for the pressure to build up and the cycle to begin again. At the start of fermentation, the autovinification cycle is relatively slow but after a few hours when sufficient carbon dioxide is being given off, the build up of pressure inside the vat is such that each cycle takes just ten or fifteen minutes to complete. By the time that the fermenting must is ready to be run off and fortified, the floating cap of grape solids has been thoroughly washed by the must at least twenty or thirty times. As alcohol forms, increasing amounts of colour and flavour are extracted from the grapes.

When they were first developed, most autovinification vats were cubic in shape and built from epoxy-lined reinforced concrete with a capacity similar to that of a traditional *lagar*. In warm years ferments continued to suffer from overheating as well as inadequate pre-fermentative maceration. Having been among the first to experiment with autovinification at Quinta do Bomfim, the Symington family remain firm advocates of the system as a means for producing premium quality Port. Wine-maker Peter Symington believes that because the system incorporates a certain amount of air, it produces structured wines that are not dissimilar in style to those made in a *lagar*.

During the 1980s a number of modifications were made to the autovinification system, the most significant of which was the introduction of temperature control. Apart from its obvious benefit during a warm vintage, temperature control enables the wine-maker to run-off each ferment as late as possible thereby prolonging skin contact. At Quinta da Cavadinha and Quinta do Sol, the Symingtons have installed a battery of stainless-steel autovinification vats all of which are conical in shape for ease of emptying (as in figure 2). These can be run-off within forty-five minutes, the solid matter being conveyed to the press by means of an Archimedes screw. The entire Quinta do Sol winery, which has a production capacity of around 10,000 pipes, will function during vintage with just six people (compared to the twenty or so individuals needed to tread a 20-pipe *lagar*!). Now that electric power is readily available, these latest autovinifiers (squat in shape for extra skin contact) are equipped with pumps that can be switched on to extract colour before fermentation begins.

In some installations (notably Croft's Quinta da Roêda), the early concrete autovinifiers have been modified to accommodate a mechanical device known as a *remontador* by which the must is sucked from the centre of the vat and sprayed over the cap, the entire operation being programmable. A number of other major producers, notably Barros and Ferreira, have built new wineries with temperature-controlled stainless-steel vats merely equipped for pumping over (*remontagem*). Although the verdict still remains open, it seems unlikely that *remontagem* alone is sufficient to provide the required levels of extraction for top quality Ports. In order to achieve necessary extraction, pumping over needs to be very regular, vigorous as well as carefully monitored and controlled.

Cockburn's addressed the problem of extraction their own way by building a central winery at Vila Nova da Foz Côa which uses thermo-vinification. Euphemistically known as the 'jam factory', the must is heated to 70–75°C for an average of fifteen minutes prior to pressing and inoculation with selected dried yeast cultures. In this way the extraction process is completed before fermentation, which takes place off the skins in any suitable vat equipped with temperature control. Jim Reader, Production Director at Cockburns, is generally happy with the overall quality of the wine but despite its capacity to produce dark, fruity wines for Ruby Port, this process has not been adopted by other shippers. In another departure, Cockburn's has also been experimenting with natural pectolytic enzymes to aid extraction and enhance colour and aroma. Enzymes help to soften skins in an under-ripe year.

Bruce Guimaraens, formerly wine-maker for Taylor and Fonseca, briefly experimented with a closed rotary fermentation tank known by the brand name of Vinimatic. Although this produced deep-coloured, aromatic Port, it was concluded that as a result of the lack of aeration during fermentation the wines lacked the structure and complexity of those made in *lagares* or autovinifiers. The Vinimatic has since been used successfully for the production of unfortified Douro wine (see Chapter 6).

Nearly forty years after they were first decommissioned, most of the major shippers have come to accept that traditional *lagares* generally produce the finest, most structured Ports although few conclusive studies have been published to prove it. During the 1990s when Vintage Port met with unprecedented success in the United States, many shippers returned to using *lagares* adapting them to the modern environment. For example at Quinta do Vesúvio, which boasts some of the largest *lagares* in the Douro, the Symington family have devised an innovative temperature-control mechanism. This consists of a matrix of stainless-steel pipes that can be lowered directly into the fermenting must. Other producers, including many independent growers, have followed suit installing heat exchangers in their *lagares*. At Quinta dos Canais, Cockburn's has recently taken the concept a stage further with its own so-called *'techno-lagares'*. These specially constructed *lagares* are roughly 1.5 metres in depth and may be either foot-trodden or pumped over according to the quality of the fruit. They are emptied with a peristaltic pump which creates a muscular wavelike movement as a gentle means of delivering both must and grape solids directly to the press without manhandling.

The preoccupation with *lagares* has led to a number of attempts to simulate the gentle action of the human foot with pistons. Cockburn's John Smithes pioneered so-called 'robotic treading' in the 1960s but Taylor's was the first to use pistons commercially. A temperature-controlled stainless-steel vat equipped with programmable pistons or *macacos* was installed at Quinta de Vargellas in the early 1990s and the idea has subsequently been taken up by a number of other shippers. In the meantime, Quinta do Noval have adapted one of their existing stone *lagares* to accommodate a robotic treading machine, which marches back and forth through the ferment attempting to mimic a traditional *roga*. In 1998 the Symington family built their own robotic stainless-steel *lagar*. The four slab-like 'feet' are themselves temperature-controlled and can be computer-programmed to 'cut' the *lagar* at a variable rhythm. Added to this the new *lagar* has a built-in hydraulic tipping mechanism, which means that it can be run off and fortified in a matter of minutes as opposed to the hours that it takes to empty a traditional *lagar*. Apart from the obvious potential saving in terms of time and labour, the robotic *'roga'* never answers back or demands a glass of *aguardente* and a cigarette!

THE USE (OR ABUSE) OF *'BAGA'*

Elderberry or *baga do sabugueiro* has been used to enhance the colour of Port ever since it became a fortified wine at the end of the seventeenth century. It was the widespread abuse of *baga* in the mid-eighteenth century that forced the Marquês de Pombal to order that all the elderberry trees in the Douro should be grubbed up. But only a few years elapsed before *baga* reappeared and by the middle of the nineteenth century its use was once more fairly commonplace. Henry Vizetelly describes the use of *baga* in the 1870s recording: 'It is quite possible that some small farmers deepen the colour of their wine in bad years – in good years it has ample colour of its own – by steeping in it a bag filled with dried elderberries . . .'

There is evidence that *baga* continues to be used in the Douro to this day in much the same way as when Vizetelly visited the region. Most of the trees are to be found in the higher peripheral areas south of the river, especially above the town of Tabuaço to the extent that *baga* is sometimes referred to covertly as the 'Tabuaço grape'. The fruit ripens in late August and can therefore be dried and stored until the vintage begins in mid-September. The trick is to conceal a sack of dried elderberry at the bottom of a *lagar* full of grapes. A lone treader will then mark time to rehydrate and extract colour from the *baga* which, provided it is used in judicious quantities, does not affect the taste or smell of the wine and is obviously quite harmless. Although *baga* produces impress-ively deep, dark young wines, the colour it imparts is apparently unstable and after a few years the pigment falls away rapidly. It is not therefore used to bolster quality wines for laying down. The major Port shippers do not admit to using *baga* themselves and I have no reason to believe that they do. However, I understand that its use (or abuse) is still sanctioned in a number of outlying *quintas* particularly in weaker years when colour is lacking. During the vintage in 1998 (which was not a particularly weak year) a Douro smallholder with a number of elderberry trees informed me that *baga* was trading at 500 escudos a kilo, roughly twice the price of Touriga Naçional. Quite understandably he described it as *bom negócio* – good business!

WHITE PORT

Compared to red, White Port has customarily been treated as something of an after-thought. White grapes (usually found inter-planted among red varieties) tend to arrive at the winery in dribs and drabs and a number of days can elapse before there is sufficient quantity to begin a fermentation. Prolonged maceration on the skins leads to the over-extraction of phenolic compounds resulting in wines that taste hard and tend to brown rapidly with age. Although there are some excellent examples of this traditional style of White Port, foot-trodden in *lagar* and aged in wood, there is a general trend towards making lighter, less extractive wines. Where possible, skin maceration is increasingly limited to the few hours prior to the onset of fermentation when the juice is run off and vinified separately. Fractions of pressings are usually mixed with the free-run juice in a process known as *meia curtimenta*. The fact that most Douro *adegas* are geared up for red wines rather than white means that pressing tends to be quite severe, accentuating the extractive character of the wine. Some producers have therefore resorted to making very light wines with little or no skin contact, the solids separated by cold settling for twenty-four hours, often aided by pectolytic enzymes. With the advent of temperature control, fermentation temperatures tend to be lower than for red Ports but not as low as they might be for an unfortified dry white wine. Lighter wines, however, are inoculated with selected yeast cultures and fermented at 18–20°C to develop and retain primary fruit character. However, most of the Douro's indigenous white grape varieties lack intrinsic character and a number of wine-makers introduce Moscatel (Muscat) to enhance aromas and flavours. Around the town of Favaios where much of the Moscatel is planted, some small producers make an aromatic varietal Moscatel by fortifying the wine prior to pressing and leaving it in contact with the skins (see page 156). This skin maceration technique is also used in southern Portugal for the production of Moscatel de Setúbal.

FORTIFICATION AND *AGUARDENTE*

With the exception of a special category of light, dry White Port known as 'Leve Seco', all Port is fortified to a strength of between 19 and 22 per cent by volume. In a process known as *encuba*, the wine is typically run off when approximately 4 or 5 per cent of natural alcohol has been produced from the fermentation and mixed with grape spirit or *aguardente* in a proportion of roughly 115 litres to 435 litres of wine thereby making up a 550-litre pipe (the standard unit of measurement in the Douro). The blending of *aguardente* with the must is generally carried out by pumping a measured quantity of spirit into a wooden, cement or stainless-steel holding tank simultaneously with the free-run juice and the pressings. The new wine is then homogenised and given a certain amount of aeration by pumping over. The action of mixing fermenting must with *aguardente* causes a rise in temperature, which can be undesirable in a young wine. One major shipper has taken to chilling the spirit down to 12°C, which helps to arrest the fermentation and ameliorates the 'thermic shock'.

Throughout the nineteenth century much of the *aguardente* was distilled locally in the Douro but since João Franco's legislation of

1907 (see page 40), shippers were forced to purchase spirit from outside the region, either from distilleries in Estremadura and the Ribatejo in central-southern Portugal or abroad. Unlike Sherry or Madeira, both of which are fortified with nearly neutral spirit of an alcoholic strength not less than 95 per cent by volume, Port producers use wine spirit (commonly and mistakenly referred to as 'brandy') with a strength of 77 per cent vol. Whereas neutral spirit has little direct impact on the flavour and character of the wine (other than raising the level of alcohol), the wine spirit used for Port contains significant levels of higher alcohols, esters and aldehydes, which have both direct and secondary effects on the character and maturation of the product. Until 1990 the distribution of fortifying spirit was controlled by a Portuguese government monopoly and the shippers themselves had little or no choice over the quality of the *aguardente* used to fortify Port. In the early 1970s the Port shippers were the subject of a major fraud, which resulted in the production of three successive years being fortified with industrial alcohol as opposed to grape spirit. The scandal is recounted in more detail on page 52.

In the 1990s the major shippers joined forces to form a company called Gruporto expressly to purchase spirit for fortification on the open market. This may originate from anywhere in the European Union but usually comes from France, Spain or southern Portugal. Samples of *aguardente* are tasted by the shippers themselves and submitted to the Port Wine Institute (IVP) for analysis and approval. Nearly all today's *aguardente* is produced in continuous stills, which produce more neutral spirit than the traditional pot stills. Consequently, the overall quality is appreciably higher than it was in the 1960s and 1970s; the somewhat dirty spirit used in the past is no longer evident today.

The style of a particular Port is determined to a great extent by the point at which the must is run off and fortified. A shipper looking to maintain a marginally sweeter house style will therefore choose to fortify slightly earlier than a producer whose wines are drier. However, shippers may also produce small amounts of sweet wine specifically for blending at a later stage (see Chapter 4). Known as *geropigas* these are wines (either red or white) with 150 g/l or more of natural sugar that have been fortified almost as soon as fermentation begins. Red *geropigas* tend to be relatively pale in colour due to the limited amount of skin contact. Conversely, some ferments may be permitted to continue for rather longer than normal to producer darker, drier wine with 20–50 g/l residual sugar, which is also used for blending and fine tuning. In a few instances, a small amount of *aguardente* may be added to musts before fermentation, raising the level to 3–4 per cent by volume to curtail the metabolism of the yeasts thereby further aiding extraction.

TIME TO PRESS

The mass of grape solids (skins, stalks and pips) remaining after a Port fermentation has been run off and fortified contains valuable must, rich in colouring matter and tannin. The traditional means of extracting this juice is to transfer the solids either to a vertical (basket) press in the centre of the *lagar*, or to a hydraulic piston press located elsewhere in the *adega*. Nowadays most wineries are equipped either with horizontal plate presses or a continuous screw press. The former is generally preferable as continuous presses can produce bitter, over-extractive juice. In spite of this, they continue to be used successfully by a number of major shippers. A large proportion of the press juice is mixed with the free-run; however, more astringent fractions may be fermented to dryness and distilled. The more gentle pneumatic presses favoured by many wine producers do not tend to be used by Port producers as they provide insufficient levels of extraction.

THE END OF VINTAGE

The vintage usually ends as noisily and cheerfully as it begins. When all the grapes have been gathered and the final *lagar* has been trodden, the *roga* or gang of pickers prepare to depart. The conclusion of a successful harvest is the excuse for a celebration by all those involved. The wife of the owner of the *quinta* is customarily presented with the *ramo*, a palm or bamboo branch that has been festooned with flowers, grapes, paper streamers and other objects (like empty sardine tins) that happen to be on hand. The significance of this ceremony has been lost to all those who take part today but it is thought to originate from a pagan attempt to ward off evil spirits. The presentation of the *ramo* is accompanied by a chorus of *'vivas'* from the *roga* followed by singing and dancing along with the libatious consumption of wine, *aguardente* and cigarettes provided by the *quinta*. The *roga* then return tired and somewhat the worse for wear to their village where they remain until the following vintage. After a month of frenzied activity, an uncanny silence settles on the Douro.

Basket press

4

Port Types

OVER-WINTERING IN THE DOURO

The onset of winter transforms the Douro into a cold, soulless place. A thick blanket of icy fog hangs over the valley for weeks on end, blotting out the sun. Houses remain shuttered up and in the *armazém* the young wines seem to shut down in sympathy. As the heady aromas and vibrant colours of the vintage begin to fade, even the finest of Ports can seem to be something of a disappointment during the winter months. All Port wines spend their first winter in the Douro, during which time they 'fall bright' as minute yeast cells, grape solids and tartrates settle to the bottom of the vat, helped by the cold weather. Left in the wine, this sediment will absorb colour and could stimulate the growth of harmful spoilage bacteria.

A month or two after the vintage, the *lota* takes place. The young wines are racked or drawn off the sediment (lees), analysed and adjusted where necessary. It is not uncommon for a Port to be fortified initially up to 16 per cent alcohol and an extra measure of *aguardente* is frequently added to bring the level up to a minimum of 19 per cent by volume. This provides the opportunity for the first selection and classification. To a certain extent this is pre-ordained. At the end of vintage, the origin, quality and quantity of the individual lots of wine will generally reflect a shipper's overall requirements. A large shipper marketing a complete range of different types of Port will end up with as many as 400–500 separate lots. Most Port producers are therefore equipped with a variety of different storage vessels in the Douro. These vary in size from the distinctive concrete *balões* (also known colloquially as 'mamas' or 'ginas' – after Gina Lollobrigida – because of their distinctive shape), each capable of holding up to 100,000 litres, through medium-sized wooden *toneis* to small, stainless-steel holding tanks in which high quality wines from different parcels of vines can be kept separate for future appraisal. However, much of the wine will remain in the custody of individual farmers throughout the winter months.

Balões . . . 'ginas', 'mamas', 'Lollobrigidas'

In the spring following the harvest, the colour begins to recover as the young Ports start to bind or 'close up'. This is the cue for much of the previous year's Port to be shipped down from the Douro to Vila Nova de Gaia before the onset of the summer heat. As the wines are prepared for shipment, they undergo a second racking from the lees and levels of sulphur dioxide are adjusted to protect the wine from undue oxidation. The fraction of wine mixed in with the gross lees used to represent a considerable loss, amounting to as much as 10 per cent of total volume. In order to keep their losses to a minimum, producers would frequently empty the lees into canvas sacks, placing boards and stones on top to squeeze as much wine as possible from the solid matter. Nowadays, this troublesome and unhygienic practice has given way to the rotary vacuum filter, which separates clean wine from the solid matter. The wine is kept to one side and blended later into lower quality Ports.

For the best part of three centuries, the new wine was shipped downstream to Vila Nova de Gaia by *barco rabelo*. These distinctive Viking-inspired boats were gradually decommissioned following the construction of the railway in the 1870s and were finally abandoned altogether when the river was dammed in the 1960s. From March through to May the Douro's winding roads are choked by spluttering articulated tankers.

MATURATION

Listen to the weather forecast for Oporto and Vila Nova de Gaia and it usually begins in much the same way. The *neblina matinal* (morning mist), which drifts in overnight from the Atlantic, often hangs around all day during the winter months obscuring the top of the Torre dos Clerigos, the tallest church tower in Portugal. An air of dampness pervades the city. It penetrates buildings so that patches of mould grow on the walls if rooms are not regularly aired. This atmosphere is eminently suitable for the maturation of wine and it is here rather than in the Douro that the Port shippers inevitably choose to set up their cellars. They are not 'cellars' in the true sense of the word for Port is generally aged above ground. The wine matures in a 'lodge', a term that derives from the Portuguese word '*loja*' meaning shop, store or cellar. The Portuguese themselves tend to use a more accurate term, *armazém*, which translates as 'warehouse' or 'storehouse'.

The long, low red-roofed buildings that stretch up from the river bank in Vila Nova de Gaia serve both as headquarters for the majority of Port shippers and storehouses for a huge quantity of Port. Most of the wine ages in wooden vats and casks ranging in capacity from *balseiros* holding as much as 100,000 litres to casks of around 600 litres (so-called 'lodge pipes'). They function as vessels for ageing where the permeability of the wood permits a gradual, controlled oxidation of the contents. Wines destined for bottling after two or three years – premium Ruby, LBV (Late Bottled Vintage) and Vintage – are partly aged in *balseiros* and partly kept in stainless steel to preserve the primary character of the fruit. Wines set aside to become old Tawnies are transferred to smaller lodge pipes to enhance the oxidative character of the wine.

Apart from a number of vats made from *macacauba* (Brazilian

1. Quinta do Vesúvio: the most stately property in the Douro. The house built by the Ferreira family is one of the largest in the region.

2. Quinta de la Rosa: the vineyards rise up from the river (at 90 metres above sea level) to an altitude of 260 metres, bringing about a range of micro-climates.

3. Explosives are used to create a new vineyard at the Symington family's Quinta do Vesúvio.

4. A Swiss 'multijyp' undergoing trials at Quinta do Noval; vineyard mechanisation has been a preoccupation among growers since the 1970s.

5. Contrasting terraces at Quinta do Bom Retiro (right) and Quinta da Corte in the Rio Torto.

6. Vertical planting (vinha ao alto) pioneered by Ferreira at Quinta do Seixo in the Rio Torto.

7. A panel of azulejos (traditional tiles) at Pinhão railway station illustrates the harvest.

8. Grapes arrive in a steel dorna at Cockburn's Tua adega. The probe is used to measure sugar content.

9. Treading grapes by foot in a granite lagar at Quinta de Foz. Richard Mayson can be seen leading the roga in the centre of the circle.

10. Purple grape must seen in the upper holding tank of an autovinifier at Quinta do Bomfim. Colour extraction is a crucial factor in Port vinification.

11. Oporto viewed from the quayside in Vila Nova de Gaia with barcos rabelos mothballed in the foreground.

12. Barcos rabelos compete in the annual race between Port shippers.

13. Port ageing in pipes at Vila Nova de Gaia. Lodge pipes may vary in size but the 550-litre pipa or pipe is the standard unit of measurement in the Douro.

14. Repairing a pipe in the cool of a lodge at Vila Nova de Gaia. New wood has no place in the maturation of Port.

15. George Sandeman prepares an al fresco tasting at Sandeman's Casa de Santa Clara, Vale de Mendiz.

16. The colour spectrum: red Port (left) turns tawny with age, white Port (right) turns amber with age until the two are almost indistinguishable. On either side are samples of the colourless spirit (aguardente) used to fortify Port.

mahogany) and a few Italian chestnut casks, nearly all the wood utilised for the maturation of Port is oak. This is favoured over other types of wood for its tighter grain, thereby reducing evaporation and enabling a more gradual oxidation. Much of the oak used for ageing Port originated from Memel and Stettin in the Baltic state of Lithuania before it was occupied by the former Soviet Union in 1939. More recently oak has been obtained from New Orleans in North America and northern Portugal although with no forest management policy to speak of, the latter is now almost non-existent. When new casks are required today, the oak is bought from the Limousin and Alliers forests of France and coopered in Portugal. Unlike a Californian Cabernet or classed growth Claret, the merest hint of new oak is extremely undesirable in Port (although I was recently alarmed to taste such a wine from a small producer in the Douro). New casks therefore have to be well seasoned (usually with unfortified red Douro wine) before they are put into use.

Although some of the larger shippers maintain their own coopers, the demand for wood is nowhere near as great as it was in the first half of the twentieth century when the majority of wine was still shipped in cask. Chestnut was generally used for shipping because it is cheaper and structurally more robust than oak. The chestnut casks that remain are left over from this period. Most coopers are now retained on regular maintenance duty, repairing a pipe when a stave has been damaged or dismantling and rebuilding a vat when it has to be moved. Many shippers have a long-term programme of wood renewal. The recent closure of lodges belonging to Royal Oporto and Borges & Irmão and the purchase of their wood by other shippers has created work for coopers as vats are dismantled, restored and reassembled.

Lesser Ports (white, Ruby and inexpensive Tawny) are generally stored in tanks made from stainless steel or cement. Many of these wines remain up in the Douro long after the premium quality wines have been shipped down to Gaia, sometimes until they are called upon to make up the final shipping blend prior to bottling (see below). Port stored in the Douro for long periods, especially at individual *quintas*, often acquires a stewed character from the ambient heat. Known as 'Douro bake', this phenomenon has as much to do with poor *élevage* as high storage temperatures. One major shipper, Quinta do Noval, has moved lock, stock and barrel

Toneis, pipas and *balseiros*

to the Douro constructing a purpose-built, temperature-controlled warehouse and bottling plant on the airy *planalto* north of the river. Cockburn, Sandeman, the Symington family and Taylor/Fonseca all maintain substantial stocks of Port in well-insulated *armazéns* to ease the pressure on their cramped quarters in Vila Nova de Gaia.

RACKING

The process of racking (or *transfega* as it is known in Portuguese) is an important but extremely labour-intensive part of the annual cycle of cellar-work. It involves the removal of clear wine from the sediment or lees that have settled at the bottom of the cask or vat. Left in the wine, the lees will generate off-flavours and, apart from aiding the process of clarification, racking also provides aeration and helps to develop the flavour of the wine.

Racking regimens vary according to the shipper and the type of wine but all Ports are typically racked three times in the first year, twice in the second and annually thereafter. Older wines like aged

Tawnies continue to precipitate solid matter as the anthocyanins (tannin and colouring matter) are deposited in the bottom of the cask. In this case pipes or casks (normally stacked four high) are decanted progressively, starting from the top row. The lees are left in the bottom of each cask, which is then removed from the stack, cleaned and replaced. The stack is effectively entirely rebuilt row-by-row. The combination of ageing vessel, the amount of air in the head space and the frequency of racking provides the wine-maker with an opportunity to influence the rate of maturation and has an important bearing on the style and character of the wine.

CLARIFICATION AND FILTRATION

Racking alone is sufficient to eliminate heavier insoluble particles from a young Port but it does not remove inherently unstable material found in solution that could precipitate after the wine has been bottled. Most wines are therefore clarified further using fining agents such as gelatin, bentonite, egg white and casein. Young Ports are no exception and it is the wine-maker's task to choose a fining agent appropriate to the type of wine. Gelatin and bentonite are normally used in tandem, with larger amounts added to round out the flavour and strip colour from a young wine (for example, a standard Tawny). Some shippers also use centrifugation to hasten deposition but many smaller producers still use gum arabic that prevents deposition and tends to produce wines with an opaque appearance and a dull colour. Casein-based products are used to stabilise and remove oxidative browning from White Ports. Unless there is a particular problem, old Tawnies and bottle-matured wines like traditional LBVs and Vintage Ports are rarely (if ever) fined.

Most Rubies and young Tawnies are cold stabilised to remove tartrates and colouring material, which could otherwise crystallise and precipitate in the bottle (particularly in colder climes like Canada and Scandinavia, both of which are important markets). Two systems are commonly used. The first involves the use of a heat exchanger to refrigerate the wine down to between −8 °C and −10 °C followed by static settling for about a week in an insulated tank. Most of the larger Port shippers have invested in continuous systems, which chill the wine and pass it continually through a crystallising tank seeded with potassium bitartrate. In each case, the wines are filtered after the stabilisation process using diatomaceous earth followed by sheet and/or membrane filters. Smaller producers like single *quintas*, which lack the wherewithal to purchase such sophisticated equipment tend to rely on metatataric acid, which merely offers short-term protection against tartrate deposition. Since the increase in bacteriological problems during the 1980s (see below), shippers have increasingly resorted to flash pasteurisation following cold treatment in order to achieve 'belt and braces' stability in volume Ruby and Tawny. Wine extracted from the lees is also pasteurised.

Needless to say, the methods of clarification and filtration outlined above inevitably strip a certain amount of character and flavour from a wine. Bottle-matured Ports are not therefore cold-stabilised and rarely filtered, leading to the formation of a heavy deposit or 'crust'. These wines need to be decanted off the sediment before serving.

QUALITY CONTROL

In the early 1980s there was a sudden increase in the incidence of bacterial problems, perhaps associated with infrequent racking but probably resulting from poorly maintained wood. Wines that appeared to be correct in the tasting room turned unpleasantly volatile (vinegary) in bottle. Lactic bacteria (predominately *lactobacilllus*), which flourish in the presence of small amounts of air, will transform naturally occurring malic acid into lactic acid and attack glucose to form acetic acid. In dry red wines and some whites, this malo-lactic transformation is perfectly natural, leading to a reduction in the overall acidity of the wine. However, in Port, where glucose levels are high and acidity is generally low in the first place, the presence of lactic bacteria is always extremely detrimental to the wine. Until the 1980s many producers believed that these lactic bacteria were unable to tolerate high levels of alcohol and (particularly up in the Douro) hygiene was perhaps not accorded the highest priority. Indeed, it was not uncommon to visit an outlying *quinta* shortly before the vintage only to find the chickens roosting inside a wooden *tonel* that would shortly be receiving the year's Port!

Since a number of shippers were caught out over the 1985

vintage, hygiene and quality control have come to the fore. Technical requirements have to be adhered to and, in response to the decline (and eventual suspension) of bulk shipments, and the trend towards bottling at source, the major shippers have all set up their own quality control laboratories. The Port Wine Institute (IVP) has a well-equipped laboratory and offers its services to smaller shippers. The IVP also has its own rigorous quality control procedures but a number of smaller shippers without their own laboratories are still sitting on a potential bacterial time bomb. The problem is most acute in the Douro where an increasing number of single *quintas* are shipping their own wine. (One property solved the problem of a tainted *tonel* by lining the inside with fibreglass to prevent the wine coming into contact with the wood!) Despite the obligatory and increasingly rigorous assessment by the IVP's much-vaunted *Câmara de Provadores* (tasting panel), a number of inconsistent and occasionally downright faulty wines continue to reach export markets.

TASTING AND BLENDING

Every major Port shipper has a tasting room with a view. Huge plate glass windows stare northwards over the River Douro and on to the kaleidoscopic city of Oporto beyond. Impressive as this

Fonseca's room with a view

sight is to visitors, there is a practical reason for capturing the panorama of Portugal's second city. Colour is axiomatic to Port and it is no coincidence that two of the most important types of Port, Ruby and Tawny, are named after different shades. A single glass held up and tilted against the cool north light may represent a blend of a thousand or more pipes of Port.

As soon as the previous year's wines (or representative samples of the wines) reach the shippers' lodges in Vila Nova de Gaia, they are reassessed. Each wine is given a name and/or number based on its origin and will be accompanied by an analysis detailing, among other things, its strength and sweetness. Relying on prior knowledge and experience, tasters have the future in their hands when they judge if a Port will stand up to ten, twenty or more years ageing or whether it is destined to form part of a younger blend. Since the 1980s, varietal lots (see page 79) have added another variable into the blending equation. With the notable exception of wines from a single year (Vintage, LBV and *Colheita* Ports), shippers generally seek to produce Port of a consistent style and age. This presents a formidable challenge, especially for younger fruit-driven styles (Ruby and premium Ruby) where the variation in harvest from year to year has to be masked in the final blend. Although many of the same principles apply, it is not possible to blend Port by means of the *solera* system used for Sherry.

Most Port is therefore the result of continuous blending, appraisal and reappraisal. Tasting is a question of memory as well as an inherent feeling for the style and character of the wines that have been put to one side. Samples are also submitted by other producers but it is usual for shippers to have contracts with the same growers year after year in order to reinforce the continuity of style. Although colour, aroma and taste will always remain paramount, nowadays quantifiable colour analysis (spectro-photometry) and computer records help to provide an *aide-mémoire*.

Shippers tend to base their blends on a series of *lotes*. These are themselves blends of wines from different years held in reserve to feed a certain pre-determined house style or brand. The *lote* is usually made up some time before it is required and a proportion of the previous *lote* is usually included in the final blend to keep the wine consonant with the last bottling. Younger or older wines may be introduced accordingly and the final sweetness may be adjusted with *geropigas* or drier wines. Sometimes both are used in order to lend complexity to a particular blend. The standard blending unit for this fine tuning is the *almude* (25.44 litres). With twenty-one *almudes* to a shipping pipe, this longstanding but apparently arbitrary measure represents the maximum amount that a man can carry on his head at one time!

Lesser quality wines destined for inexpensive Ruby and Tawny blends tend to be classified early on and their *lotes* are made up first, usually within six months of the vintage. Many shippers purchase large volumes of wine from co-operatives (predominantly in the Baixo Corgo) in order to augment these wines. Later in the year blends of differing but complementary wines will be formed, perhaps with a particular brand of premium Ruby in mind. The small quantities of wine set aside to become old Tawnies may remain for several years before further blending whereas potential vintage *lotes* are kept separate and classified as late as possible. They are regularly reassessed before the decision is finally taken as to whether or not to declare roughly eighteen months after the harvest.

The rules and regulations that govern the various different types of Port are covered below.

PORT: A BASIC CATEGORISATION

Despite the proliferation of numerous different commercial styles of Port since the end of the 1960s, there are two fundamental categories:

Wood-matured: All Ruby, Tawny and White Ports (including old Tawnies, *Colheitas*, so-called 'Vintage Character' Port and most LBVs) are aged for varying periods in bulk (either in wood and/or stainless-steel or cement vats) and are only bottled when they are judged to be ready for drinking. Once in bottle most of these wines will keep for a year or more but they are not intended to be kept over the medium or long term. Having been fined and filtered before bottling, they do not need to be decanted. So-called 'wood Ports' are generally bottled with a stopper cork.

Bottle-matured: Vintage, single-*quinta* Vintage, Crusted Ports and some LBVs are bottled when relatively young and the wines continue to age and develop in the bottle over the medium to long term. Compared with wood Ports where the maturation takes place in a controlled, oxidative environment (see above), bottle-matured Ports age in reductive conditions largely isolated from the air. Bottle maturation therefore slows down the ageing process. This can be seen just by comparing the colour of a twenty-year-old Vintage Port with a twenty-year-old *Colheita*. Bottle-matured Ports are not generally subject to any fining or filtration and therefore throw a sediment or 'crust' in bottle and should be decanted. They are mostly bottled in opaque, dark glass with driven corks and should be stored lying down in cool conditions to keep the cork elastic and prevent the ingress of air.

Aside from this, the Port Wine Institute have their own categorisation, which is written into the statutes. Anything other than standard Ruby, Tawny and White Port, which together account for around 90 per cent of the trade in volume terms belongs to a *Categoria Especial* or 'Special Category'. This embraces Vintage Port, LBV, Vintage Character, Port with the year of vintage stated (i.e. single-*quinta* Vintage and *Colheita*), and Port with the age indicated on the label (i.e. most old Tawnies). The rules that accompany the Special Categories are considerably more exacting. The wines are regularly and randomly monitored by the IVP and shippers are required to maintain a current account for each *lote*. At the time of writing the legislation governing different styles of Port is under review and the changes are due to be published in 1999.

A detailed appraisal of the multifarious types of Port follows on pages 154–85.

PORT: A BASIC CLASSIFICATION

The world seems to have an obsession with class and classification. Not content with the continuum in which we mostly inhabit and interact, for the sake of convenience we divide ourselves into socio-economic groups (sometimes attaching names like 'sloane ranger' or 'preppie')! The classification of wine took hold in the nineteenth century with the 1855 Classed Growth system in the Médoc although Pombal had attempted a similar (but more complex) classification of Port vineyards when the Douro was demarcated nearly a century earlier. The latter has long been superseded by Moreira da Fonseca's vineyard points system (see page 64). Needless to say, no classification system is ever perfect and various categorisations of Bordeaux and Douro vineyards have been subject to vociferous criticism over the years. Because most Ports are complex blends from a number of different properties and *terroirs*, the Douro's vineyard classification system has not filtered through to the consumer.

In the 1980s and 1990s, high-profile North American wine critics have taken wine classification a stage further with their points scoring systems. Based on the US examination system, a wine can score a minimum of 50 points (in which case it will be totally and utterly undrinkable) and a maximum of 100. Most scores are massaged to fall between 80 and 100 and in reality there is very little difference between a wine that is awarded say 90 as opposed to a wine with 95 points. Apart from common wine faults and the agreed expectation of a particular style of wine, in the end all classification is a matter of personal taste.

It is therefore with some trepidation that I put forward my own classification for general guidance in this book. Taking each style of Port separately, I have categorised the best wines as either 'Premier League', 'First Division' or (in the case of Vintage Port) 'Second Division'. I make no apology for the fact that the classification is inspired by the UK football leagues! Producers whose wines have not, in my opinion, made the grade are not listed. Unlike the American points system this categorisation is not based on a single showing but repeated tasting of Port wines over a decade or more. It is inevitably subjective but it takes consistency into account and this is fundamental both to the reputation of individual Port shippers and Port wine in general. With one notable exception, I have limited the classification to the wines that belong to the Port Wine Institute's officially designated Special Categories.

STANDARD STYLES

Ruby

Named after its youthful colour, Ruby is the simplest and often one of the most satisfying styles of young Port. The wines chosen to make up a Ruby usually present a deep colour, straightforward fruity aromas, some body and structure but not too much in the way of tannic grip. Ruby blends are generally made up from more than one year, aged in bulk for up to three years and bottled young to capture the strong, fiery personality of young Port. The wines are either aged in large wooden *balseiros* or more usually in lined cement or stainless-steel vats. Racking is kept to a minimum in order to prevent any oxidative character entering the wine. Some Rubies have a coarse but rather hollow character as a result of heavy-handed stabilisation but there is something honest and entirely admirable about a good, down-to-earth Ruby, packed with raw, primary fruit. A glass of fiery Ruby Port can be extremely satisfying outdoors on a cold day or on a winter's night, accompanied by a slice of strong cheese. Beware of wines with qualifying adjectives like 'fine old' or 'full rich' on the label: Cockburn, Dow, Sandeman and Smith Woodhouse all bottle good, reliable Ruby Port.

For much of the nineteenth and twentieth centuries, Ruby was the bread and butter for the Port trade. In the years that followed the First World War, Ruby Port was drunk in huge quantities by the British and became strongly associated with the archetypal 'Rover's Return' street-corner pub. It was frequently used as the basis for a long drink, 'Port and lemon', poured over ice and let out with fizzy lemonade but the fashion faded in the 1960s and poor old Ruby was rather left on the shelf. Having been hijacked by the manufacturers of so-called 'British wine', it is a shame that the term 'Ruby' has taken on somewhat pejorative connotations. As a result the focus for many shippers has shifted away from Ruby towards Ports with more prestigious-sounding titles like Vintage Character and LBV. Even so, many of these wines are little more than jumped-up Ruby.

Tawny

The word 'Tawny' is attached to two very different styles of Port. It implies a wine that has been aged in wood for longer than a Ruby until it takes on an amber-tawny hue. But much of the Tawny Port that reaches the shelves today is no older than the average Ruby and it is not uncommon to see the two wines standing side by side at the same price. These inexpensive Tawnies are merely made from lighter wines from the Baixo Corgo, often further diluted with some White Port so that they appear pink. Heavy fining is also used to adjust the colour and some shippers add a little *mosto torrado* (basically caramelised grape must), which lends a coarse but artificially mature colour, aroma and flavour to the blend. This form of tinkering is not a particularly new practice. At the beginning of the twentieth century Ernest Cockburn relates that it was not uncommon to use 'brown finings', which 'certainly removed the pinkness of a wine, but produced in its stead an unpleasant yellow, greenish colour . . .' Fining is still used as a means to tinker with the colour but today's young Tawnies are rather more natural in appearance than they were in Ernest Cockburn's day. Many wines spend a summer up in the Douro being *estufado* (stewed) in cement *balões* by the ambient heat and, as one shipper admitted candidly, these Ports see wood by accident rather than by design! The resulting wines usually display a slightly brown tinge on the rim but lack the freshness and vibrancy usually associated with young Port.

Often drunk as an aperitif, these so-called 'Tawnies' have a popular following in France. They have largely filled the gap at the bottom end of the market left behind by the demise of 'Port and lemon'. In order to distinguish them from 'boot-Tawny', most wood-matured Tawnies are labelled with an indication of age (see section below) although the words 'old', 'very old' or 'velho' may be applied to a wine showing the characteristics of seven years ageing in wood. Niepoort bottle two such wines with the complementary names of 'Junior' and 'Senior'.

White Port

There is an old adage that Port has two duties: the first is to be red and the second is to be drunk. Having tasted so many dull, insipid White Ports, I am more than inclined to agree. Although handling has improved in recent years, characterless grape varieties and heavy-handed vinification methods are still largely to blame. Nowadays, much White Port is produced merely to cut inexpensive Tawny blends and in the wake of the vineyard replanting scheme of the 1980s that focused on five red grape varieties, there is a shortage of white grapes.

Wood-ageing lends character to White Port but most wines are left in lined cement or stainless steel and bottled after eighteen months to two years. The honourable exceptions are Barros, Churchill, Niepoort and Quinta de la Rosa, all of whom bottle excellent traditional dry White Ports, which have turned golden amber with age and have picked up an incisive, nutty character from the wood. Rare white *Colheitas* like the 1952 from C. da Silva or Niepoort's exceptional wine from 1895 present a rich, honeyed complexity comparable to well-aged Tawny. White Ports are produced in a number of different styles ranging from the unctuous wines labelled 'Lagrima' (meaning 'tears' because of their viscosity) with a baumé reading of 4.8 to 6.6 through 'sweet', 'medium sweet', 'dry' to 'extra dry' (around zero baumé). With the exception of a special category known as *'leve seco'* (light dry), which is bottled at 16.5 per cent alcohol by volume (abv), White Ports are normally fortified to between 19 and 22 per cent alcohol by volume.

White Port is usually served chilled as an aperitif, either on its own or with a twist of lemon peel to sharpen up the flavour, accompanied by a bowl of salted almonds. Some shippers pour White Port over ice and advocate a long drink let out with tonic water and served with a mint leaf, although a long, cool Super Bock (the local beer) is a better quencher at the end of a hot day in the Douro. At Factory House lunches where a decanter of dry White Port stands alongside a decanter of Fino Sherry, the latter is usually more popular! White Ports nevertheless continue to find a market in Portugal (where Sherry is a virtual anathema) and in Holland, France and the Benlux.

Moscatel de Favaios

There are pockets of Moscatel (Muscat) all over the Douro but the greatest concentration is to be found on the *planalto* around the towns of Alijó and Favaios. So far it has escaped the attention of the legislators and no DOC has ever been created although a special sub-region (Moscatel de Favaios) has been under discussion for some years. Made in much the same way as Port, production is centred on the local co-operative, which ages the wine for around three years in wooden *toneis* and *balseiros* ranging in size from 10,000 to 33,000 litres. Most Favaios wines share a similar rustic, oxidative style although Quinta do Portal bottles a paler, fresher wine, which is sweet to the point of cloying. Outside the Favaios sub-zone, Niepoort make limited quantities of a rich, balanced Moscatel, which is amber-brown in colour from prolonged ageing in cask.

Vintage Character/Premium Ruby

Vintage Character is Port's great misnomer. These wines are not the product of a single year and few share much of the character or concentration of a true Vintage Port. The style is none the less highly laudable and results from the blending of young Ports of a higher quality than those used for standard Ruby, with an average age of between three and five years. The greater part of the blend is likely to be aged in wood although shippers are looking to select well-structured wines with a ripe, primary fruit character that have mellowed more than a standard Ruby. Like Ruby, Vintage Character is ready to drink as soon as it is bottled and is not intended for laying down. 'Premium Ruby' is therefore an apt description for this style of Port.

'Vintage Character' was first recognised by the IVP in 1973 and, partly due to its marketing cachet, the style has been extremely successful in the United Kingdom where sales of standard Ruby have been steadily declining. The category is now well established and a number of leading shippers have removed the words 'Vintage Character' from their labels in favour of their own brand names (Taylor's First Estate or Dow's Trademark for example). Reflecting the tendency to 'trade-up', Cockburn's Special Reserve has taken over from Cockburn's Ruby as the United Kingdom's best-selling brand (although for obscure technical reasons these branded wines like Cockburn's Special Reserve and Warre's Warrior are not officially included in the Vintage Character category).

Premier League	*First Division*
Fonseca Bin 27	Dow's Trademark
Graham's Six Grapes	Cockburn's Special Reserve
Warre's Warrior	Ferreira, Vintage Character
	Quinta de la Rosa, Finest Reserve
	Sandeman Signature
	Smith Woodhouse, Lodge Reserve
	Taylor's First Estate

Late Bottled Vintage (LBV)

Unlike Vintage Character, LBV means as it says: a wine from a single year bottled between four and six years after the vintage (compared to a maximum of two years for Vintage Port *per se*). The style evolved largely by default. In the lean years from the 1930s to the 1950s, it was not uncommon for a Vintage Port to remain in wood for rather longer than normal while the wine was awaiting a buyer. Under subsequent legislation many of these Vintage Ports were technically 'late bottled'. A number of shippers therefore claim to have invented LBV but it was in 1955 that Taylor's introduced a new style of wine, which they termed 'Vintage Reserve'. Taylor's owned the rights to this name but with a clear gap in the market, a new designation – Late Bottled Vintage – was officially sanctioned by the IVP in the mid-1960s. Consequently the first such wine to appear on the market was Taylor's 1965 LBV, which was launched in 1970.

Adopted by most shippers, LBV proved to be hugely successful, first in the United Kingdom and subsequently in North America where the word 'Vintage' undoubtedly commands a premium. In order to prevent too much oxidative character from entering the blend, wines destined to become LBVs are kept in large vats (either wood or stainless steel) until they are bottled between 1 July in the fourth year after the respective harvest and the 31 December in the sixth year. Two very different styles of wine have now evolved. Most producers of LBV followed Taylor's, fining and/or filtering and cold-stabilising their wines before bottling in order to prevent the formation of a sediment thereby removing the need to decant. This has proved popular both with restaurateurs and consumers but both the size of some of the *lotes* and heavy-handed filtration have conspired to strip much of the character from the wine. As a result many LBVs are no more than premium Ruby with a date attached.

In the 1990s there has been a growing trend towards so-called 'traditional' LBV, bottled without any filtration or treatment. Usually produced from a good, undeclared harvest, in order to qualify for the traditional/bottle-matured designation the wine must spend an extra three years in bottle before being released. Bottled with a driven cork (as opposed to the stopper corks used for fined/filtered LBVs) these wines will often continue to improve in bottle for another four to six years and the best share something of the depth and intensity of a true Vintage Port. Like a Vintage Port, an unfined and unfiltered LBV will throw a sediment and should be decanted prior to serving.

Premier League	*First Division*
Churchill	Burmester
Graham	Croft
Niepoort	Dow
Quinta do Noval	Ferreira
Quinta de la Rosa	Fonseca
Smith Woodhouse	Taylor
Warre	

Crusted Port

So-called because of the deposit or 'crust' that the wine throws in bottle, Crusted Port is a twentieth-century creation that has earned itself the epithet of 'poor man's Vintage Port'. Although the coveted word 'Vintage' does not appear anywhere on the label, Crusted Ports are much closer in style to Vintage Port than either Vintage Character or most LBVs, presenting a dense, concentrated wine for a fraction of the price. Wines from two or three harvests are aged in wood for up to two years and bottled without any fining or filtration. The only date that is of any significance is the year of bottling, which appears on the label. The wine may only be released after spending at least three years in bottle, by which time it is usually quite approachable having developed the ripe aromas characteristic of a Vintage Port as well as a substantial crust. Some will keep for nearly as long as a fully-fledged Vintage Port as I found recently on opening a bottle of Noval crusted from 1961! Most Crusted Port was shipped in bulk and bottled in the United Kingdom and with the suspension of bulk shipments in 1996, the legal status of Crusted Port was challenged by the IVP. Thankfully it has been redefined and, although sales are small, Crusted Port is a valid style which is here to stay.

Premier League
Dow
Churchill

Tawny with Indication of Age

The majority of 'true' Tawny Ports are bottled with an 'indication of age'. 'Ten', 'twenty', 'thirty' and 'over forty years old' are the designations officially permitted by the IVP. These are merely approximations as all Tawny Ports (with the exception of *Colheita* below) are complex blends of wines from a number of different years.

Wines set aside to become part of this chain of aged tawnies are selected from among the finest Ports only after making up the potential Vintage or single-*quinta* Vintage *lotes*. By their very nature, the component wines are mostly sourced from 'A/B' grade vineyards in the Cima Corgo or Douro Superior. Individual shippers look to maintain different house styles but on the whole the young wines destined to develop into mature Tawnies combine stature and structure with elegance and finesse.

The ageing process is of crucial importance to the style and character of Tawny Port. In small casks of 600–640 litres the wine undergoes a gradual process of oxidation and esterification as the colour fades and ethyl esters and acetals develop in the wine. The formation of these volatile components (sometimes known colloquially as *vinagrinho* – 'little vinegar') is directly influenced by the ambient storage temperature and rate of evaporation. Consequently, Tawny matured in the Douro undergoes a different (and more rapid) maturation process than that aged in the cooler lodges of Vila Nova da Gaia where annual evaporation (mainly of alcohol and water) is between 1 and 2 per cent. Provided the wines are well nurtured, a degree of so-called 'Douro Bake' can be a positive advantage in a mature Tawny. A slightly higher rate of evaporation (around 3 per cent) concentrates the natural, residual sugars and the higher temperature produces wines with a distinctive toasted richness. One single *quinta* making their own ten-year-old Tawny estimates that keeping the wine up in the Douro accelerates the ageing of the wine by around 30 per cent. Many shippers use a component of Douro-matured wine in their aged Tawnies.

The racking regimen is also very influential in the development of the wine and provides the tasting room with a regular opportunity to monitor the character and evolution of each *lote*. The tasting and blending of Tawny Port is a continuous process, the aim being to produce a wine that not only conforms to the house style but is also consistent over time. Wines set aside initially are often marked with the year of the harvest but as the shipper makes up new blends followed by blends of blends, the characteristics of the individual wines gradually meld into the house style. Lighter, earlier maturing wines will go towards a ten-year-old blend with richer, more structured wines reserved for older Tawnies (see individual styles below). Stocks of old Tawny Port are largely driven by anticipated sales and the onus is on the shipper to put the correct quantity of wine aside. If there is a run on stock, the house style may waver and it is not unknown for shippers to trawl the Douro in search of old wine. Occasionally a slightly caramelised *rancio* character can enter a wine that was otherwise a text book Tawny. The final *lote* may be made up of anything between ten and fifty different component wines with younger, fresher, fruit-driven Ports balancing older, mature styles that have gained more in the way of secondary complexity from extended ageing in wood.

I am by no means alone in my admiration for the delicacy and intricacy of a glass of well-aged Tawny, and the Port shippers themselves often drink a good Tawny in preference to any other style of Port. The refined complexity of a well-aged Tawny befits the climate and temperament of the Douro better than the hefty, heady character of bottle-matured wines, which are better suited to cooler climes. Indeed a glass of Tawny served cool from the fridge is positively refreshing either as an aperitif or after a lunch in the heat of the day.

Ten-Year-Old: still brick-red in the centre of the glass but developing an amber-tawny rim, these wines tend to retain a rich, raisin and sultana character with a touch of toasty complexity. Smooth in texture, with a vestige of peppery tannin on the finish.

Premier League	*First Division*
Delaforce, His Eminence's Choice	Barros
Fonseca	Burmester
Ferreira, Quinta do Porto	Dow
Offley, Baron Forrester	Graham
Niepoort	Ramos Pinto, Quinta da Ervamoira
	Taylor
	Warre

Twenty-Year-Old: the epitome of balance combining freshness and delicacy with the secondary toasted almond and brazil nut complexity from ageing in wood. Generally slightly sweeter than a ten-year-old owing to the greater concentration of sugars. Colours vary alarmingly according to house style ranging from tawny-pink to amber-orange.

Premier League	*First Division*
Burmester	Barros
Ferreira, Duque de Bragança	Cockburn
Fonseca	Croft
Niepoort	Delaforce, Curious and Ancient
Sandeman	Dow
Ramos Pinto, Quinta do Bom	Graham
Retiro	Krohn
	Martinez
	Noval
	Taylor
	Warre

Thirty Years Old: amber-tawny to mahogany in colour. Marked torrefaction character (roasted coffee) and raisin-like richness and sweetness. Some wines heading downhill with distinctly rustic, high-toned, *vinagrinho* (not to say acetic) aromas. Bottled in very small quantities (a few hundred cases a year).

Premier League
Barros
Niepoort

Over Forty Years Old: mahogany in colour, often with an olive-green hue on the rim. Typically mature and roasted – coffee and burnt toast – *rancio* character often evident. Some wines overblown and cloying. Tiny quantities and needless to say: expensive!

Premier League
Burmester
Fonseca
Taylor

Colheita

Often misunderstood, the Portuguese word '*Colheita*' (pronounced col-yate-a) means 'harvest' and by extension can be confused with 'Vintage'. Like Vintage Port, *Colheitas* are the product of a single harvest but the wines are aged in wood for a minimum of seven years by which time they have begun to take on an oxidative, Tawny character. In practice most *Colheitas* are aged for considerably longer, the casks or vat being racked and topped up periodically (in theory with the same wine) to replace that lost by evaporation. The wines take on secondary aromas and flavours, losing colour and gaining in richness, sweetness and intensity the longer they mature in wood. Without recourse to blending and refreshing, some *Colheitas* look distinctly tired by the time they come to be bottled and in comparative tastings they tend to fare less well than aged Tawnies. Two dates appear on the label: the date of the harvest (the '*Colheita*') and the date of bottling. The latter is significant as the wine will not generally improve in bottle (although after prolonged oxidative ageing in wood it won't deteriorate that quickly either). It is not uncommon to find *Colheitas* from the early years of the twentieth century on sale in grocers' shops in Lisbon and Oporto but wines from post-war years tend to be more reliable. A number of shippers continue to maintain *Colheitas* dating back prior to the 1930s, many of which have distinct overtones of *vinagrinho*. Breaking from the ranks, Warre's *Colheita* goes under the title of 'Reserve Tawny'.

Premier League	*First Division*
Barros	Cálem
Burmester	Dalva
Kopke	Krohn
Noval	
Niepoort	

Garrafeira

The term *garrafeira* meaning 'private wine cellar' or 'reserve' is usually associated with Portuguese light wines rather than Port. In fact it does not even form part of the Port Wine Institute's official lexicon and, to my knowledge, has only been used by one shipper – Niepoort – to designate a unique style of Port. Wines from a single year are aged for five years or so in wood before spending a longer period in 5- or 10-litre glass demi-johns known colloquially as bon-bons. After twenty, thirty, even forty years or more in glass, the wine is decanted off its sediment and rebottled in conventional 75 cl bottles. For example, Niepoort's 1967 Garrafeira was 'bottled' (i.e. put into glass demi-johns) in 1972 and 'decanted' (i.e bottled) in 1981. Garrafeira wines combine the oxidative character and complexity of Tawny with the more reductive bottle-ageing of Vintage Port. Not surprisingly, the wines bridge the gap in terms of weight and style.

Vintage

For many shippers, Vintage Port represents the very pinnacle of achievement. The British-owned shippers in particular have built their individual reputations on Vintage Port and, in spite of the reluctance of some Portuguese firms, the category has become a flagship for the entire trade. But all the approbation that surrounds Vintage Port belies the fact that it is one of the most straightforward of all Ports to produce. Wines from a single year are bottled, without treatment or filtration, after spending a maximum of two years ageing in bulk. The skill in producing a Vintage Port is in the selection of the finest grapes, picked at optimum ripeness after a successful growing season. To a certain extent this is predetermined as most shippers know their own *quintas* intimately as well as those belonging to their long-term suppliers. Many of the most successful Vintage Ports are therefore based on grapes from the same plots of vines in the same properties, year after year. The grapes need to be very well worked during vinification, usually either foot-trodden in a *lagar* and/or turned over in an autovinifier (see Chapter 3). After the harvest these Ports are put to one side and monitored as potential Vintage *lotes*. The wines have traditionally been kept in large wooden vats (*balseiros*) in order to prevent undue oxidative ageing but since the microbiological scare of the mid-1980s a number of shippers have resorted to stainless steel. As one well-known shipper of Vintage Port remarked, 'handling and hygiene are more important than the material from which the vessel is made'.

Under the rules set out by the IVP, the shippers have up to two years to decide whether to 'declare' the wine as vintage. As most of the major shippers inhabit premises cheek-by-jowl with each other in Vila Nova de Gaia, there is inevitably a certain amount of debate about the overall quality of the harvest and the weekly

Wednesday lunch at the Factory House is often a forum for discussion. But contrary to popular opinion, the declaration is a purely independent decision that isn't taken lightly. More often than not there is a natural consensus but there are a number of recent examples of so-called 'split declarations' where some shippers have opted for one year and others have plumped for another (for example, 1982–1983 or 1991–1992). As hard as some speculators might try, there is no law of averages about the regularity of vintage declarations. As a rule of thumb, three or four years are declared in a decade. Expectation mounts when there are long gaps between declarations as happened, for example, between 1985 and 1991.

With the steady investment in temperature-controlled vinification that has taken place since the early 1980s, the production of high quality Port is much less hit-and-miss than it was in the past. Unless the harvest happens to be a complete washout (as in 1993), wines of potential vintage quality are now made nearly every year. Port shippers have consequently been faced with a dilemma of how to market wines from good, interim years without undermining or diluting the reputation of Vintage Port *per se*. In the past a certain amount of wine that was good but not quite up to vintage standard was bottled as Crusted Port, usually accompanied by both the date of harvest and bottling. Since the 1960s, the collective solution to this problem has either been to declare these wines under a second label (Fonseca Guimaraens for example) or, more commonly, to bottle a single-*quinta* Vintage Port.

The IVP treats second labels and single *quintas* in exactly the same way as fully declared Vintage Ports. In order to obtain approval for the description 'Vintage', a sample of the wine must be submitted to the Institute between 1 January and 30 September in the second year after the harvest. The amount of stock must be registered and, pending its approval by the *Câmara de Provadores* (tasting panel), a current account will duly be opened for the wine. In the past, approval from the tasting panel used to be a rubber-stamping exercise but in 1994 one or two shippers were taken aback when their wines were rejected and samples had to be resubmitted! The wine may be bottled as soon as it has been approved by the IVP until 30 June in the third year after the harvest. In practice most Vintage Ports are now bottled earlier than they were in the past, usually during the second spring after the harvest to avoid the hot summer weather. They may only be shipped after 1 July in the second year after the harvest.

Once a Vintage Port has been bottled, it continues to develop and evolve over a period of fifteen or twenty years before it is considered as being ready to drink. After an initial burst of youth, the wine tends to shut down and go through ten to fifteen years of spotty adolescence before it re-emerges as a mature and graceful adult. Wines from the very finest vintages will continue to develop over half a century or more (see notes on 1963, 1945, 1927 and 1896 below). However, the accepted practice in the British market of 'laying down' Vintage Port to mature has been overturned by the Americans who, perhaps because of their familiarity with Californian Cabernet, are prepared to broach their Vintage Ports almost as soon as they have been shipped. A young Vintage Port can be extremely satisfying (if mouth-numbingly tannic) but I am firmly of the opinion that a good vintage is well worth the wait. It remains to be seen whether some shippers will change their style of wine-making to appeal to the powerful American market but there can be little doubt that some Vintage Port samples are 'freshened up' in order to appeal to impressionable journalists!

By the very nature of the beast, there should be no excuse for poor quality Vintage Port but there is a considerable variation between the great and the good (and occasionally the bad and ugly as well). Individual shippers and different vintages have their own character and style, which put some in the premier league while others fall below par. The following guide to Port vintages takes each year in turn, noting relevant weather conditions, market considerations, the overall style of the wines, and highlights particularly successful shippers. I have endeavoured to assess each and every year back to 1960, which roughly coincides with the emergence of single-*quinta* Vintage Port in between fully-fledged declarations. Prior to this, only the more prominent vintages are listed. As an indication of overall quality, the following years are rated with stars (up to a maximum of five) with ageing potential rated in brackets:

***** an outstanding vintage
**** very good, some outstanding wines
*** good, all round vintage
** an average year; wines generally sound but unexciting
* generally indifferent
No stars: poor

Note that there is often considerable variation between different bottlings of the same wine from vintages prior to and including 1970 when Vintage Port was frequently shipped in pipe and bottled by individual UK wine merchants. It was not unknown for a wine to languish in wood for an extra year or more thereby increasing the amount of oxidative maturation before bottling or for unscrupulous merchants to stretch the blend with a generous slug of Ruby!

1998*(**) Challenging year: tiny crop with some good, concentrated wines

Blighted from the start by a poor spring that reduced yields catastrophically and brought on an attack of oidium and mildew, 1998 looked set to produce some small quantities of potentially outstanding wine after unrelenting summer heat. Picking began in the Douro Superior on 14 September and by 24 September the harvest was underway throughout the region. Sadly this coincided with the onset of unsettled weather with periodic heavy showers diluting sugar levels. The exception was Quinta do Noval, who stopped picking in September and resumed again in clear weather at the beginning of October. Although the grapes arrived cool and there was very little need for temperature control, a potentially 'great' vintage became merely 'good' in terms of quality. Small quantities of excellent single-*quinta* wines are likely to be produced.

1997*(***) Good, potentially excellent wines.

An extraordinarily warm spring gave way to cool, wet weather in June and July. This retarded development but the heat returned in August and by mid-September grapes were registering high baumés and picking began in earnest. Apart from the occasional isolated thunderstorm, the harvest continued under clear skies. The wines are by no means as opulent or ripe as the 1994s but they do not have the rather ponderous burnt character of the 1995s. In short, 1997 produced some extremely elegant, balanced Ports with a sinewy tannic structure that should make them last (1983 springs to mind as a comparison). Nearly all the leading shippers declared in the spring of 1999, marking up their prices by around 30 per cent on the 1994s. From early tastings I found some wines tending to be rather lean and one-dimensional but Dow, Fonseca, Graham, Niepoort and Noval are certainly in the premier league. Noval

Nacional is the best for three decades – perhaps since their remarkable duo of wines from 1966 and 1963. Rather like 1963s and 1966s, the 1994 vintage will inevitably cast a shadow over the 1997s.

1996*(*) Huge crop, some stretched wines

After one of the wettest winters on record and a mild spring, there was an abundance of fruit with the result that picking began quite late (end of September/early October). Yields were huge (leaving plenty for producers of unfortified Douro wine) but sugar levels were generally on the low side with the result that many wines taste stretched and dilute. Some growers picked too early and better wines tended to be made towards the middle or end of the vintage. This was a good year for replenishing premium Rubies and LBVs but, perhaps playing up to an American audience, a handful of single *quintas* declared some attractive, forward fruity wines for the medium term. Quinta do Noval Naçional, Quinta de la Rosa and Quinta do Vesúvio are among the most successful as are Churchill's Quinta da Agua Alta and Burmester's Quinta Nossa Senhora do Carmo.

1995*(**) Concentrated but somewhat burnt

Had it not come hard on the heels of the exceptional 1994s, 1995 might just have been a fully-fledged declaration. In the event, Barros Burmester, Krohn, Osborne, Noval, Rozès and Poças declared outright with the remainder opting for second label or single-*quinta* wines. After a generally cool spring and early summer, August provided four weeks of intense and unrelenting heat. Up in the Douro Superior some growers began picking in mid-August and by 7 September the harvest was underway throughout the region. The extreme heat raisinised grapes and produced some rather coarse, burnt wines but the sheer jammy concentration of flavour justified the declaration for some. Well received by the American market, in the United Kingdom 1995 will provide some pleasurable Ports for drinking over the medium term. Fonseca Guimaraens, Quinta do Noval, Osborne, Quinta de la Rosa and Quinta de Vargellas Vinha Velha and Quinta do Vesúvio are the pick of the vintage.

1994*(****) Outstanding wines, with flesh disguising structure
It was clear almost from the first snip of the secateurs that 1994 would be a fully-declared Port vintage. A wet winter put an end to three consecutive years of drought and when the sun began to shine in March–April, the vines were sprouting in all directions. Heavy rain in May served to check the overall size of the crop but from then on it was plain sailing all the way through to the harvest. Cloudy skies and a little light rain in mid-September rekindled memories of 1993 when the heavens opened during vintage. A few growers panicked and picked too early but the majority kept their nerve and by 20 September the harvest was well underway. Wine-makers were helped in their task by clear skies and cool night-time temperatures. *Lagares* took plenty of work and long, slow fermentations gave rise to prolonged skin contact and good extrac-tion. As the wines were run off and fortified, the big guns could hardly conceal their glee at the prospect of a major vintage declar-ation. The shippers were helped in their decision by the healthy state of the market. Having tested the water successfully in 1991–2, they knew that there was enough support for a large declaration with the Americans particularly receptive to Vintage Port. Opening prices rose considerably and in some cases continued to soar, over-taking mature vintages like 1970. Tasting the 1994s from an early stage, they are characterised by super-ripe fleshy fruit, which tends to cover up the underlying tannic grip. But this somewhat deceptive puppy fat will eventually fall away to reveal some outstanding wines that will last the test of time. Dow, Fonseca, Graham, Taylor and Warre are in the premier league as always with Burmester, Croft, Quinta da Eira Velha, Gould Campbell, Martinez, Quarles Harris and Quinta do Vesúvio nudging them from behind. The wines are unusually approachable in their youth but will repay keeping at least until 2008 and beyond.

1993 A near disaster from start to finish
An utterly miserable year with a damp spring and cool summer followed by a thorough drenching at vintage. The pickers had a terrible time and grapes were rotting on the vines. Yields were low. No one in their right mind declared although there are one or two rather washed out LBVs.

1992*(***) Rich, concentrated wines from those who picked late
Declared by a handful of shippers in preference to 1991, it remains
to be seen which is the better year but I have a hunch that 1992
has the edge. The winter was unseasonably dry and the drought
continued through until June when a few days' rain proved to be
very beneficial. Fortunately, the flowering was early and was not
harmed. The summer was dry but not unduly hot and a few
short, sharp rainstorms in August helped to swell the grapes. Most
growers began picking on 21 September but those who held off
for another week or so probably made better wines. Fonseca,
Niepoort (who also declared 1991) and Taylor are rich and
impressive with some promising single-*quinta* Ports such as
Churchill's Agua Alta, Quinta do Passadouro and Quinta do
Vesúvio. Approach from 2003.

**1991*(***) Classic, foursquare wines with power, backbone and
grip**
A watershed vintage in that for the first time in history, the United
States purchased more Vintage Port than the British. Growing
conditions were good: a wet winter was followed by a settled, dry
spring and hot summer with very high temperatures at the end of
August and early September. The hot spell ended when timely rain
fell in mid-September but when picking began ambient temperatures were still high, presenting problems for those without
adequate temperature control. Cooler weather arrived during the
harvest and when the last grapes reached the *adegas* some producers were having to heat the must in order to kick-start ferments.
The grapes tended to be small with little juice, resulting in deep,
dense well-structured wines with powerful tannic backbone and
grip, not dissimilar in style to 1983. Not declared by Taylor or
Fonseca but some massive, well-structured wines from Dow,
Graham, Niepoort and Warre, with Croft back on form after more
than a decade in the wilderness. Approach with caution around
2005; some wines may take considerably longer to soften up.

1990**(*) Unusual year: quantity matched by reasonable quality
A prolific year with a very hot July and August. Rain in early
September saved the day. There were problems during the harvest
when shippers ran out of fortifying *aguardente* only to find that
the unruly Casa do Douro had issued permits in excess of the

annual *benefício*. No declarations but some rich, ripe single *quinta* and LBVs sometimes tending towards jamminess. Dow's Quinta do Bomfim, Graham's Malvedos and Warre's Quinta da Cavadinha will all be good in the medium term.

1989** Attractive wines for the short to medium term

A dry winter was followed by sporadic rain throughout the spring. This gave way to extreme heat in July and August by which time some vineyards were showing signs of stress. Yields were thankfully up on 1988 but still below average. Picking began early but in retrospect better wines would have been produced if the harvest had been delayed for a week or so as heavy rain fell on the Pinhão and Rio Torto areas on 8 and 9 September. The vintage continued under warm, clear conditions and some appealing, full-bodied single-*quinta* wines were produced, most of which are now fully ready to drink.

1988* Tiny crop of rather one-dimensional unbalanced wines

A very challenging year in all respects. Bad weather in the spring and early summer and a comparatively cool July and August gave way to intense heat in early September when the thermometer rose to over 40°C. Yields were tiny and grapes shrivelled in the heat leaving the stalks green and under-ripe. Temperatures fortunately moderated for the vintage, which began towards the end of September. Some single-*quinta* wines were bottled, many of which look stewed and somewhat unbalanced.

1987*** A handful of dense wines for the medium term

One of those 'nearly but not quite' years when a number of shippers declared (Ferreira, Martinez, Niepoort) but the majority held off and bottled single-*quinta* wines. Perhaps wet weather during the vintage provided a deterrent although the market for Vintage Port was also looking distinctly shaky by the time of the would-be declaration in 1989. Despite the weather problems in September, grapes were healthy after a hot dry summer. The heat may have contributed to the ponderous, roasted character now evident in some of the wines although dried up grapes provided some dense, concentrated Ports. Niepoort and Quinta da Eira Velha are both thick-set for the future. Now – 2010.

1986** Attractive, open fruity wines

The growing season began with a cold snap in April followed by a hot, dry summer. The weather broke in mid-September and picking began with low sugar readings amidst heavy rain and the fear that rot was setting in. In the event, the clouds cleared and most of the harvest took place in perfect conditions. After the universal 1985 declaration there was never much prospect of a declared vintage in 1986 but attractive single-*quinta* Ports were bottled, with an exceptional trio from Dow's Quinta do Bomfim, Graham's Malvedos and Warre's Quinta da Cavadinha matched by a good wine from Fonseca Guimaraens. Now – 2005.

1985**(**)? A few outstanding, fleshy wines but caveat emptor

The question mark over this unanimous declaration vintage concerns the alarming number of seriously faulty wines. It was a textbook growing season with a wet winter followed by a cool spring but from June onwards the weather was magnificent. Michael Symington wrote in his vintage report that 'never can the grapes have been gathered under better weather conditions' and I recall Bruce Guimaraens remarking that it was clear from the aromas of the fermenting must that 1985 would be a high quality year. It certainly started out that way and some impressively rich, full-bodied wines were declared and bottled in 1987, not dissimilar in some ways to 1994. Since then 1985 has thrown up some rather nasty surprises. Wines that seemed to be exemplary at the outset (e.g. Cockburn) soon turned volatile (vinegary) in bottle. Cockburn are by no means alone and from recent tastings of the 1985 vintage Cálem, Churchill, Niepoort, Quarles Harris, Ramos Pinto and Sandeman all appear to be experiencing varying degrees of difficulty as well. A question mark even hangs over Taylor's. The cause is still not entirely clear but a combination of hot weather during the vintage, over-use of chemical fertilisers producing musts of low acidity, and poor handling and hygiene, are probably collectively to blame. Another theory put forward is that the wines were not fully fortified at the outset, making them even more vulnerable to bacterial spoilage. When it became evident that there was something seriously wrong with many 1985s, it provided the impetus for shippers to clean up their act. The power and concentration of fruit that was the hallmark of the vintage continues to live on in some of the wines. With a good, ripe tannin structure to support them Fonseca, Dow, Graham and Warre will be ready to drink in the early years of the twenty-first century and have a twenty- or thirty-year life thereafter. Gould Campbell and Martinez will be good for drinking slightly earlier.

1984** Straightforward single-*quinta* wines

Despite an unstable spring and early summer, the flowering was successful and July and August were hot and dry. The fine weather continued through until picking when the heavens opened. The grapes none the less withstood a certain amount of dilution and there was no rot to taint the wines. Sandwiched between 1983 and 1985, no one declared but there are some well-rounded single-*quinta* wines like Dow's Quinta do Bomfim and Delaforce's Quinta da Corte, which continue to stand the test of time.

1983***(*) Firm, powerful, lasting wines

Having been overshadowed early on by the plump 1985s, 1983 is at last starting to come into its own. The year began badly with a long, cold winter and spring. Snow fell on the Serra do Marão as late as 20 May! During the early part of the summer the weather was hot but unsettled and the vines were three or more weeks behind. A fine September saved the day. Michael Symington reported that the sugar graduations in the Douro Superior were on average at least 1.5 degrees baumé above 1982 and that despite hot fermentation temperatures 'above average wines have been made throughout the Douro Superior and we are sure that some will prove to be outstanding'. Dow, Gould Campbell, Graham, Smith Woodhouse, Quarles Harris and Warre proved him right and stand alongside Taylor and Niepoort as the finest examples of the vintage. Initially these powerful muscular wines were much less easy to taste than the 1985s but the best 1983s certainly have a cast-iron backbone and the fruit seems to have fleshed out with age. Drink from 2003. Cockburn (which started out well) is very variable and Fonseca is disappointing.

1982** Soft, early maturing

A handful of shippers chose to declare 1982 in preference to 1983 leading to a so-called 'split vintage'. In retrospect they clearly made a mistake for the wines are generally light and inconsequential. After a burst of heat in August and early September the grapes were fully ripe and healthy and this is reflected in the soft, sweet raisiny character of the wines. The best (Churchill, Sandeman, Niepoort and Quinta do Noval) are no more than useful wines to drink while waiting for the 1983s to come round and they lack the backbone to last much beyond 2005. Croft and Delaforce both declared poor wines that fell apart within a decade and did nothing for their reputation. Those who decided not to declare bottled some successful single-*quinta* wines.

1981*
An extraordinary year in all respects. A severe drought began in the autumn of 1980 lasting all the way through the winter. The spring and early summer were unusually cold, giving way to searing heat in mid-June. The hot, dry weather continued through the summer, delaying the development of the vines and turning grapes to raisins. But by mid-September, when the growers could wait no longer and picking began, the weather broke and the mother and father of storms swept through the Douro. Gales brought down electricity pylons, leaving Pinhão without power for fourteen hours. Better wines were made in the Baixo Corgo (where picking began later) than in the Cima Corgo, where a small crop produced dark wines that tended to taste cooked and lacking in freshness. No declaration but some good LBVs were bottled. Niepoort continues to stand the test of time.

1980*** Open, fresh, attractive and fruit-driven
Perhaps deterred by a hike in prices, the 1980s were largely overlooked by the trade and the year subsequently became a 'Cinderella vintage' overshadowed by 1977, 1983 and 1985, the last of which turned out to be something of an ugly sister. The growing season was variable and sugar readings relatively low when picking began in late September. Temperatures were high during the harvest and the *lagares* fermented furiously fast and therefore took little work. In spite of these difficulties, the wines are generally very well balanced. Fonseca is on the light side but Dow, Graham, Niepoort, Offley, Smith Woodhouse, Taylor and Warre all produced open, attractive wines that are drinking very well indeed and will continue to develop through the first decade of the twenty-first century.

1979*
No declaration but a handful of straightforward single-*quinta* wines, most of which are now fully mature. Drink soon.

1978**
Preferred by some (Ferreira, Krohn and Noval) to 1977 with Niepoort and Kopke declaring both years. The wines are generally soft, quite rich and approachable although Noval is weak. The year was notable for the number of single-*quinta* Vintage Ports, some of which appeared on the market for the first time. Drink now – 2005.

1977****(*) Huge, concentrated, long-lasting wines but some developing faster than expected
A wet winter followed by a disappointingly cool summer provided an inauspicious start to a year that has subsequently been hailed as 'a classic'. Michael Symington records that sugar readings were as low as 10.5 baumé at the beginning of September but hot weather held on into October for a late harvest. Even then sugar readings were not all that high but it was clear from the colour and flavour of the musts that some outstanding wines would emerge. All except Cockburn, Noval and Martinez decided to declare. From early on, the 1977s were compared in stature to the 1963s. This is praise indeed and although there are some extremely impressive wines, overall the 1977s have not quite lived up to expectations. One or two are already beginning to show their age. There can, however, be no doubt that Fonseca is an all-time great, very nearly matched by Dow, Graham, Taylor, Smith Woodhouse and Warre. These wines retain their monumental tannic core wrapped in layer upon layer of powerful, ripe, fleshy fruit. Still somewhat impenetrable, they would be better kept until 2003 or longer and will last for decades to come. Anyone born in 1977 probably has a wine for life!

1976**
A variable year that produced a brilliant, dense, lasting Port from Fonseca Guimaraens to beat all the declared 1975s and Fonseca's 1980 and 1983 as well! Otherwise the wines tend to be light and early maturing; Graham's Malvedos and a 'traditional' LBV from Smith Woodhouse are the best of the rest.

1975** Soft and early maturing; drink soon

Christened the *Verão Quente* (hot summer) both because of the heat and the political temperature at the time, 1975 has always been a controversial declaration. There is absolutely no truth in the tale that the wines were only declared due to the revolution and the threatened nationalisation of the Port industry because by the time the shippers chose to declare (in the spring of 1977) Portugal had settled down as a mild-mannered democracy. Reading vintage reports from the time, the majority of shippers talked themselves into a declaration but the wines clearly failed to live up to their early promise. Even Quinta do Noval Naçional is disappointing. In general the 1975s are now soft and rather hollow but have none the less been attractive to drink while waiting for the 1970s, 1966s and 1963s to mature. Cálem, Delaforce, Dow and Graham are still drinking well but should not be kept for anything other than academic interest!

1974*

Good traditional LBVs from Smith Woodhouse and Warre and single-*quinta* Vintage from Taylor's Vargellas. Most wines tend to be quite light and simple. Drink soon.

1973

Unusually heavy demand for wines caused prices to rise by as much as 150 per cent on the previous year. Early September was wet and cold, and when picking began under clear skies around 20 September, sugar levels were surprisingly low and the intial feeling was that the harvest had begun too early. In the event, wet weather returned in early October. High yields produced undistinguished wines. I have never seen or tasted a 1973.

1972* A curiosity

A number of shippers made attractive wines in 1972 in spite of heavy intermittent rain during the harvest. The vintage was blighted early on by the alcohol scandal that broke shortly after Dow, Offley and Rebello Valente declared. Although rarely seen, many of the wines are still curiously attractive, retaining their simple, fresh fruit character.

1971

A cool, cloudy summer necessitated regular spraying against mildew. By early August, growers in the Rio Torto could not recall a year when the grapes were so far behind. Nothing of any consequence was made and no wines were declared.

1970***** Classic, tight-knit wines; the best with a long future ahead

Early tastings tended to play down the 1970s and the wines are only now being judged in their true light. The summer was dry and temperatures were high at the start of the harvest with a high incidence of raisinised grapes that may have led to some early doubts about the wines. A few wines have developed burnt, high-toned aromas and, this being the last vintage to be bottled both in Gaia and in the UK, there is inevitably a certain amount of variation from bottle to bottle (see my qualifying note on page 167). The overall quality is by no means as uniformly high as in 1963 but there are wines that deserve to be ranked among the century's greats. Dow and Graham certainly deserve this accolade followed up by some undeniably impressive wines from Cálem and Kopke. Delaforce, Fonseca, Niepoort, Noval Naçional and Taylor are also very good, displaying the tight-knit concentration that is the hallmark of this vintage. I suspect that many of the 1970s have been drunk too early for the best are only just reaching their peak. With a life-span that will take the wines to 2020 at least, it will be a long plateau.

1969*

Desavinho (millerandage) in May and an attack of mildew in early June cut down potential production ensuring that 1969 would not be a high-yielding year. A hot summer followed but by early September the vines continued to be very backward. Rain fell in mid-September, bringing on rot in some districts. A late harvest produced wines that were much better than was previously thought possible. Taylor's produced an attractive wine from Quinta de Vargellas but otherwise no one declared.

1968*
Heavy rain just before harvest led to rot. Early-maturing wines represented by Fonseca Guimaraens, Taylor's Quinta de Vargellas and Graham's Malvedos. Drink soon.

1967** Middle-weight, middle distance; fading
Four shippers declared in preference to 1966 with Cockburn and Martinez following their own rather idiosyncratic hunch that 1967 was a better year. Certainly the weather was good but many picked too early. At best 1967 produced good, gentle, middle-distance wines, which are starting to look tired around the edges. Even Quinta do Noval's Naçional is starting to fade.

1966***** Power and elegance; complete
History has been rather unkind to the 1966s and until quite recently they were completely overshadowed by 1963. A wet winter prepared the vines for a hot, dry summer and the grapes were small but developed well without undue raisining. The rain finally arrived during the harvest but yields were well down on average and some deep, dark, powerful wines were made. Although the standard is not as high across the board as in 1963, there are a number of really stupendous Vintage Ports combining structure and quintessential 'bitter chocolate' intensity. Quinta do Noval Naçional typifies the vintage matching its cast-iron tannic backbone with supreme elegance. Dow and Fonseca are two of my all-time favourites followed by dense, brooding wines from Delaforce, Graham and Taylor. Cálem is also very fine. The 1966s may be drunk now but the best will keep for a lifetime or more.

1965**
A hot summer produced some deep, powerful Ports. No fully-fledged declaration apart from Wiese & Krohn but some fine second-string wines from Taylor's Quinta de Vargellas and Graham's Malvedos which have developed well. Drink fairly soon.

1964
Exceedingly hot weather during the vintage produced some round, full-blown jammy wines that are either fully mature or fading. Coincided with the introduction of autovinification. Drink up.

1963***** A classic vintage, ready now and with years ahead
A textbook growing season in northern Portugal: a long, warm summer followed by a little rain in mid-September that helped to swell the grapes just before the harvest. Picking took place under ideal conditions with warm days and cool nights. Ronald Symington reported at the time that *'mostos* [musts] look very nice indeed and seem to have plenty of flavour and colour even if perhaps lacking a little in "guts" '. He need not have worried for the 1963s have evolved very well indeed and the vintage has subsequently become a benchmark for the trade. Good across the board, the wines have layer upon layer of rich, ripe fruit backed up by a powerful tannic streak which stands them in good stead for years to come. Some are only just ready to drink. With the exception of Quinta do Noval, nearly every shipper produced an impressive Vintage Port in 1963 and this consistency is reflected in today's auction prices. The superstars of the vintage are Croft, Fonseca and Quinta do Noval Naçional. Cockburn, Delaforce, Dow, Graham, Taylor and Warre all produced superb wines. No other vintage since 1963 has such an extensive roll of honour.

1962**
Catastrophic winter floods, followed by long summer drought. Some wines tasting burnt. Not generally declared but some good second-string wines and a rich, lasting Quinta do Noval Naçional.

1961**
I take a particular interest in this vintage because it is my own birth year. Some successful wines (Graham's Malvedos, Quinta de Vargellas, Wiese & Krohn and Noval's 1961 so-called 'Crusted' (bottled in 1964) generally drinking well although not for long-term keeping. Bordeaux better. Drink fairly soon.

1960*** Gentle wines that have reached their peak
This beguiling vintage seemed to peak in the late 1970s–early 1980s but many wines continue to stand up quite well. Mostly midweight and lacking in backbone, the best wines of the vintage are still soft, sweet and open. Some were diluted by rain during the harvest. Cockburn, Dow and Graham showing particularly well. Drink fairly soon.

1958*
A good summer followed by rain during picking. A handful of shippers declared although the wines were always one-dimensional and are now declining. Sandeman is still good for a few years but otherwise drink up.

1957
Apart from isolated examples, not generally declared. A soft, sweet *Colheita* from Cálem and an unusually impressive Vintage Port from Royal Oporto are almost all that remain.

1955*** Outstanding, concentrated wines for the long-term**
After a fine summer and very high temperatures in early September, warm, dry weather continued right through the harvest. Reading Ronald Symington's notes from the time, it was clear that he thought a fine vintage was on the cards. So it has turned out and the best 1955s are still complete wines retaining wonderful balance and masses of concentrated fruit. They are now quite hard to find but anyone with bottles remaining need be in no hurry to drink up. With so much of the vintage bottled in the UK, even the Port shippers lack stock. Croft, Dow, Graham and Niepoort are very impressive.

1954?**
Tiny vintage, now a rarity. I have only ever tasted one 1954 (an elegant wine from Sandeman) but the vintage had a good reputation at the time. Most shippers opted for 1955 but there were a number of successful second-string wines.

1950 Soft and early maturing**
After a challenging growing season, conditions were apparently ideal during the harvest and a number of shippers declared despite the difficult market conditions. Graham's Malvedos continued to display good fruit and acidity into the 1990s but Dow, Sandeman, Ferreira and Cálem (tasted in 1998) are looking hollow and pale. Drink up.

1948**? Rich, sweet but hard to find**
Declared by a handful of shippers in the face of post-war quotas and an impossible market at the time, it is now very difficult to

find a 1948. By all accounts the wines are outstanding (probably better than 1947). Francis Warre noted 'slow fermentation even after a tremendous amount of work'. The grapes were extremely sweet and beautifully ripe after a hot growing season and this is reflected in one of the few 1948s that I have tasted, Dow's Quinta do Bomfim, which is almost syrup-like but still retains a touch of spicy grip. Drink now or keep.

1947****
Reluctantly declared by a number of shippers, 1947 was a small vintage that produced some finely poised, balanced wines (Sandeman a good example). Few examples remain but those which have continue to hold up well.

1945***** Victory vintage: wonderful, lasting wines
'This being the first vintage spent in peace after the defeat of Germany and Japan it is disappointing that conditions may not allow a 1945 Victory Vintage' wrote Ronald Symington at the time. With a summer drought and high temperatures during the harvest, 1945 was certainly challenging but in the end it proved to be a superb vintage declared by everyone except Cockburn. Due to shipping restrictions, the wines were mostly bottled in Oporto (often in brown sherry bottles due to lack of glass) and have developed well. Some are starting to look rather frayed (e.g. Quinta do Noval) but Croft, Dow and Niepoort are bolt upright, reflecting the depth and concentration of this small but exceptional vintage. There is obviously considerable variation between bottles but the best 1945s will continue to evolve well into the twenty-first century.

1942***
Wartime vintage. Some good wines but very little shipped. Niepoort is outstanding.

1935***** Classic wines that continue to develop well
A split vintage: some shippers went for 1934 while others went with 1935. The crop was smaller in 1935 but weather conditions were similar and there is little to choose between the two years. If anything the wines seem to be slightly softer and more refined in 1935 making up in balance and harmony for what they lack

in structure. None the less, the best 1935s (like Sandeman and Delaforce) have plenty of life in them yet.

1934***** Rich, well-structured

It is difficult to generalise with wines of this age but, allowing for significant bottle variation, the 1934s seem to have the edge over 1935 in terms of structure. Fonseca and Sandeman still look quite powerful but Dow is soft, sweet and delicate with age. Niepoort have an impressive 1934 *Colheita*.

1931*****? An outstanding year – overlooked

Bypassed by the majority of shippers because it coincided with the world-wide Depression, 1931 is almost certainly the best year never to have been declared. Ernest Cockburn records 'that demand this year was unusually small and the produce of some *quintas* could be bought at very low prices which hardly paid the farmer's expenses . . .' The weather was atypically cool during the summer months but a challenging growing season was redeemed by a blast of heat in September. The only major shipper to declare was Quinta do Noval, which has built its reputation on the vintage, especially the Naçional, which fetches an astronomical price on the rare occasions that the wine reaches auction. At 5,900 US dollars for a bottle in 1988, it holds the record for the most expensive Port ever sold. Niepoort also declared a deep, dense 1931, which was effectively 'late bottled' and in 1998 I tasted one of the last remaining examples of Cockburn 1931, a small quantity of which was bottled for private consumption. Not as rich or dense as either Noval or Niepoort, it retains the balance and elegance of an outstanding but nearly forgotten vintage.

1927***** Classic, concentrated wines

Embraced by most shippers, 1927 has stood the test of time and remains a truly monumental vintage. It was one of those rare years that combined both quality and quantity: both Cockburn and Croft declared between thirty and forty thousand cases. So dark and dense are some of the wines that they will still continue to improve in bottle! Although I have tasted individual samples more recently, I was fortunate to taste eleven 1927s side by side in 1989. Fonseca, Niepoort and Taylor are still incredibly powerful and concentrated, retaining the bitter chocolate and liquorice-like intensity that is the hallmark of a really fine Vintage Port.

1924****? High quality wines, keeping well

It was clear from the start that 1924 would be out of the ordinary and the wines were well received by a buoyant market. Gordon Cosens noted at the time 'that the 1924s will turn out to be a better than ordinary vintage . . .' Small quantities were produced due to *queima* (burn) in the early part of the year but the wines did not seem to suffer. On the contrary, if Dow's is anything to go by (tasted in 1998), 1924 produced some extraordinary wines, which have retained their colour, structure and intensity.

1912*****? Classic vintage of the era

Generally declared, 1912 was considered to be a great vintage (perhaps one of the greatest of the early twentieth century). Ernest Cockburn notes that 'the wines showed a good average percentage of sugar and had considerable flavour but the yield was on the short side; as they developed, however, they showed good colour and the year produced some extremely fine wines for bottling'. The 1912 Dow is now rather dry and maderised but Sandeman retains its texture and soft, elegant fruit. Others may also be holding up.

1908***** Fine, long-lived post-phylloxera vintage

Both Ernest Cockburn and John Warre concur. 'It seemed probable from the start that the year would be declared a Vintage Year,' wrote the former; 'Everything points to 1908 turning out to be the best year since phylloxera swept away all the Portuguese vines,' according to the latter. Cockburn, Graham and Offley reputed to be fine but I can certainly vouch for Dow, which retains a deep amber-tawny colour and succulent texture and complexity. Outstanding by any standards. Cálem is now looking slightly fragile but still quite impressive.

1904****? Light wines; waning

A large crop of ripe grapes none the less produced some fine, delicate wines that are now on the decline and have faded into old Tawny. Sandeman is still just about alive. The harvest was so abundant that the fortifying *aguardente* was in short supply and had to be rationed.

1900**** Fine, delicate wines – now fragile

The century began with a fine vintage that turned out well in spite of an initial lack of body and colour. Ernest Cockburn wrote that 'the vintage lots shipped showed wines of great delicacy with appreciable breed, and although lighter in colour than many previous vintages they appealed to connoisseurs of Port Wine'. I have tasted Ferreira, Noval and Dow, which are fading fast but are still up to a millennium celebration!

1896***** Watershed year: the first great post-phylloxera vintage

The turning point for Port: the best vintage since phylloxera struck the Douro in the 1870s. By July the grapes were quite forward and by mid-September the harvest was well underway and continued amid favourable weather conditions although Ernest Cockburn – who seems to be quite pessimistic about most vintages – wrote that 'the grapes were not as ripe as they should have been'. This is certainly not born out by Dow's 1896 which, when tasted at their bicentennial celebration in 1998, retained its deep, youthful colour, firm peppery tannins and berry fruit. It was still a remarkably bold wine after 102 years!

Based on tasting over a century of Vintage Ports, I put forward the following classification with the addition of a 'second division':

Premier League
Dow
Fonseca
Graham
Niepoort
Quinta do Noval Naçional
Taylor

First Division
Churchill
Cockburn
Croft
Delaforce
Quinta do Noval
Sandeman

Smith Woodhouse
Warre

Second Division
Ferreira
Fonseca Guimaraens
Gould Campbell
Martinez
Offley

Single Quinta Vintage Port

Premier League
Quinta do Bomfim (Dow)
Quinta dos Malvedos (Graham)
Quinta de Vargellas (Taylor)
Quinta do Vesúvio

First Division
Quinta da Agua Alta (Churchill)
Quinta da Cavadinha (Warre)
Quinta do Crasto
Quinta da Eira Velha (Martinez)
Quinta da Foz (formerly Cálem)
Quinta do Panascal (Fonseca)
Quinta do Passadouro (Niepoort)
Quinta da Terra Feita (Taylor)
Quinta de la Rosa

Second Division
Quinta dos Canais (Cockburn)
Quinta da Corte (Delaforce)
Quinta da Roêda (Croft)
Quinta do Tua (Cockburn)
Quinta Nova de Nossa Senhora do Carmo (Burmester)

STORING AND AGEING PORT

So much has been written about the rituals of storing, serving and drinking Port that some people are deterred from opening a bottle. In reality there are no hard and fast rules, just practical suggestions that help to enjoy a wine to the full. So-called 'wood-matured' Ports (Ruby, premium Ruby, all Tawnies, *Colheitas*, White and filtered LBVs) are bottled ready for drinking and should be stored upright. They do not benefit from keeping and will begin to deteriorate with age in bottle. But given the correct storage conditions bottle-matured Ports (Vintage, Crusted and 'traditional' LBV) will evolve in bottle over the medium to long term, gaining character and complexity with age.

The ideal cellar for all types of wine is a cool, dark space with a reasonably even temperature of 10–12°C; winter to summer, day to night. Port is more resilient than many wines but will still be damaged by excessively high or fluctuating temperatures. Seepage around the cork and capsule is often a symptom. Bottles should be laid on their side to maintain the elasticity of the cork with the label uppermost so that the sediment or crust falls to the underside. Older bottles of Vintage Port are often marked with a splash of whitewash that survives even after the label has disintegrated. If the bottle is moved for any reason it should be returned to its original position with the white splash facing upwards (see section on decanting below).

SERVING PORT

With the exception of Vintage, Crusted and traditional LBV, all Port can be poured directly from the bottle into the glass. White Ports should be served chilled, straight from the refrigerator. Tawny Ports also benefit from being served 'cellar-cool', especially during the summer months. Be careful not to over-chill the wine (an hour or two in the fridge will suffice) as this tends to mask the delicacy of the aromas and flavours. All other Ports should be served on the cooler side of room temperature remembering that rooms in modern, centrally heated houses are considerably warmer than those of yesteryear. A Port that is too warm will appear unbalanced and excessively spirity on the nose.

Once a bottle has been opened, all Ports begin to deteriorate after a short period of time. Rubies and filtered LBVs begin to lose some of their freshness and vibrancy a week or so after opening and should be drunk within three weeks. Having matured for longer in cask, aged Tawnies will stay in good condition for up to a month or more after opening. Like all great wines, Vintage Ports (along with Crusted and bottle-matured LBV) should be consumed within two days. Older wines tend to be more fragile and are likely to lose any vestige of freshness and complexity after a relatively short period of time. Ideally these should be drunk within an hour or two of decanting.

The pleasure gained from a great wine is all too often marred by the use of an inappropriate glass. I recall the occasion when a senior Port shipper received the *Wine* magazine Fortified Wine-Maker of the Year award and a major London hotel served the Vintage Port in thimble-sized glasses, filled to the brim. Although Port is generally served after a meal and therefore drunk in smaller quantities than the average red or white wine, it should still be served in capacious glasses, filled to a maximum level two-thirds from the brim. This leaves plenty of space for the Port to be swirled and aired in the glass so that the aromas can be appreciated to the full. The Port Wine Institute have their own recommended glass shaped like a small Paris-goblet, which is used by the majority of Port shippers. These are well suited for most types of Ports but tend to be too small to appreciate a venerable Vintage to the full. Tulip-shaped ISO glasses are better but Austrian glass producers Riedel have developed the ultimate Port glass: one for Tawny, another for Vintage.

DECANTING PORT

Vintage Port is one of the few wines to be bottled without any fining or filtration. Consequently, after around five years in bottle, a substantial amount of sediment begins to form. This is not like the fine-grained sediment that appears in a bottle of mature Claret or Burgundy but a heavy 'crust' that sticks to the side of the glass or slides slowly to the base of the bottle when stood upright.

Decanting Vintage Port (along with Crusted and bottle-matured LBV) is a relatively straightforward procedure requiring only a steady hand and reasonably good light. The traditional use of a candle to illuminate the neck of the bottle adds a certain romance but as most Vintage Ports are bottled in opaque, black glass to protect the wine from the light during storage it is of limited effect. Good background light is, however, useful to illuminate the neck of the decanter as the wine is being poured.

Ideally, the bottle should be stood upright some two or three hours before decanting (although there are many spontaneous parties at *quintas* in the Douro where a bottle of Vintage Port is opened and decanted at short notice without detriment to the wine). If a wax seal covers the cork a few solid raps with the handle of the corkscrew will cause it to break away and fragment. More challenging are the thick plastic capsules used in the UK in the mid-1960s, which require a Stanley Knife and a great deal of patience to remove!

The cork should then be eased slowly from the bottle causing the minimum of disturbance to the wine. In the case of older vintages this can be quite difficult as the cork will often break where it fans out about three-quarters of the way down the neck of the bottle. It may therefore take two or more attempts to remove the cork in its entirety and fragments will fall into the wine. A decanting funnel equipped with a fine mesh screen or a nylon stocking (previously rinsed with a little Ruby Port) will catch the pieces of cork but avoid using a coffee filter which could taint the wine. Always use a good corkscrew with a sharp point and an open helix as cheaper examples with a solid 'worm' will pull the core from a soft or spongy cork.

If the bottle has been shaken and the crust disturbed, leave it standing upright for thirty minutes after pulling the cork for any loose sediment to settle. Then, keeping the label or splash of white-wash uppermost, pour the wine steadily and slowly into a clean, freshly rinsed decanter. Many wines are tainted by musty decanters and either the Port or the cork takes the blame. Tilt the decanter as you pour. As the level of wine in the bottle falls, tiny particles of sediment will start to appear on the side of the decanter. This is the cue to stop pouring immediately. The remaining crust along with a very small quantity of Port can be poured into a glass and may usefully be used in cooking if the wine has been decanted before a meal. Younger Vintage Ports will benefit especially from two or three hours exposure to the air before serving so a limited amount of pre-planning is recommended.

A great deal of unnecessary ritual surrounds the use of Port tongs which, at first sight, look rather like a medieval instrument of torture. The tongs are meant to be heated in an open fire until red-hot before being clamped around the neck of the bottle. Subsequently, a damp cloth is applied whereupon the neck is supposed to break cleanly. Contrary to perceived opinion, Port tongs are almost never used in Vila Nova de Gaia and have mostly been mothballed as museum pieces. Another myth surrounds the use of a specially made, ornamental decanting machine. This apparatus (usually made from brass) has a cradle for the bottle, which is controlled by a screw device and handle. However, once the first sediment starts to appear you have to rewind the handle quite fast, a feat that is beyond the mechanism that controls the bottle's incline. A steady hand is always the safest option!

PASSING THE PORT

Port, either in bottle or decanter, is traditionally passed from right to left or clockwise around the table. There are a number of explanations for this, one of which is an ancient Celtic superstition that all left hand turns were an ill omen. A much more practical reason is that the majority of people are right-handed making it easier to pour the wine with the right hand and pass it on with the left.

With the lively conversation that usually follows a meal, it is not unusual for someone to neglect to pass the Port and for the decanter to come to a complete standstill. Rather than ask directly and rather abruptly for the Port, the customary question frequently used by members of the trade at Factory House lunches is to turn to the person on your right and say 'Do you know the Bishop of Norwich?' The origin of this expression is obscure but upon this gentle reminder the Port should immediately continue its clockwise course around the table. There is, however, a story about lunch at the Factory House when the new British Chaplain was asked by a Port shipper if he knew the Bishop of Norwich. He replied that he certainly did as the then Bishop of Norwich was his brother-in-law. The decanter of Port stayed where it was!

5

Port Producers and Shippers

STRUCTURE OF THE TRADE

The Port trade is dominated by brands. It has been to a greater or lesser extent since the eighteenth century when many of the famous Port-shipping firms came into being. But household names like Sandeman, Cockburn, Graham and Taylor represent the apex of a much larger pyramid. There are around 38,000 individual growers in the Douro, the vast majority of whom farm too little land to justify investment in a modern winery. A few continue to produce wine in the time-honoured fashion, but the vast majority sell their grapes either to one of the major shippers or to a co-operative winery.

The shippers often have long-term contracts with individual growers. 'Contract' is perhaps too strong a word, for these are mostly gentleman's agreements based on mutual trust, which stretches back for generations. A senior member of the shipping firm (usually the wine-maker) will visit his growers at least once a year, usually just prior to the harvest. Deals are invariably done over a glass of ancient Tawny from the farmer's own stock followed by a handshake. In the past it wasn't unknown for the farmer's daughter to be offered as part of the bargain!

Until 1986 all Port wine had to be traded through the *entreposto* or bonded area of Vila Nova de Gaia. The legislation that came into force in June of that year opened the way for wines to be exported directly from growers in the demarcated Douro region. Although a number of leading *quintas* and some co-operatives have begun to market their own wine, the pre-eminence of the established brands has meant that their share of Port wine sales has not passed one per cent. The twenty-two co-operatives in the region produce around 35 per cent of all Port, most of which is bought by the shippers as the basis for their standard Ruby and Tawny.

The term 'shipper' dates from the era when Port companies were little more than agents taking a commission on the wines they shipped abroad. Nearly all shippers are now intimately involved in the production of Port with their own *quintas*, centralised wine-making and bottling plants as well as ageing facilities in Vila Nova de Gaia. The mechanics of these are covered in detail in Chapters 3 and 4.

Ponte D. Luíz and Gaia

The shippers themselves are also subject to a certain amount of categorisation. Despite (or perhaps because of) the sale and amalgamation of shipping firms following the Second World War, companies, which are alternately Portuguese, British, multinational and family-owned, form an increasingly complex Venn diagram. To complete the picture there are also companies of Dutch, German, Norwegian and Spanish extraction.

At the time of writing, 108 companies are registered with the Port Wine Institute. The following directory of Port producers and shippers is by no means exhaustive but includes all those with a significant presence on export markets. A few of the names that follow have been extinguished but merit inclusion because their wines continue to be sold at auction. Shippers and producers are listed in alphabetical order by brand name with the full company name and address below.

BARROS

Barros Almeida & Ca. – Vinhos SA, Rua D. Leonor de Freitas, 180/2, Apartado 39, 4401 Vila Nova de Gaia
Barros is the principal brand in a somewhat unwieldy group of companies belonging to the Barros family. The company is among the largest shippers and deserves to be better known but tends to be obscured by a multiplicity of brand names – Feist, Hutcheson Feuerheerd, Kopke, Rocha, Douro Wine Shippers and Growers Association, Vieira da Souza, A. Santos Pinto – all of which form part of the group. A certain amount of welcome rationalisation has taken place in recent years with the number of companies reduced from seven to four. Nevertheless, confusion still exists not just among consumers but with the wine trade as well (see separate entries for Feist, Kopke and Hutcheson Feuerheerd).

Barros Almeida itself is a relative newcomer to the scene having been founded in 1913 when Manoel de Almeida left the firm of Motta & Vaz to create his own independent company – Almeida em Comandita. His sister married Manoel de Barros, who reputedly started out as an office boy and then entered the firm as a partner, altering the name to Barros Almeida. Barros weathered the Depression of the 1930s and used it as an opportunity to buy up a number of ailing firms. The last acquisition was Kopke (founded in 1638 and purchased by Barros in 1953), which still retains a measure of independence within the group.

Barros Almeida owns two major properties in the Douro, Quinta Dona Matilde by the Bagauste dam just upstream from Régua, and Kopke's Quinta de São Luíz on the way to Pinhão. This is its principal vinification centre making just under half the company's needs. It was substantially revamped in the late 1990s, concrete autovinifiers being replaced mainly by pumping over in temperature-controlled stainless steel. Barros has maintained *lagares* at Dona Matilde.

The bulk of Barros wines are young Rubies and Tawnies destined for the Netherlands, France, Belgium, Germany and the home market. However, its strength at the quality end of the market lies not in Vintage Port but in aged Tawnies and *Colheitas*. Barros Almeida maintains substantial stocks of these wines in Gaia dating back to the 1930s. With wines like its finely tuned 1966 *Colheita*, a rich, concentrated 1937 *Colheita* and a beautifully lifted thirty-year-old Tawny, Barros Almeida is firmly in the 'premier league'. Barros also produces one of the few good, wood-aged, dry White Ports. Although its Vintage Ports can be open, supple and attractive (1995, 1987, for example), Barros declares on a frequent basis and the wines tend to be relatively light and early maturing. 1995, 1994, 1992, 1991, 1987 and 1985, 1983 and 1982 were all declared.

BORGES

Sociedade dos Vinhos Borges & Irmão, SA, Avenida da Republica, 796, 4431 Vila Nova de Gaia
After years of deeply damaging uncertainty, Borges & Irmão (one of the best-known names in the Portuguese wine trade) has been virtually wound up. The company was founded in 1884 by two brothers, who began trading in tobacco, matches, textiles and wine. They also established a high-street bank, making Borges & Irmão one of the best-known names in Portugal. In 1975, a year after the 25 April revolution, all Portuguese-owned banks and insurance companies were nationalised. Subsidiary companies like Borges & Irmão Vinhos went with them. In the ensuing confused political situation, Borges faced an uncertain future as successive governments talked about ways of returning Portugal's moribund state sector to private ownership. The quality of the wines suffered accordingly although by the mid-1990s, under the auspices of wine-maker Anselmo Mendes, there were encouraging signs of improvement. For a time there was talk of a management buy-out but eventually Borges & Irmão was stripped of its principal assets to realise capital. Much of the stock and two of the company's *quintas*, Junco and Casa Nova, were purchased by Taylor's in 1998. Only Quinta da Soalheira remains independent.

BURMESTER

J.W. Burmester & Ca., Lda, Rua de Belmonte, 37, 4050 Porto
Chancing upon Burmester is rather like coming across a well-kept

secret. Hidden up a narrow alley in the heart of the Vila Nova de Gaia *entreposto*, Burmester's small, immaculately kept lodge is the source of some remarkably high quality wines. The company's head office is to be found in an elegant eighteenth-century *solar* or manor house in the old part of Oporto.

The Burmesters are a large family who came to Portugal from Germany in 1730 and began to specialise in Port twenty years later. The name is a corruption of *Burgmeester*, who was effectively mayor of a town or city in the middle ages. One of the family's ancestors was the *Burgmeester* of the town of Moelln near Luebeck in northern Germany. There are nine branches of the family altogether, one of which settled in the United Kingdom, forming the company Burmester Nash & Co. with offices in both London and Oporto. Frederick Burmester subsequently became a founding director of the Westminster Bank (precursor of Natwest) and the family name is still represented by 'Burmester Road' in the London suburb of Wimbledon.

In 1834 Johann Wilhelm Burmester arrived in Oporto to work for the family company. On becoming sole owner in 1861 the name was changed to J.W. Burmester and Ca. The firm remains in family hands represented by Arnold Gilbert, Fatima Burmester, Henrique Burmester Silva and Fernando Formigal. The company traditionally sourced grapes from around Castedo do Douro and the Sabrosa area, owning no vineyards of its own. In 1991 Burmester purchased the 120-hectare Quinta Nova de Nossa Senhora do Carmo in the district of Sabrosa, a magnificent 'A' grade estate on the north bank of the Douro. With three traditional *lagares* alongside autovinification and pumping over in stainless steel, Quinta Nova now serves as Burmester's vinification centre. It has also been hived off as a separate company producing a full range of wines parallel to Burmester.

Since Burmester acquired Quinta Nova, its Vintage Ports have improved considerably and although they do not quite belong as yet to the 'first division' the wines are dense and fleshy with the structure to last in the medium term. Where Burmester really scores is with its supremely good old Tawnies and *Colheitas*. Being a relatively small firm, it is able to maintain a consistent quality more easily than large companies saddled with well-known brands. Burmester's ten-year-old is delicate but rich while its twenty-year-old is soft, high-toned and beautifully balanced. The Tawny range includes an unusual wine which, registering 2.5 baumé (as opposed to around 4 baumé), they describe as 'half-dry'. The company also maintains outstanding old *Colheitas* dating back to 1890 and 1900, both bottled in 1977. In 1998 it was able to present an intriguing vertical tasting covering a century of its *Colheita* Ports.

With Souham's, Jem's and McPhersons as subsidiary brands, Burmester has a strong presence in the Netherlands, followed by Belgium, France and Germany. Gilberts is a subsidiary company belonging to Burmester (see page 209).

BUTLER NEPHEW

The company was founded by Nash of Burmester Nash & Co. (see above), who took James Butler into partnership in 1789. He in turn was joined by his nephew, Robert Butler, and the name of the firm became Butler Nephew. The firm had a good reputation before the Second World War. It has since been consigned to relative obscurity, first by Gonzalez Byass (see below) and subsequently by Vasconcelos. Butler Nephew was disbanded in 1989.

CÁLEM

A.A. Cálem & Filho, Lda, Rua de Reboleira, 7, 4050 Porto
Cálem was closely identified with the family of the same name until 1998 when it made history by becoming the first shipper in Gaia to be bought out by a company from the Douro. For Joaquim Manuel Cálem, who fronted the firm with considerable dexterity, it must have seemed an inglorious end to a long family tradition. The company was founded in 1859 and grew into one of Portugal's leading brands. Facing mounting debts in the 1990s, the Cálems were forced to sell and (after much speculation on the Douro 'grape vine') the firm was bought by a consortium established by Manuel Saraiva (whose road tankers ship Port down to Gaia from the Douro) and Rogerio Silva (ex-Rozès). Saraiva has since left the consortium. In the process the company was separated from the *quinta* that had been the backbone of Cálem's Vintage Ports for over a century. At the confluence of the Pinhão River with the Douro, Quinta da Foz has remained with the family and is currently supplying grapes to Noval. The vinification centre at São

Martinho d'Anta near Sabrosa has been retained as part of the new company.

Cálem produced a superb Vintage Port in 1966 but subsequent wines from the 1980s and 1990s have been very inconsistent, such that three vintages (1985, 1990 and 1991) have been withdrawn from the market. Aged Tawnies and *Colheitas* dating back to 1957 (the latter bottled to order) look much better. The company's main brand is Velhotes, a standard Tawny which is brand leader on the home market. The company's stocks are split between four separate lodges in Vila Nova de Gaia. Located by the lower tier of the Ponte Dom Luíz, Cálem has initiated an energetic public relations campaign. It receives over 100,000 visitors a year.

CHURCHILL

Churchill Graham, Lda, Rua da Fonte Nova, 5, 4400 Vila Nova de Gaia
Churchill's gravitas as a Port shipper belies its youthful age. Deprived of its own Port house by the sale of W. & J. Graham to the Symington family in 1970, Churchill Graham was established as recently as 1981 by brothers Johnny, Anthony and William Graham. The birth of the first new British Port shipper in half a century was not without acrimony. Named after Johnny's wife (née Churchill) and his own surname, he clashed with the Symingtons (who own Graham) over the use of the family name on the label. Eventually a compromise was established whereby the company was called Churchill Graham but the brand was curtailed to 'Churchill's'.

With a lodge rented from Taylor and a shoe-string budget, Johnny Graham quickly gained a reputation for small quantities of high quality wines pitched mainly at the UK market. The company had no *quintas* to call its own and bought in wines from properties belonging to the Borges de Sousa family. Since 1982 Quinta do Fojo, Quinta da Manuela and Quinta da Agua Alta have provided the backbone for some ripe, plump Vintage Ports. Quinta da Agua Alta with its own distinctive *terroir* has been bottled as a single-*quinta* wine in good interim years. Churchill's deep, dense, unfiltered LBV is without doubt one of the best on the market.

With few stocks of old wine to draw on, the Churchill range

has gradually developed to include a ten-year-old Tawny and a well-aged dry White Port. The latter is exceptional. Deep amber in colour with complex toasted/candied aromas, it resembles a dry Tawny and, unlike so many White Ports, makes a deliciously incisive aperitif.

Churchill's now has its own sturdy granite-built lodge with an excellent view of the river and in 1999 purchased a *quinta*. William Graham lives in Brazil but Johnny and Anthony are already part of the Port establishment.

COCKBURN

Cockburn Smithes & Ca. SA, Rua das Coradas, Apartado 20, 4400 Vila Nova de Gaia
The butt of many a pun over its pronunciation, Cockburn is one of the best-known names in the Port trade. But the story of Cockburn's success is an intriguing tale of five enterprising families and a multinational. The firm was established in 1815 by George Wauchope and Robert Cockburn (whose younger brother Henry, Lord Cockburn, was a Scottish judge). Originally called Cockburn Wauchope & Co., the name was extended to Cockburn Wauchope & Greig when the two founding partners were joined by Captain William Greig in 1828. Casks branded with the initials 'C.W.G.' can still be seen at Cockburn's lodges in Gaia.

The company has always looked outwards and in 1829 (just fourteen years after it was formed) Archibald and Alexander Cockburn established an office in London. The family was joined in 1845 by Henry and John Smithes and the firm was renamed Cockburn Smithes, the name which survives to this day. John Smithes subsequently married Eleanor Cobb whose brother, Charles, joined the London office in 1863. The Smithes continued to work for Cockburn until 1971 and Peter Cobb, who retired in 1999, is still associated with the company.

In the slump that followed the Second World War, Cockburn's became prey to outsiders. The company was initially taken over by Harvey's of Bristol in 1962, a year after Harvey's had acquired arch-rivals Martinez Gassiot. Harvey's was subsequently bought by Allied-Lyons (now Allied-Domecq) making Cockburn's an increasingly small cog within a very big wheel. But with the support of a multinational, Cockburn's has become the leading Port brand on the UK market. Clever television advertising playing on the pronunciation of the name shot Cockburn into the limelight at a time when many other Port shippers were resting on their laurels. Huge amounts of capital have been poured into new vineyards and an impressive bottling plant at Quinta de Santo António at the back of the *entreposto* in Vila Nova de Gaia.

Much of Cockburn's success must be attributed to its wide range of good, consistent wines. Until his retirement in the mid-1990s, wine-making at Cockburn was overseen by Gordon Guimaraens, the tall, lean brother of portly Bruce, formerly wine-maker at Fonseca. The responsibility has now been devolved to another Englishman, Jim Reader. He is supported in the vineyard by Miguel Corte Real, one of the foremost viticulturalists in Portugal. Cockburn's has always maintained a talented team.

The company owns a number of substantial properties in the Douro. Quinta de Santa Maria on the outskirts of Régua relieves the pressure on the lodges in Gaia. Upstream, Quinta do Tua serves as one of the company's principal vinification centres and has long formed part of Cockburn's vintage blend. Cockburn has always favoured the Douro Superior as a source for its fruit and has long-established vineyard holdings at Val Coelho and nearby Telhada. In 1978 it pioneered the move further east, planting its own 250-hectare vineyard on relatively flat land at Vilariça (Quinta do Atayde). In 1989 it added the spectacular Quinta dos Canais to its vineyard portfolio. Facing Taylor's Quinta de Vargellas on the opposite side of a broad curve in the river, Canais is set to become one of the great *quintas* of the Douro. Wines from both Tua and Canais are bottled as single-*quinta* Vintage Ports in good, interim years.

Cockburn's has set its store by Special Reserve, now deservedly the best-selling Port in the United Kingdom and one of the most consistent premium Ruby Ports on the market. During the 1970s and early 1980s, the company had a decidedly eccentric view about vintage declarations missing out both 1977 and 1980 to build up stocks for Special Reserve. Cockburn returned to producing Vintage Port in 1983 but, after an extremely promising start, bottles of this and the subsequent 1985 have gone awry. More recent Cockburn's vintages have been sound but not nearly as impressive as the years prior to and including 1963 when Cockburn definitely belonged to the 'premier league'. Perhaps it is the emphasis on fruit from the Douro Superior that gives Cockburn's recent Vintage Ports a somewhat coarse, cooked character. They are sometimes beaten in blind tastings by wines from the supposedly 'second-string' house of Martinez Gassiot. A soft, easy-going LBV named 'Anno' and good well-aged ten- and twenty-year-old Tawnies completes Cockburn's line up.

QUINTA DA CASA AMARELA

Laura Maria Valente Barreto Regueiro: Riobom, 5100 Cambres
Named after the well-proportioned yellow house at the centre of this eight-hectare vineyard, Quinta da Casa Amarela has been in the hands of the same family since 1885. Laura Regueiro sells much of the estate's production to Cockburn but, since 1979, she has retained a small quantity of wine to bottle as a round if slightly rustic ten-year-old Tawny. As soon as stocks permit, she plans to extend the range to include a twenty-year-old.

QUINTA DO CÔTTO

Montez Champalimaud, Lda, Cidadelhe, 5040 Mesão Frio
Miguel Champalimaud is a controversial figure in the Douro. Since taking responsibility for the wine-making at Quinta do Côtto in the mid-1970s, he has been vociferous in his criticism of the status quo. Champalimaud's principal bug-bear is that the official system of vineyard classification rates the Cima Corgo and Douro Superior higher than the Baixo Corgo where his own family's properties happen to be situated. With some justification, he reminds visitors that this was the part of the Douro where Port first began, but as part of a perpetual tirade against the establishment his stock phrase is that the shippers are 'shitting on the consumer'!

Perhaps for this reason it has been difficult to take Montez Champalimaud's Ports seriously, and the firm has become much better known for its range of red and white Douro wines. Although it has only declared three vintages to date (1982, 1989 and 1995), Montez Champalimaud produce Port every year from 50 hectares of mainly 'C' grade vineyard in and around Régua. Champalimaud has done much to advance the cause of the 'single *quinta*' (and perhaps much to damage it). In 1986 Quinta do Côtto became one of the first properties to take advantage of the new legislation, which permitted Port exports directly from the Douro whereas previously it had to be shipped from the *entreposto* in Vila Nova de Gaia.

Miguel Champalimaud has now retreated to the safer haven of property development near Lisbon leaving the wine-making at Quinta do Côtto in the capable hands of Carlos Agrellos. None the less, a rather quirky philosophy remains with the 1995 vintage made in a much drier style than is the norm (2.8 baumé as opposed to around 4 baumé). With a concentrated raisin-like aroma and a flavour akin to bitter chocolate, the wine bears a strong resemblance to an Italian Recioto. Filtered before bottling, it is enjoyable to drink young but it remains to be seen whether the wine will develop in the same way as other Vintage Ports.

QUINTA DO CRASTO

Sociedade Agricola da Quinta do Crasto, Rua de Gondarem, 834, 4150 Oporto
Perhaps best known for its unfortified red Douro wines, this well-situated *quinta* midway between Régua and Pinhão also produces both Vintage and unfiltered LBV Port. Unusually, many of the best grapes from the older, low-yielding vineyards are used to make Douro wine and Port is often relegated to second place. Nevertheless, Quinta do Crasto produces some attractive firm, middle-weight Ports, entirely foot-trodden in *lagares* in the traditional manner. Both Crasto's 1997 and 1994 Vintage Ports are relative heavyweights and compare favourably with many shipper's wines but it is still some way from matching the truly exceptional 1950 vintage of which painfully few bottles now remain.

CROFT

Croft & Ca. Lda, Largo Joaquim Magalhaes, 23, Apartado 5, 4400 Vila Nova de Gaia
Croft is one of the oldest and most distinguished names in the Port trade having been founded as far back as 1678. It began as a partnership called Phayre & Bradley, the trading name changing frequently as partners joined, retired or died. The Crofts became involved through the Thompsons, a family of merchants from York who began trading with Portugal in around 1660. Thomas Croft

married Frances Thompson and it was their grandson, John Croft, who joined the firm in 1736 taking the name to Tilden Thompson & Croft. The most famous member of the Croft family was another John (born in 1732), who commuted between York where he was Sheriff and Oporto where he was a member of the British Factors. John Croft wrote a *Treatise on the Wines of Portugal* (published in 1788), which provides a valuable insight into the evolution of the Port trade.

By 1827, Croft & Co. was the fourth largest Port shipper. The firm continued to grow steadily during the nineteenth century and in 1875 it purchased Quinta da Roêda near Pinhão, which remains as Croft's flagship property. In 1911 Croft became part of Gilbey Vintners, who were subsequently taken over by International Distillers and Vintners (IDV). In the corporate merry-go-round, Croft is now owned by UDV (United Distillers and Vintners), itself a subdivision of drinks and fast-food multinational, Diageo.

All the latter-day corporate talk of 'return on assets employed, synergies and centres of excellence' has not been that good for Croft, who, for a time in the 1980s, seemed to lose its way. Croft's reputation for fine Vintage Port, built on the back of two outstanding wines in 1955 and 1963, was largely squandered. Its 1982 vintage was simply not worthy of the name. Croft appears to be determined to make amends and both the 1991 and 1994 declarations reflect the strong, muscular character of the Ports from Quinta da Roêda balanced by wines from Vale de Mendiz and the Ribalonga valley. The success of the latter vintage can be ascribed to Nick Delaforce, who joined the company in 1992 having graduated from Roseworthy in Australia. He is exactly what Croft needs: a hands-on wine-maker.

The bulk of Croft's production is represented by Triple Crown, a young Ruby, and fine Tawny destined for France. Its filtered LBV is sound but somewhat gutless and, on past form, Quinta da Roêda tends to be a rather inconsistent single-*quinta* Vintage Port (although the 1997 is very promising). Apart from recent vintages, the best wine of the range is Croft's twenty-year-old Tawny, which is mostly aged in Gaia and retains its fruit-driven freshness and delicacy.

DALVA

C. da Silva (Vinhos) SA, Rua Felizardo de lima, 247, Apartado 1530, 4401 Vila Nova de Gaia

Founded in 1862 by Clemente da Silva, C. da Silva maintains a huge stock of wine at lodges in the less-fashionable part of Gaia. An eighteenth-century house at the centre of the complex is thought to have belonged to Baron Forrester. Spaniard José Ruiz Mateos, better known for his connections with the former Rumasa empire in Jerez, is now one of the principal shareholders.

The company owns a winery at Quinta de Avidagos near Régua and sources grapes from over seven hundred growers thereabouts. The bulk of C. da Silva's wines are standard Rubies and Tawnies destined for Germany, Belgium, Holland and France, sold under the Dalva, Presidential, Saint Clair or Armada labels. *Colheitas* dating back to the 1930s are mostly well kept and used for blending into a competent range of aged Tawnies. A deliciously rich 1952 white *Colheita* forms part of an unusual, mature, honeyed Branco Velho blended to an average age of about fifteen years. Other *Colheitas* can occasionally be found on the home market. Vintage Ports, which tend to be light and early maturing, sometimes show quite well in comparative tastings.

DELAFORCE

Delaforce Sons & Ca – Vinhos Lda, Largo Joaquim Magalhães, 23, Apartado 6, 4400 Vila Nova de Gaia

The Delaforce family were Huguenots who fled from France to London in order to escape religious persecution in the seventeenth century. Their connection with Portugal began in 1834 when the young John Fleurriet Delaforce went to Oporto to set up a new Port-shipping company for the partners of Martinez Gassiot. John's son, George Henry Delaforce, founded his own firm of Port shippers in 1868 and rapidly established strong trading links with countries as far-flung as Russia, Scandinavia, Germany and the UK. By the end of the nineteenth century, George Delaforce was purveyor to the Portuguese kings, an unusual honour for a non-Portuguese citizen. In spite of the proclamation of a republic in 1910, the royal coat-of-arms still appears on the label of Delaforce Vintage Port.

Delaforce remained in family hands until 1968. Unable to finance the *lei do terço* (two-thirds stock ratio) during those bleak years, they sold out to IDV who already owned Croft. The firm still has a strong family input with father and son David and Nick Delaforce representing the fifth and sixth generations to work for the firm.

Although the family continue to own Quinta de Foz do Temilobos, Delaforce is the only major Port shipper to be without a vineyard of its own. Instead it has maintained a long-term agreement with the owners of Quinta da Corte, well located in the lower reaches of the Torto valley. Alongside wines from the Roncão and Tavora valleys, Corte provides the basis for their Vintage Ports and, since 1978, has been the source of a single-*quinta* Vintage. In the 1980s, Delaforce Vintage Ports suffered in much the same way as those of its sister company, Croft. Although the wines have improved substantially in the 1990s (Delaforce produced a full, fleshy 1992), you have to go back to 1970 to find a big, concentrated wine in the classic mould. Delaforce produces two excellent Tawnies that are among my personal favourites: 'Curious and Ancient' is an apt title for a particularly fine, delicate twenty-year-old and 'His Eminence's Choice' is a richer ten-year-old. At the other end of the spectrum, Germany is the company's principal market with a 'Medium Tawny' formerly known by the brand name 'Paramount'.

DOW

Silva & Cosens Ltd, Travessa Barão de Forrester, Apartado 26, 4401 Vila Nova de Gaia

Dow's is the brand name for Ports shipped by the firm of Silva & Cosens. I have to admit to an in-depth interest in Dow having written a book, *The Story of Dow's Port*, to commemorate the company's bicentenary in 1998. The story is an intricate tale of five families, each of whom have contributed significantly to the history of Port.

The business was established by Bruno da Silva, who left Oporto for London in 1798. He imported a wide range of Portuguese goods (including Port) and quickly built up a thriving trade in England. Bruno da Silva was joined in the business by one of his sons, John J. Silva, who brought in Fredrick William Cosens as a partner. Silva & Cosens was then joined by George Acheson Warre, the only son of George Warre, who was then a partner in the firm of Warre. Warre became a driving force both in Silva & Cosens and in the Douro where he was among the pioneers in the restoration and replanting of vineyards that followed the phylloxera epidemic in the 1870s. Dow & Co., a company with roots dating back to the late eighteenth century, merged with Silva & Cosens in 1877, and James Ramsey Dow took charge of the London side of the business. Although considerably smaller than Silva & Cosens, Dow's had a fine reputation for its Vintage Ports and it was decided to attach the name to the company's entire range of wines. Professor George Saintsbury later wrote 'there is no Shipper's wine that I have found better than the best of Dow's, 1878 and 1890 especially'.

It was in 1882 that Andrew James Symington came to Oporto from Glasgow and began working for the Graham's textile firm. Taking a greater interest in Port than cloth, he became a partner in the firm of Warre & Co. in 1905 and within a few years had become its sole proprietor. In 1912 George Acheson Warre returned to London and offered Symington the opportunity to manage the Portuguese end of the business with a partnership in Silva & Cosens. This bi-partisan arrangement continued until 1961 when the Symington family took control.

The Symington family (which now also owns Graham, Warre, Smith Woodhouse, Quarles Harris and Gould Campbell) has been careful to maintain a separate identity for Dow's Port. The wines are closely linked to Quinta do Bomfim at Pinhão, which was bought for the company by George Warre in 1896. Until 1996 it served as the firm's main vinification centre but in order to relieve pressure on the *adega*, production is now shared between Bomfim and a new winery downstream at Quinta do Sol. Wine from Bomfim's vineyards, supported by Quinta do Zimbro and Senhora da Ribeira, has formed the backbone of Dow's Vintage Port for over a century. Since 1978, Quinta do Bomfim has been released as a single-*quinta* Vintage Port in good years between fully-fledged declarations.

Dow's Ports are made in a slightly drier style than most. In some years the wines can verge on austere with a rather bony structure showing through. This is not to denigrate them in any way for Dow's Vintage Ports are among my personal favourites. In ripe years like 1994, 1977, 1970, 1966 and 1963 the wines have tremendous appeal with a cast-iron tannic backbone offset by intense, fleshy fruit. Dow also performs exceptionally well in lesser years like 1980 and 1975. A tasting in London organised to celebrate the company's bicentenary in 1998 brought together an array of Dow's Vintage Ports with stupendous wines from 1945, 1924, 1908 and 1896, all of which are still drinking extraordinarily well.

The other wines in the Dow range share a similar hallmark, right down to its fine Ruby. 'Trademark' is a dense, full-bodied premium Ruby and its LBV is a structured wine packed with berry fruit. Aged Tawnies tend to be rich and seemingly on the youthful side – not as delicate as some. Dow's Crusted Ports present much of the breadth and concentration of a declared Vintage Port at a fraction of the price.

FEIST

H & C.J. Feist – Vinhos SA, Rua de Serpa Pinto, 183–191, Apartado 42, 4400 Vila Nova de Gaia
In 1836, two cousins left Germany and established themselves in London as Port merchants. By the 1870s, the business had expanded to the extent that Carl Feist left London for Oporto to establish a new branch of the business. The company remained in family hands during the first half of the twentieth century, run by the founder's son-in-law and grandson. During the Second World War, the London headquarters were completely destroyed in an air raid and the family retreated to Oporto. Feist was subsequently taken over by Barros Almeida and is now an integral part of the group. At the quality end of the spectrum Feist tends to focus on *Colheitas* but somehow these never seem to be quite as good as those shipped under the Barros or Kopke labels.

FERREIRA

A.A. Ferreira SA, Rua da Carvalhosa, 19–103, 4400 Vila Nova de Gaia
During the 1980s, Ferreira built itself into the market leader in Portugal with the simple but effective slogan *'Foi você que pediu ('was it you who asked for') Porto Ferreira'*? The company remained with the descendants of the redoubtable Dona Antónia Adelaide Ferreira until it was sold to Sogrape, Portugal's largest

wine-makers, in 1987. Founded in 1751 by José Ferreira, it was his great-granddaughter, Dona Antónia, who effectively built the company up into the force it is today. She was nicknamed Ferreirinha (little Ferreira), an affectionate Portuguese diminutive, which continues to be used on some of Ferreira's labels and in the local vernacular. Until 1999 the company was managed by Vito Olazabal, Dona Antónia's great-great-grandson, who represented the eighth generation of the Ferreira family. His son Francisco is wine-maker at the family property, Quinta do Valado, which produces its own Douro wine as well as Port for Ferreira. Vito Olazabal himself owns Quinta do Vale do Meão, the spiritual home of Portugal's most prestigious red wine, Barca Velha.

The company owns four superb properties in the Douro. Quinta do Porto was purchased by Dona Antónia in 1863 whereas Quinta do Seixo was acquired in 1979 and now houses Ferreira's main vinification centre. Quinta da Leda is situated high up in the Douro Superior close to the Spanish border and a fourth vineyard, the 15-hectare Quinta do Caedo, was purchased in 1990. Ferreira's properties have been the subject of considerable research and development in the 1980s. Under the auspices of the late Jorge Maria Cabral Ferreira (to whom this book is dedicated), they pioneered the *vinha ao alto* or vertical system of planting. Ferreira also purchase both grapes and wine from properties owned by members of the family. Until 1989, it had the use of Quinta do Vesúvio, one of the largest and most stately properties in the Douro, which used to belong to the Ferreira family before it was sold to the Symingtons.

Ferreira's Vintage Ports are frequently underrated. Although not quite in the heavyweight mould, wines from the 1980s and 1990s are well structured with richness and staying power. In good, interim years between declarations single-*quinta* Vintage Ports are produced from Quinta do Seixo and Quinta da Leda. The company began producing an excellent unfiltered LBV in 1987, and in subsequent years the wines have been consistently solid, dense and fruit-driven. They count among the best of the genre.

Ferreira makes some of the very finest aged Tawnies. Quinta do Porto is a refined, well-developed ten-year-old made from grapes grown on the estate. Blended from a number of properties in the Cima Corgo and Douro Superior, the twenty-year-old Duque de Bragança is a benchmark Tawny that combines perfect delicacy and complexity. It belongs firmly in the 'premier league'. With an average age of around six years, Ferreira's Dona Antónia Reserva Pessoal falls rather between two stools combining a hint of true Tawny character with summer fruit and a peppery finish. Sound, well-made Vintage Character, Ruby and Tawny (the latter popular in Portugal) complete a remarkable range of Ports.

Hunt Roope and Constantino are brands belonging to Ferreira. They have now been amalgamated in a single subsidiary firm: Hunt, Constantino Vinhos Lda.

FEUERHEERD

(see under Hutcheson Feuerheerd & Associados – Vinhos SA)

FONSECA

Fonseca Guimaraens – Vinhos SA, Rua Barão de Forrester, 404, Apartado 13, 4401 Vila Nova de Gaia
Catch a Port shipper in a candid moment and many will admit that, apart from their own, Fonseca is their favoured Port. Few other shippers can flaunt quite such an accomplished range of wines.

The company was founded by Manuel Pedro Guimaraens. Born near Barcelos north of Oporto in 1798, he began as a trader exporting cloth and a range of comestibles to Brazil both on his own behalf and for an associated company, Fonseca & Monteiro. In 1822, Guimaraens acquired the majority shareholding in the firm with the caveat that Fonseca should remain the brand name no matter who owned the business.

Manuel Pedro was a controversial character. He took the side of the liberal Dom Pedro in the 1820s conflict with the absolutists and was forced to leave the country on a number of occasions. In one incident he was smuggled on board a ship bound for England, hidden in an empty pipe of Port! Despite the liberal victory in 1832 he remained in London until his death in 1858. Under his stewardship, Fonseca Monteiro & Guimaraens (as it became known) grew into one of the largest Port shippers. The company continued to be based in London until 1927 when it was repatriated to Oporto.

In the slump that followed the Second World War, the Guimaraens family consolidated their holdings with those of Taylor Fladgate & Yeatman. The Guimaraens family nevertheless continued to steer the firm. Frank Guimaraens, followed briefly in the mid-1950s by Dorothy Guimaraens and then Bruce Guimaraens, are collectively responsible for every one of Fonseca's remarkable Vintage Ports from 1896 to 1991. The family mantle has now been taken on by Bruce's son David who, having graduated from Roseworthy in Australia, is now the company's wine-maker.

The chairman and managing director of Fonseca is Taylor's Alistair Robertson, who owns the majority of shares in both companies. The two houses have none the less succeeded in maintaining their own separate identities and produce different styles of Port. Fonseca's wines are based mainly on two enviable *quintas* in the Pinhão valley, Cruzeiro and Santo Antônio, both of which were acquired in the 1970s but have long formed the basis for Fonseca's Vintage Ports. Viticulturalist Antônio Magalhães, who trained with Miguel Corte Real at Cockburn's Vilariça, justifiably describes Cruzeiro as 'a showpiece *quinta*'. A third property, Quinta do Panascal, is open to passing visitors who want to experience a working *quinta*. Down in Gaia, Fonseca's labyrinthine lodges serve as the work-a-day production centre for the group, whereas Taylor's lodge has been restored as a showpiece. Just occasionally one senses that Fonseca has been rather lent upon by its larger sibling.

Fonseca's best-known wine is Bin No. 27, a ripe, hearty premium Ruby wine that is based on grapes from Quinta do Panascal. The company also bottles a small quantity of filtered LBV. But Fonseca reigns supreme with its fine ten- and twenty-year-old Tawnies and some outstanding Vintage Ports, which manage to combine both power and finesse. Leaving aside 1983 and 1980 – both of which are light and rather disappointing – 1985, 1977, 1966, 1963 and 1927 are classic rapier-like wines that tower above others in comparative tastings. Recently declared vintages like 1997 and 1994 are also on a par. Wines from good, in-between years are sold under a second label, Fonseca Guimaraens. Lacking the verve of great Fonseca Vintage Port, they are similarly well made, with Fonseca Guimaraens 1976 consistently outscoring other fully declared vintages, notably some 1977s!

Fonseca's wines are inevitably compared with those produced by Taylor but the markets are surprisingly different. Whereas Taylor's strength is in the UK, Fonseca's main market is across the Atlantic in the USA.

FORRESTER & CA.

(see under Offley)

GILBERTS

Gilberts & Ca., Lda, Rua de Belmonte 39, 4050 Porto
Gilberts began life as a small Portuguese company known as Alcino Correia Ribeiro. In 1962 it was acquired along with its fine stock of old Port by J.W. Burmester & Ca. and renamed after Karl Gilbert, a former partner and director of Burmester. Since Burmester purchased Quinta Nova de Nossa Senhora do Carmo in 1991, both companies' Ports have come from the same stable. Gilberts mainly ship small quantities of wine for the German market. Tawnies tend to be aged for slightly longer in cask than those sold under the Burmester label but are a little sweeter and more rustic in style.

GONZALEZ BYASS

Sherry giant Gonzalez Byass maintained a strong presence in Oporto from 1896 until its stocks of Port were sold to Vasconcelos in 1983. From the turn of the twentieth century until the 1930s, Gonzalez Byass had an arrangement with the van Zeller family to buy the production of Quinta do Roriz. Fearing that Spain would be invaded by Hitler in 1940, Manolo Gonzalez, the third son of the Marquês de Torre Soto and a director of Gonzalez Byass, was sent to Portugal. After the Second World War, he continued to divide his time between Jerez and Oporto. Some good Vintage Ports were declared by Gonzalez Byass as late as the 1970s. With no reputation to uphold, they are frequently undervalued at auction.

GOULD CAMPBELL

Gould Campbell, Travessa Barão de Forrester, 85, Apartado 26, 4401 Vila Nova de Gaia
This is one of six companies belonging to the Symington family,

now collectively the largest single Port shippers (see also Dow, Graham, Quarles Harris, Smith Woodhouse and Warre). The company was founded in 1797 when Garret Gould left Ireland for Portugal and established Messrs. Gould Brothers & Co. with offices both in Lisbon and Oporto. Messrs. James Campbell, merchants and bankers, joined the partnership after the end of the Peninsula War. It was acquired by the Symingtons in 1970.

Gould Campbell is still relatively unknown and is often thought of (rather unfairly) as a *sous-marque* of the more famous Symington brands. The company has no vineyards of its own and sources its fruit from independent *quintas*, mainly in the Covas area downstream from Pinhão. The name is used mainly for big, beefy Vintage Ports, which are often excellent value for money. In both 1985 and 1983, Gould Campbell produced two wines with more depth of flavour than many of its better-known peers.

GRAHAM

W & J Graham & Ca., SA, Travessa Barão de Forrester, 85, Apartado 19, 4401 Vila Nova de Gaia
Graham is indisputably one of the great names of Port. The company is of Scottish origin and began as a Glasgow-based textile concern. With an office in Oporto, the firm entered the wine trade by accident in 1820 after accepting twenty-seven pipes of Port in lieu of a bad debt. The Graham family name has a strong presence in Oporto, linked to Port, construction and textiles. There is even an area of the city at the western end of the Avenida da Boavista known as 'Graham'. W. & J. Graham continued to belong to the family until 1970 when, like so many others, the business fell on hard times and was sold to the Symingtons. Deprived of their family firm, brothers William, Anthony and Johnny Graham founded a new Port shipper known as Churchill Graham in 1981.

Graham's Ports are closely identified with Quinta dos Malvedos overlooking the Douro near Tua, which was bought for the company in 1890. Following the Second World War, the vineyard went into decline and the property was sold off, only to be repurchased in a poor condition in 1982. In the interim, much of Graham's finest Port was sourced from Quinta das Lages in the Rio Torto and this continues to be an important component in the Vintage blend. Malvedos has now been completely replanted and a new winery is being built on the site, equipped with robotic *lagares*. Although the Malvedos name has been used purely as a brand in the past, a Vintage Port from the *quinta* is now bottled in good, undeclared years under the Malvedos label.

Graham's Ports are generally richer, sweeter and rather more fleshy than wines from the other houses belonging to the Symington family. The company boasts a phenomenally good range of wines. Six Grapes is an upmarket, premium Ruby, which always does well in comparative tastings, putting it firmly in the 'premier league'. Graham's powerful, fruit-driven LBV is also consistently good; richer than most and invariably satisfying. Fined before bottling, it counts among the best of the modern genre and has deservedly become brand leader in the UK market. Perhaps not quite as finely poised as some, Graham's ten- and twenty-year-old Tawnies have a sumptuous, mellow texture that make them all too easy to drink.

The house style is best illustrated by Graham's exceptional Vintage Ports, which are consistently rich and fleshy, yet backed by a rod of tannin, which is often concealed behind the fruit. Among recent vintages, 1997, 1994 and 1991 are wines in the classic mould, balancing intensely sweet, concentrated fruit with beguilingly firm, broad tannins. Graham's 1970, 1963 and 1945 are among the finest Vintage Ports declared this century.

GRAN CRUZ

Gran Cruz Porto, Sociedade Comercial de Vinhos SA, Rua José Mariani, 390, 4400 Vila Nova de Gaia
Almost an unknown on English-speaking markets, Cruz is a best-seller in France making it among the leading brands of Port. It is owned by the French group Martiniquaise, who run Cruz as a commodity trader rather than a producer, although the company has recently purchased a *quinta* in the Douro Superior. Cruz Ports are mostly the light, young, Tawny-style wines favoured by the French, who drink them mainly as an aperitif.

HOOPER

Richard Hooper & Son: see Royal Oporto
Hooper is an old name in the Port trade revived by Real Companhia Vinicola (Royal Oporto), who bought the company in 1951.

Most of the wines are in the same league as those of Royal Oporto (see below).

HUNT CONSTANTINO

Hunt Constantino, Vinhos Lda, Apartado 16, 4401 Vila Nova de Gaia

Better known under its former title of Hunt Roope, this firm has one of the longest and most colourful histories in the Port business. It was established by a number of the Dartmouth and Devon families of Newman, Roope, Holdsworth, Hunt and Teage. The Newmans carried out a thriving trade in dried cod (*bacalhau*) with their own ships as far back as the fifteenth century.

In 1735 Hunt Roope opened lodges in Vila Nova de Gaia and Viana do Castelo, the former for wine, the latter for fish. The company's ships had a number of escapades and adventures. Their brig named *Jenny*, *en route* to London with a cargo of Port, beat off a French privateer with eighteen guns. This is commemorated in a panel of *azulejos* on the wall of the *adega* at the Newmans' family property, Quinta da Eira Velha.

Ferreira bought the firm of Hunt Roope in 1956 and the Newman family retained the *quinta*. For a time the name Hunt Roope virtually disappeared but it has recently been revived and merged with Constantino, the latter better known in Portugal for brandy. Quinta do Caedo, the property that has supplied Hunt Roope for over a century, has recently been acquired to ensure its continued presence in vintage blends. Nowadays the wines are bottled under the brand names of Hunt's or Tuke Holdsworth.

HUTCHESON

Hutcheson Feuerheerd & Associados – Vinhos SA, Apartado 39, 4401 Vila Nova de Gaia

Hutcheson Feuerheerd is the result of the fusion of two long-established Port shippers in 1996 under the Barros Almeida umbrella. Feuerheerd is the older of the two companies having been founded in 1815 by a German, Diedrich M. Feuerheerd. The firm used to own Quinta de la Rosa, but the property remained with the Feuerheerd family when the shipping company was taken over by Barros Almeida in the 1930s. The Bergqvists, who now own and run La Rosa, are descendants of the Feuerheerds.

Hutcheson was founded in 1881 by English-born Thomas Hutcheson and Alexander Taylor. Neither of the founders had any heirs and the company was acquired by Barros Almeida in 1927. The merger of Hutcheson and Feuerheerd brought together a number of diverse brands including Vieira de Souza, A. Pinto Santos Junior, The Douro Wine Shippers and Rocha. The majority of these wines are basic Rubies and Tawnies but there are also some lightweight vintages, rather rustic *Colheitas* and aged Tawnies.

QUINTA DO INFANTADO

Quinta do Infantado, Vinhos do Produtor, Lda, 5085 Pinhão
Centred on the village of Covas do Douro just downstream from Pinhão, Infantado was the first of the new generation of Port *quintas* to bottle and market its own wine, having previously sold wine to Taylor. The estate belongs to the Roseira family, who attempt to farm Infantado's forty-five acres of vineyard using the minimum of pesticide and herbicide. Two plots are completely organic (farmed in accordance with Agrobio, Portugal's association of organic farming) and Quinta do Infantado bottles a small quantity of powerful, concentrated Organic Vintage Character Port. Well established on the local market, Infantado produces a full range of Port, from Ruby, through aged Tawny to LBV and Vintage. These wines have been rather variable in the past but over recent years Infantado has shown considerably more character and class. In 1991 Infantado produced a varietal Vintage Port made entirely from Touriga Naçional, to my knowledge the first such Port on the market.

CASAL DOS JORDÕES

Arlindo da Costa Pinto e Cruz, Casais do Douro, 5130 São João de Pesqueira
One of the few producers of organic Port, Casal dos Jordões comprises 50 hectares of vineyards in the Torto valley. This family concern produces a premium Ruby/Vintage Character Port as well as Douro wines under the Casal dos Jordões and Quinta da Esteveira labels. An organic olive oil is also bottled on the estate.

KOPKE

C.N. Kopke & Ca. Lda, Rua de Serpa Pinto, 183–191, Apartado 42, 4401 Vila Nova de Gaia

Established by a German, Cristiano Kopke in 1638, this is the oldest company of foreign origin in Portugal. Little is known of the intervening period as much of the company's heritage was destroyed by a fire in 1882. The firm was bought by Barros Almeida in 1953 but is still run as a separate entity with its own cavernous lodge in Gaia. The administration has been transferred to Barros, and Kopke's offices, kept much as they were in the 1950s, are in a time warp.

Kopke boasts a fine range of Tawnies and *Colheitas* with stocks going back to 1938. Vintage Ports can also be impressive, particularly the 1970, which has developed as well as many of the big names. Recent vintages like 1994 and 1995 also look very promising. The wines are based on Quinta de São Luíz, which was acquired by the company in 1922 and now serves as the main vinification centre for all the companies belonging to the Barros Almeida group.

KROHN

Wiese & Krohn Sucrs, Lda, Rua de Serpa Pinto, 149, Apartado 1, 4401 Vila Nova de Gaia

Norway is not a country usually associated with Port, until that Portuguese delicacy, *bacalhau* (salt cod), enters the equation. Theodor Wiese and Dankert Krohn were in the business of selling fish to Portugal and shipped Port back to Norway, setting up their own firm in 1865. In 1906, an English family by the name of Arnsby briefly entered the business but the company came under the control of Edmundo Augusto Carneiro in 1937. Wiese & Krohn is currently run by the third generation of the Carneiro family, represented by José Falcão Carneiro and his sister Iolanda.

Wiese & Krohn has developed a good reputation for *Colheitas* and aged Tawnies. It maintains remarkable stocks of old Port with one wine dating back to 1863, two years prior to the foundation of the company. This is almost undrinkably concentrated with an aroma and flavour of black molasses. Such wines are occasionally used to add complexity to younger blends. Krohn's twenty-year-old Tawnies and *Colheitas* from the 1950s and 1960s generally combine a high-toned, *vinagrinho* character with the sweetness and concentration that comes from ageing in wood. I have, however, found one or two alarmingly oxidised wines.

Krohn's frequent vintage declarations are often overlooked. Although lighter than the mainstream, in many years the wines are soft and elegant for drinking in the mid-term. In 1989 Krohn bought a small vineyard; Quinta do Retiro Novo in the Torto valley, which serves as the company's main vinification centre. Krohn is unusual in that the wine-making is overseen by two women: Maria José Aguiar and Iolanda Carneiro.

MARTINEZ

Martinez Gassiot & Co., Ltd, Rua das Coradas, 13, Apartado 20, 4401 Vila Nova de Gaia

Martinez belongs to the category of old established Port firms who now have a relatively low profile both in Portugal and on export markets. The company was founded in 1790 by Sebastian Gonzalez Martinez, who sold Port, sherry and cigars from an office in Mincing Lane in the City of London. In 1822, Martinez was joined by an Englishman, John Peter Gassiot. They acquired a lodge in Vila Nova de Gaia in 1834 and entrusted the management to John Fleurriet Delaforce, founding father of the Delaforce dynasty in Portugal.

By the time Sebastian Martinez retired in 1849, the company was the largest shipper of Port and sherry to the UK. The business passed to the Gassiots. Charles Gassiot (John Gassiot's son) was a governor of St Thomas's Hospital in London and built a nurse's home, Gassiot House, in 1906. A plaque commemorating Charles Gassiot remains in the hospital. His brother John Paul Gassiot Jnr. left a portrait of Sebastian Martinez to the Vintners Company where it now hangs in the main hall.

By the turn of the twentieth century, the Gassiots had no successors and Martinez Gassiot became a public company in 1902. In 1961 it was taken over by Harvey's of Bristol. A year later Harvey's acquired Cockburn and two of the keenest rivals in the Port trade found themselves under the same umbrella. Both companies now form part of Allied-Domecq with Cockburn's taking the upper hand.

Martinez has largely been relegated as a vehicle for 'own label' sales. Nevertheless, a small amount of Port is bottled under the Martinez label and the wines often represent good value for money as the brand is much less well known. Martinez bottles a complete range of Ports, the best of which are an elegant, pale twenty-year-old Tawny and some fine, middle-to-long distance Vintage Ports. Past Martinez vintages (like 1963) were relatively lightweight but wines from 1994, 1991 and 1985 score more highly than Cockburn in comparative tastings. Both wines are sourced from much the same vineyards but Martinez has the additional support of Quinta da Eira Velha, which is also bottled as a single-*quinta* Vintage Port. With firm, ripe 'bitter chocolate' concentration, the 1994 Eira Velha is outstanding.

MONTEZ CHAMPALIMAUD LDA

(see under Quinta do Côtto)

MESSIAS

Sociedade Agricola e Commercial dos Vinhos Messias SA, Rua José Mariani, 139, Apartado 1566, 4401 Vila Nova de Gaia
The Messias family entered the Port business in 1934 and now runs it in tandem with a winery in Bairrada. The company has a substantial vineyard holding in the Douro with two properties, Quinta do Cachão and Quinta do Rei at Ferradosa, adding up to 130 hectares of vines. The company's main markets are Belgium, Holland and Portugal and, reflecting demand, the majority of its wines tend to be light and insubstantial young Tawnies. Messias has a rather quirky approach to vintages declaring years like 1979, 1984, 1989. From 1989 to 1994, Quinta do Cachão underwent substantial replanting and no vintages were declared. In the 1970s and 1980s, Messias Vintage Ports have proved to be very variable in quality but I have tasted some attractive wines from the 1960s, among them the fresh, floral Cachão 1960.

MORGAN

Morgan Brothers, Lda, Largo Joaquim Magalhães, 23, Apartado 1318, 4401 Vila Nova de Gaia

Morgan dates back to 1715 and the company remained in family hands until 1952 when it was bought by Croft. The company had a strong reputation for Tawny Port in the nineteenth century and the old Morgan brand of 'Dixon's Double Diamond' is mentioned by Dickens in *Nicholas Nickleby*. Morgan now serves mainly an 'own label', supplying large retailers in the United Kingdom. Small quantities of Morgan Vintage Port are sourced from the Pinhão valley.

NIEPOORT

Niepoort (Vinhos) SA, Rua Infante D. Henrique, 39, 4050 Porto
For five generations this Dutch-owned family firm has been hoarding wines in a cramped lodge in the heart of Vila Nova de Gaia. The firm was founded in 1842 and, for many years, Niepoort lay virtually undiscovered. It remains one of the most under-appreciated of all Port shippers by all but a few *aficionados*. Dirk Niepoort, who is gradually taking over the reins from his father Rolf, is doing all he can to promote the family name at the same time as maintaining and building on the quality of the firm's wines. Although single-minded about wine, his interests extend way beyond Port and the Douro. Dirk Niepoort has been dabbling in wine throughout northern Portugal and has built up an eclectic cellar of wines from around the world. His commitment to quality is total.

Until relatively recently the company possessed no vineyards of its own. Instead Niepoort built up strong contacts with small farmers, mainly in and around the Pinhão valley. In 1988 and 1989 Niepoort bought two adjoining properties, Quinta de Napoles and Quinta do Carril overlooking the River Tedo, giving them a total of 50 hectares of grade A vines. These have been joined by Quinta do Passadouro, which belongs to a Belgian industrialist Dieter Bohrmann whose passion for wine equals that of Dirk Niepoort. The property has been completely restored and is now being bottled as a single-*quinta* Port under the Niepoort label.

Niepoort earned its reputation for some fine Tawnies and *Colheitas*, but from simple Ruby to great Vintage Ports, Niepoort ship small quantities of excellent wines. Vintage Ports tend to be solid and foursquare in their youth, not as 'showy' as some, needing time for that surly façade to break down to display underlying fruit and finesse. Niepoort 1970, 1955 and 1927 count among the very best of those vintages: huge, concentrated wines with the power and depth to develop further in bottle (even the 1927!). With the exception of 1985 (a year when a number of shippers faced problems), recent vintages are always impressive with a ripe, tannic underbelly supporting dense, concentrated fruit. LBVs produced in larger quantities from interim years are bottled unfiltered (although the word 'traditional' has never appeared on the label). Given sufficient bottle age, they can be more impressive than some shippers' fully declared vintages!

The company bottles a fine array of aged Tawnies, graduating from so-called 'Junior', through 'Senior' to ten-, twenty- and thirty-year-old wines, all of which belong in the premier league. Stocks of *Colheitas* date back to 1935, becoming increasingly maderised with age and I was recently presented with a half-bottle of extraordinarily rich dessert White Port dating back to 1895. Niepoort is unique in maintaining a stock of 'Garrafeira' Ports, which age in wood followed by glass demi-johns before being 'decanted' into bottles. In an era when many Port shippers have become prey to economies of scale and standardisation, Niepoort is a welcome idiosyncrasy.

QUINTA DO NOVAL

Quinta do Noval – Vinhos, SA, Avenida Diogo Leite, 256, Apartado 57, 4401 Vila Nova de Gaia
Noval has brought the word *quinta* into the international lexicon. The property first appeared in the land registries in 1715 and passed through the hands of the Rebello Valente family and Visconde de Vilar d'Allen in the eighteenth and nineteenth centuries. Having been ravaged by phylloxera in the 1880s, Noval was sold in 1894 to Port shipper António José da Silva. The estate was thoroughly renovated and the major part of the vineyard was replanted on phylloxera-resistant American rootstock. It seems, however, that da Silva planted a small parcel of vines on their own roots, thoroughly fumigating the soil in advance. This marked the beginning of Quinta do Noval's now legendary Naçional Port, produced entirely from ungrafted vines (see below).

António José da Silva was followed into the business by his son-in-law Luís Vasconcelos Porto, who ran Noval for nearly three decades. Vasconcelos continued where da Silva left off, transforming many of the narrow terraces into the wider inclined terraces that made better use of the space and allowed more exposure to the sun. He also did much to build Quinta do Noval's reputation in the UK, targeting Noval's sales on Oxford and Cambridge colleges as well as private clubs.

Vasconcelos retired in 1963 and his grandsons, Fernando and Luís van Zeller, took over the running of the company. In 1981 the company suffered a disastrous fire at its lodges in Vila Nova de Gaia, which destroyed 350,000 litres of stock as well as the company's archives. This combined with a long-running family dispute eventually brought the company to its knees. In 1993 the van Zeller family sold out to the French insurance company AXA. Quinta do Noval is now part of AXA Millesimes, a group that includes a number of Bordeaux châteaux and owns Disnoko in the Tokay region of Hungary. The company is overseen from France by Jean-Michel Cazes, and an Englishman, Christian Seely, has been put into the driving seat in Portugal as Managing Director of Noval. In 1999 it was announced that Seely would take over from Cazes in Bordeaux following his retirement in 2001.

Taking advantage of the change in legislation in 1986, Noval has moved lock, stock, and barrel from the Vila Nova de Gaia *entreposto*. A new lodge has been constructed on the estate with air-conditioning to mitigate against the summer heat and a bottling plant has been set up on the *altos* above Alijó. About one third of the company's production originates from Noval's own vineyards, which include the neighbouring Quinta de Silval and Quinta das Canadas. Nowadays wines bearing the name 'Quinta do Noval' are produced entirely from grapes grown on the estate whereas 'Noval' signifies a wine sourced from a number of growers. Around half the *quinta*'s production is foot-trodden in *lagares*. The latest addition to Noval's technological make-over is a robotic treader.

In the 1970s and 1980s, Quinta do Noval had a somewhat patchy record for Vintage Port, preferring to declare 1978 and 1982 to 1977 and 1983 respectively. Since AXA took over, this slightly idiosyncratic approach to vintage declarations has continued with declarations in both 1994 and 1995 and a Naçional wine in 1994 and 1996 (see below). But the overall quality of Noval's Ports has improved considerably under the new regime and the 1995 (which includes grapes from the Naçional vineyard at the heart of the blend) is one of the leading wines of the vintage. The name 'Silval' is attached to a second-string Vintage Port sold mainly in the USA and Holland. Noval has also entered into a long-term contact with the van Zellers at Quinta do Roriz to make and market a single-*quinta* Vintage Port.

Noval's prestige as a Port shipper in the 'premier league' emanates from the Naçional. The vineyard is planted on traditional terraces either side of the main drive to the house and amounts to about 6,000 vines mainly comprising Tinta Francisca, Touriga Naçional and Souzão. The name is derived from the fact that the vines are planted on their own roots ('attached to the soil of the nation') without recourse to American rootstock. Vines are generally replanted on an individual basis when they become weak from age or disease. The age of the vineyard therefore averages around thirty-five years so it is a complete misnomer to describe them as 'pre-phylloxera vines', a phrase that appeared on the label as recently as 1994! The Naçional vines are much less vigorous than the surrounding vineyard and berries tend to be small, yielding around 15 hectolitres per hectare (compared to an average of 30–35 hectolitres per hectare elsewhere on the estate). The grapes are worked hard with five men treading for five days in a small *lagar* (capacity no more than five pipes). The must is fortified when the sugar levels decline to about 8 baumé and run off into stainless steel where it spends the winter before being racked into well-used pipes. Over a two-year-period, the wine is regularly retasted and if it is not of a sufficiently high standard it is blended into the other *lotes*. Quinta do Noval Naçional is one of the most concentrated of all Vintage Ports with a deep, opaque colour when young and an almost overpowering intensity of liquorice and bitter chocolate fruit. It is not merely confined to generally declared vintages, a trait established in 1931 when just three shippers had the temerity to declare. The 1931 Naçional is legendary for being the most expensive bottle of Port, fetching $5,900 (c. £4,000) at the Graycliffe Restaurant in the Bahamas in 1988. The wine is all the more remarkable for the fact that the vines were around five years old at the time. The 1962, 1963, 1966 and 1970 Naçional are among the finest Vintage Ports that I have tasted: massive wines, tight and intensely ripe, with flavours of liquorice and all-spice shrouded in tannin. Noval's Naçional is only available on a strict allocation basis and bottles rarely come to auction. In 1997, when Noval

Naçional was one of the leading wines of the vintage, the entire declaration amounted to just 250 cases.

The remainder of Noval's range is extremely competent and well made. From the vibrant 'Old Coronation' Ruby through a full-flavoured premium Ruby known as 'LB' to a ripe, unfiltered LBV, the wines all retain freshness and depth. Bolstered occasionally by declassified Naçional, Noval's aged Tawnies are attractively rich, with a hint of tannic grip still lingering in the ten-year-old. Noval also maintains small stocks of *Colheita* Port dating back to 1937. *Colheitas* and LBVs are made entirely from fruit grown on the *quinta*.

OFFLEY

Forrester & Ca. SA, Rua Guilhereme Braga, 38, Apartado 1309, 4401 Vila Nova de Gaia
Offley Forrester, as it used to be styled, is a company with a long and distinguished history, which has been kicked from pillar to post in recent years. Fortunately, the quality and reputation of the wines has not suffered greatly in the process.

The firm was established in 1737 by William Offley, one of whose ancestors was Lord Mayor of London, another sheriff of Stratford. In 1803 he was joined by Joseph Forrester whose nephew became Baron Joseph James Forrester, the great nineteenth-century dilettante cartographer and artist who did so much to open up the Douro before he drowned at Cachão de Valeira in 1862. Offley bought Quinta da Boa Vista from the Barão de Viamonte in the 1820s. In a complicated restructuring of the company involving litigation a century later, Boa Vista became separated from Offley only to be repurchased in 1979. It now serves as the company's main vinification centre.

In 1962 Offley Forrester was bought by Sandeman, who then sold half the shares in the company to Martini & Rossi in 1965, who picked up the remainder of the business in 1983, only to pass it on again in 1996 to Portugal's largest wine-makers Sogrape, who also own Ferreira. The company was renamed Forrester & Ca. SA but the wines continue to be sold under the Offley label. Sogrape's acquisition of Offley was a shrewd move, reinforcing its position as brand leader on the domestic market with an inexpensive Ruby and Tawny duo known as 'Duke of Oporto'. Ten-, twenty- and thirty-year-old Tawnies under the Baron de Forrester label are made to a high standard and since 1988, Offley has been producing a good, unfiltered LBV, which is slightly drier in style than the norm. Offley's Vintage Ports have been bottled under the name 'Boa Vista' for much of the twentieth century even though the *quinta* was outside the company. A certain amount of confusion was created in 1987 when Offley declared two Vintage Ports, Offley *per se* and Offley Boa Vista, because of demand from the USA. In spite of this, Boa Vista is a brand rather than a single-*quinta* Port. It is rarely a massive, long-lived wine but it does have huge appeal, developing wonderful violet-like aromas after a few years. This is already evident in the 1989, 1983, and 1980, whereas the 1995, 1994 and 1985 have further to go. For some reason neither 1991 or 1992 were declared.

Rainha Santa, Rodrigues Pinho and Diez Hermanos are *sous-marques*.

OSBORNE

Osborne (Vinhos de Portugal) & Ca. Lda, Rua da Cabaça, 37, 4400 Vila Nova de Gaia
Osborne's instantly recognisable black bull – strategically placed along roadsides in Spain – is rarely seen in Portugal. Founded in 1772 by Thomas Osborne, the company only came to Portugal in 1967. Although Osborne purchased Port shipper Duff Gordon in the nineteenth century retaining only the brand name, the company is still much more closely identified with sherry and brandy than it is with Port.

Between 1967 and 1988 Osborne moved in with Noval taking over their entire lodge in Vila Nova de Gaia when the van Zellers retreated to the Douro. The company has no vineyards as yet and rents an *adega* at Moncorvo in the Douro Superior. All their grapes are sourced from the Cima Corgo and Douro Superior; nothing is bought from the Baixo Corgo. The company's quality-conscious Managing Director, José Teles, has already established a talented technical team and despite a lack of aged stock, this is evident in the entire range of wines. Premium styles begin with an aged Tawny labelled 'Special Reserve – Master of Port' and continue through a ten- and twenty-year-old Tawny. Quinta do Ventozello provides the backbone for Osborne and Duff Gordon 1994 and 1995

Vintage Ports, both of which are solid and well made for keeping in the medium to long term. An LBV, bottled without filtration, has plenty of body and structure. Osborne is a welcome newcomer to the Oporto scene: it deserves to succeed.

POÇAS

Manoel D. Poças Junior – Vinhos SA, Rua Visconde de Devesas, 186, 4400 Vila Nova de Gaia

The Poças family is a relative newcomer to Port, having set up in business as a brandy trader in 1918. This lucrative business ceased abruptly in 1934 when the Salazar regime imposed a monopoly on the distribution of the *aguardente* used to fortify Port. The company was forced to sell its distilleries for a paltry sum and the founder's grandson, Manuel Poças Pintão, who now runs the company, has been vehemently opposed to the authoritarian politics of the *Estado Novo* ever since.

Helped by the acquisition of Quinta das Quartas near Régua, the Poças family began to export wine. In spite of the Depression in the early 1930s, sales grew and Poças captured lucrative markets. However, they never declared a vintage until 1960 preferring to concentrate on *Colheitas* and Tawnies instead. The company's founder, Manoel Poças Junior, firmly believed that Vintage Port was the preserve of the English houses but this did not stop him from bottling small quantities for his own consumption. When he died in 1976, his grandson found 142 bottles of 1927 Vintage Port stashed away in the cellar!

Since 1960 Poças has made up for lost time, declaring 1964, 1978 and 1990, as well as all the mainstream vintages. In good years like 1963, 1970, and 1995, the wines are rich, medium-bodied, middle-distance Ports. The majority of their exports are destined for Belgium, Holland and Denmark. This is reflected in the sweet, slightly jammy style of standard Rubies and Tawnies, shipped either under the Poças, Pousada or Seguro brands according to the market. LBVs are rich and concentrated, bottled without filtration. Aged Tawnies and *Colheitas* tend to be similarly full and sweet in style, often retaining a smattering of tannin on the finish.

QUINTA DO PORTAL

Sociedade Quinta do Portal, SA, Rua Guilhermina Suggia, 200, 4200 Oporto

The Mansilha family has owned vineyards in the Favaios area for over a century and has recently begun producing its own Port at a well-equipped winery near Celeirós. Aged in the Douro, the wines tend to be sweet but somewhat rustic in style, marred I fear by poorly maintained wood. I noticed that at least one vat on the property had been attacked by woodworm!

PRESIDENTIAL

(see under Dalva)

QUARLES HARRIS

Quarles Harris & Ca. Lda, Travessa Barão de Forrester, 85, Apartado 26, 4401 Vila Noa de Gaia

Founded by Thomas Dawson in 1680, Quarles Harris is among the oldest of all the Port houses. The Harris family was a wine supplier in the City of London and entered the company when Quarles Harris married Dorothea Dawson in 1752. The firm grew substantially during the latter part of the eighteenth century and by 1792, Quarles Harris was the second largest Port shipper. It remained independent until the 1920s when Reginald Quarles Harris sold the firm to Andrew James Symington, who was related by marriage.

The Symington family continues to manage Quarles Harris in tandem with Dow, Graham, Warre, Smith Woodhouse and Gould Campbell. Alongside Gould Campbell, it is the least well known of all the Symington houses and the name is often incorrectly pronounced ('Quarles' rhymes with 'squalls'). The company has no vineyards of its own and is principally a wine-making operation whose purpose is to supply the French market. At the upper end of the spectrum, Quarles Harris produces some fine Vintage Ports which are well made and often well priced. Vinified and blended to a firm, dry style that often resembles Dow, recent vintages have been truly excellent and on a par with the best of the big names. Quarles Harris 1994 is a mainstream wine that will be

Bacalhau

approachable perhaps five or so years before the wines from the top tier of Symington companies. Although the 1997 Quarles Harris is much lighter than other wines from the Symington houses, it is worth keeping a keen eye open for previous vintages.

RAMOS PINTO

Adriano Ramos Pinto (Vinhos) SA, Avenida Ramos Pinto, 380, 4400 Vila Nova de Gaia

Ramos Pinto has always been a company with foresight. In 1880 Adriano Ramos Pinto founded a Port shipper in his own name with the idea of tapping into the competitive Brazilian market. Most wine was shipped in bulk at the time and little attention was paid either to marketing or presentation. Ramos Pinto backed his sales drive with a series of rather *risqué* posters depicting the female form. *Tentação* (temptation) was the byword – the US Bureau of Alcohol, Tobacco and Firearms would certainly draw the line at such advertising today! The campaign succeeded and Ramos Pinto managed to sell its wines at twice the price of Ports normally shipped to Brazil.

The firm suffered more than most when the Brazilian market collapsed in the 1920s, but continued in family hands. In the early 1970s José Ramos Pinto Rosas was among the first to enter the brave new world of the Douro Superior when he purchased Quinta de Santa Maria (now Quinta da Ervamoira) for the company. Throughout the late 1970s and early 1980s, Ramos Pinto was at the forefront of research and development in the Douro, while its ornate, brightly painted lodge on the waterfront at Gaia remained in a time warp without a computer in sight. In 1990 the champagne house Louis Roederer stepped in to purchase a controlling stake in the firm and began introducing some necessary changes in the management of the company as well as maintaining a commitment to continued investment in the Douro. Wine-maker João Nicolau d'Almeida (son of Fernando Nicolau d'Almeida of Barca Velha fame and a direct descendant of the founders) exudes enthusiasm for all the work that has been carried out at Ramos Pinto's four widely spread Douro *quintas*: Bom Retiro and Urtiga in the Rio Torto and Bons Ares and Ervamoira in the Douro Superior. The latter, threatened for many years by a hydro-electric dam project, has been saved following the discovery of palaeolithic rock engravings in the Côa valley. In 1998 it was declared a World Heritage Site.

Ramos Pinto tends to be better known for its wood Ports than for Vintages which, though generally attractive and well made, tend to be midweight and fairly forward in style. Fruit from Quinta da Ervamoira provides the basis for a rich, candied ten-year-old Tawny with Bom Retiro producing one of the finest of all twenty-year-olds: pale, delicate and supremely refined. Urtiga is a ripe, spicy, premium Ruby and the company also produces a rich, unfiltered LBV, which has the capacity to age. A 1927 LBV from Bom Retiro (bottled in 1932) was still alive though soft and creamy with age when the cork was drawn in 1998.

In line with its forward-thinking approach, Ramos Pinto is one of the few major Port shippers to have spent time and effort in producing unfortified Douro wines (see Chapter 6).

REBELLO VALENTE

(see under Robertson)

ROBERTSON

Robertson Bros. & Ca. Lda: c/o Sandeman
Established in 1847, Robertson Bros. owned the famous Quinta do Roncão upstream from Pinhão. In 1881 the company took over Rebello Valente, which it reserved as a brand name for its renowned Vintage Ports. After a number of changes of ownership, Robertson in turn was taken over by Sandeman in 1953. It continues to use the name, mainly for sales to the Netherlands. Since 1970, Rebello Valente Vintage Ports have been a pale shadow of their former selves.

ROMARIZ

Romariz – Vinhos, SA, Rua de Rei Ramiro, 356, 4400 Vila Nova de Gaia
With a strong presence in Portugal and on the continent of Europe, Romariz is almost unknown in English-speaking markets. The company was founded in 1850 by Manoel de Rocha Romariz and spent many years trading with South America, especially Brazil. In

1987 a British consortium closely associated with Taylor's bought the firm and began developing the brand. The company is managed by Albino Jorge, who is also Production Director for Taylor. Without its own vineyards but sharing a winery with Taylor and Fonseca at Quinta da Nogueira, Romariz produces large volumes of reliable standard Tawny sold under the Reserva Latina label.

QUINTA DE LA ROSA*

Quinta da Rosa (Vinhos do Porto) Lda, 5085 Pinhão
Father and daughter, Tim and Sophia Bergqvist, are leading pioneers of single-*quinta* Port. This 'A' grade property near Pinhão has been in the family since 1906, but by the early 1980s the Bergqvists felt that the wines were under-performing. Helped by a change in the legislation in 1986, the family wrested control of the wine-making from Sandeman (who used La Rosa for Robertson/ Rebello Valente) and began to produce their own single-*quinta* Vintage Port. Despite being soft and relatively early maturing, their first vintage (1988) was a significant improvement on wines from the 1970s and early 1980s. All the grapes for La Rosa's Vintage Port are now trodden in stone *lagares* before fermentation whereas Sandeman used the ill-fated *movimosto* system. With increasingly rigorous selection, recent vintages have gained in stature, 1994 being the most successful wine to date. La Rosa works on the 'château principle', declaring a vintage in all but the poorest of years. At the time of writing, 1993 is the only year to have been bypassed. With one of the largest traditional *armazéns* in the Douro, La Rosa also acts increasingly like a Port house in its own right. The Bergqvists ship an increasingly broad range of wines spanning standard Ruby and Tawny, a robust premium Ruby known as 'Finest Reserve' and a ten-year-old Tawny. Apart from Vintage Port, La Rosa's most fulfilling wines are a firm-flavoured, unfiltered LBV and a properly wood-aged, dry, White Port. All the wines are aged on the property, which reinforces the house style.

Quinta de la Rosa began producing a red Douro wine in 1990 (see Chapter 6). They also sell olive oil from the property.

---

*The estate is called Quinta de la Rosa but the trading name is Quinta da Rosa, 'de la' not being recognised in the Portuguese language!

Real Companhia Velha SA, Rua Azevedo Magalhaes, 314, 4430 Vila Nova de Gaia

Better known outside Portugal as 'Royal Oporto', the Real Companhia Velha has a controversial history having been established in 1756 by Royal Charter as the Companhia Geral da Agricultura das Vinhas do Alto Douro, a monopoly controlled by the then Prime Minister, the Marquês de Pombal. With its headquarters at Régua, the Companhia continued to enjoy numerous privileges and regulatory powers into the nineteenth century. It was briefly dissolved but in 1865 Real Companhia Velha was re-established as a public company.

The firm grew quickly in the twentieth century becoming the largest single Port shipper before being pushed into second place by the Symington family. For many years the fortunes of the company have centred on one man, Manuel da Silva Reis, who began as an office boy in the firm of Souza Guedes and by the early 1970s owned twelve wine-producing companies including Pombal's former monopoly. Then came a set-back. Following the 1974 revolution, Real Companhia Velha was occupied by its workforce and nationalised by the government. In an effort to keep afloat, much of the company's better quality Port was sold off to other shippers. The company was returned to the Silva Reis family in 1978, stripped of its most important asset. Manuel da Silva Reis has never forgiven the other shippers for purchasing Royal Companhia Velha's stock and a certain amount of friction is still in the air.

In 1990 a substantial share of the company changed hands twice. Forty per cent of the firm was bought by Cofipsa, a subsidiary of the Italian financier Carlo de Benedetti. While the ink of the signatories was still wet, Benedetti's share was acquired by the Casa do Douro, one of Port's quasi-official controlling bodies. This insider-dealing sent a wave of protest through the establishment. The government nevertheless consented to the sale before acting to withdraw many of the Casa do Douro's regulatory powers. The acquisition of 40 per cent of Real Companhia Velha has virtually bankrupted the Casa do Douro and, at the time of writing, Benedetti is still trying to obtain payment for the sale of his shares.

With its sister company Real Vinicola, Real Companhia Velha

is itself the largest single vineyard owner in the Douro with land holdings adding up to over 2,000 hectares. The company's principal estate is Quinta das Carvalhas, which covers an entire hill opposite Pinhão, crowned by the famous round house. Quinta dos Acipretes faces Tua, Quinta do Sidró is on the plateau near São João de Pesqueira, and Quinta Casal da Granja on the north side of the river serves as the company's main vinification centre. Real Companhia Velha continues to occupy Pombal's original headquarters in the centre of Régua.

During the 1980s and early 1990s Real Companhia Velha tended to put quantity before quality. Frequently declared vintages were weak and the company's main focus lay in shipping large volumes of standard Tawny to France at bargain-basement prices. The wines were sold under any number of different names, among them Silva Reis, Souza Guedes, Pitters, Hooper's, Real Companhia Velha and Royal Oporto. In the late 1990s, under the auspices of Pedro da Silva Reis (Manuel's second son), the company seems to be undergoing a welcome retrenchment. Aged Tawnies (particularly the twenty-year-old) are balanced, refined and delicate. After a let up in vintage declarations in the early 1990s, the Royal Oporto's 1997 Vintage Port shows a return to form perhaps not seen since the 1950s. It is almost certainly symbiotic with their return to using *lagares*.

Under the name of Real Vinicola, Real Companhia Velha is also an important producer of an increasingly good range of Douro wines (see Chapter 6).

ROZÈS

Rozès, Lda, Rua Candido dos Reis, 526–532, 4400 Vila Nova de Gaia
The fortunes of Rozès have been linked inextricably with those of France since the firm was founded by Bordeaux wine merchant Ostende Rozès in 1855. His son Edmond developed the brand name 'Rozès' and established a lodge in Vila Nova de Gaia. During the Second World War, the company ceased trading when the partners returned to France to take part in the *Resistance*. Activities only resumed again in 1956 when Guy and Yves Rozés returned to Portugal. The company was sold by the family in 1974 and,

after a number of changes of ownership, Rozès was bought by the French luxury goods conglomerate LVMH (Louis Vuitton Moet-Hennessey) in 1987. Rozès has been supplied with Port at various times by Ferreira, Cockburn and Taylor but is now building up stocks of its own. Much of the company's production is standard Tawny made for the French market but the range includes a 'Special Reserve' Tawny with six years in wood, an LBV, and a decent ten-year-old Tawny. Vintage Ports are satisfying if somewhat simple and straightforward.

SANDEMAN

Sandeman & Ca., SA, Largo de Miguel Bombarda, 3, Apartado 1308, 4400 Vila Nova de Gaia
The Sandeman don is one of the most instantly recognisable of all logos. It was devised in 1928 by George Massiot Brown and helped to make Sandeman into one of the largest single Port brands. Perhaps the don doesn't quite compare in recognition terms with McDonald's 'golden arches' but Sandeman claims that it is the fifth best-known logo all over the world.

The company was formed by a Scotsman, George Sandeman, in 1790. He was lent £300 by his father and began selling Port from Tom's Coffee House off Cornhill in the City of London. The business flourished and by 1792 Sandeman was representing the sherries of James Duff of Cadiz (forerunner of Duff Gordon). In the same year he shipped and bottled one of the earliest Vintage Ports – Sandeman 1790. As the business grew, Sandeman moved from the coffee house and eventually established a headquarters at St Swithin's Lane in London. The company remained there until the lease finally expired in 1969.

On his death in 1841, Sandeman was followed by his nephew, George Glas Sandeman, who enlarged the company to include insurance and the export of British linen and textiles. The firm even ran its own schooner, the *Hoopoe*, which plied the high seas under the company flag until 1875. George Glas Sandeman was the first in a long line of Sandemans whose direct descendants continue to manage the firm today. Under his son, Albert George Sandeman, the firm began to promote its own brand name and in 1880 the House of Sandeman became the first Port shipper to export wine bottled and labelled in Oporto.

In the early years of the twentieth century, the firm began a high profile marketing and advertising campaign based on the Sandeman partners. 'Three Star', 'Picador' and 'Partners' were the Sandeman Port brands of the day. The don, dressed in a Portuguese student's cape and a wide-brimmed hat, served to reinforce Sandeman's pre-eminent position at a time when other shippers were still selling Port in bulk. It is fair to say that Sandeman paved the way for the modern Port shipper.

The Sandeman family lost control of the company after it was forced to go public in 1952. For the late David Sandeman, who chaired the firm from London in the 1980s, this marked 'the beginning of the end'. The company became easy prey for a take-over. Forestalling an unfriendly bid from Rumasa, chief predator in the sherry trade of the 1970s, the firm was sold to drinks multinational Seagram in 1980. The famous don rather lost his way during the 1980s. With control of the company remote from both Jerez and Oporto, Sandeman seemed to wander directionless and the wines lacked something as a result. Vintages shed much of their depth and dimension while Founder's Reserve, one of the best-selling brands of Port in the USA, became a pale relic of its former self.

In 1990 Sandeman celebrated its bicentenary. It proved to be something of a milestone in the company's history, marking the beginning of a period of retrenchment. George Sandeman was appointed the managing director in Oporto, bringing back the direct involvement of the family. Quinta do Confradeiro, a relatively low-grade vineyard, was sold and over three hundred farmers were laid off, leaving the firm with Quinta do Vau, an 'A' grade riverside vineyard, which the company purchased in 1988. During the 1990s Sandeman has been the object of corporate 'downsizing', leading to an overall improvement in the quality of the wines. The range was streamlined to focus on a soft plummy Ruby (surprisingly popular in France), a ripe premium Ruby known as 'Signature' for the UK, and Founder's Reserve, now back on form as a richer, sweeter premium Ruby styled for the US market.

After a run of rather light Vintage Ports in the early 1980s, Sandeman decided not to make a declaration between 1985 and 1994. Based on Quinta do Vau, which was extensively replanted at the end of the 1980s, Sandeman's Vintage Ports have changed in style, the 1994 being a much richer, sweeter and perhaps a more forward wine than in the past. Blending is the responsibility of Eduardo da Costa Seixas, who owns Quinta de Santa Julia above Régua, and wine from this property also forms part of the Vintage *lote*. On its own, Quinta do Vau produces a midweight single-*quinta* Vintage Port in good, interim years. Possibly playing up to the American market, Sandeman is one of the only shippers actively to encourage consumers to drink young Vintage Port, perhaps because, unlike its wines from the 1950s and 1960s, the wines are no longer built to last?

One style of wine, which never suffered during the years of upheaval is aged Tawny. Sandeman's Imperial, now designated an 'Aged Reserve Tawny', is pale, gentle and could easily pass as a ten-year-old. Sandeman's best wine is undoubtedly its twenty-year-old, a delicate, refined style of Tawny with a slightly roasted finish. The company maintains substantial stocks of these wines at Cambres in the Douro, which perhaps helps to explain this overtly mature style of wine.

Sandeman has invested a great deal in public relations, setting up a fascinating museum both at its waterfront lodge in Gaia and the Museu dos Lagares in the village of Vale de Mendiz in the Douro. For further information on the latter, see page 107.

CASA DE SANTA EUFÉMIA

José Viseu Carvalho e Filhos Lda, Parada do Bispo, 5100 Lamego
Not to be confused with Quinta de Santa Eufémia (below), which belongs to a branch of the same family, this estate lies on the south bank of the Douro with forty hectares of vineyard (mostly on *patamares*) overlooking the Bagauste dam. The wines are made on the property in a small but modern *adega*. Wood Ports are the speciality here, with old White Ports and aged Tawnies making up the range. Some are rather rustic in style but all the wines share a certain richness and concentration from having been aged in the Douro. The granite-built house on the estate has been turned over to *turismo de habitação* and now receives paying guests.

QUINTA DE SANTA EUFÉMIA

Sociedade Vitivinicola da Quinta de Santa Eufémia, Parada do Bispo, 5100 Lamego

Established in 1984, Quinta de Santa Eufémia sold wines to shippers until 1994 when it began bottling and marketing its own wines. Thirty-five hectares of vineyard are now managed by the fourth generation of the Viseu family and the wines are made on the property in stone *lagares*. Santa Eufémia produces a wide range of Ports, from a rather simple Vintage Character to some gentle, refined aged Tawnies. Vintage Port and Douro wines are also planned. An unusual White Port bottled as 'Very Old Reserve' is a blend of wines with around twenty-five years of age, seemingly with a very high proportion of rather cloying Moscatel (Muscat). Quinta de Santa Eufémia has recently opened to *turismo de habitação* and has bedrooms available for paying guests.

C. DA SILVA

(see under Dalva)

SILVA & COSENS LTD

(see under Dow)

SKEFFINGTON

Skeffington Vinhos Lda, Rua do Choupelo, 250, Apartado 24, 4401 Vila Nova de Gaia

Charles Neville Skeffington was a nineteenth-century partner and vineyard manager in the firm of Taylor Fladgate & Yeatman. Facing increasing competition from own-label sales in the 1980s, Taylor's created a new associate company, adopting the name Skeffington for the purpose. Since the suspension of bulk shipments in 1996, Skeffington has increasingly become a brand in its own right with a full range of Ports from a fruity Ruby through to a good but relatively early-maturing vintage. The wines are by no means as impressive as those from the parent firms of Taylor and Fonseca but neither do they command the same price. None the less, Skeffington produces sound middle-market Ports.

SMITH WOODHOUSE

Smith Woodhouse & Ca. Lda, Travessa Barão de Forrester, 85, Apartado 19, 4401 Vila Nova de Gaia

Sometimes considered to be a second-string shipper, Smith Woodhouse produces Ports that are often in the premier league. The company was founded in 1784 by Christopher Smith, a British Member of Parliament who went on to become Lord Mayor of London. His sons were joined by the Woodhouse brothers in 1818 and the firm acquired its present-day name. In the late nineteenth century, Smith Woodhouse Vintage Port gained a high reputation, with Professor Saintsbury claiming in *Notes on a Cellar Book* that 'I have never had a better '87 than some Smith Woodhouse...' The brand was taken over by Louis Gordon & Sons Ltd of London in 1956 and the wines were shipped by W. & J. Graham. When Graham was sold to the Symington family in 1970, Smith Woodhouse became part of the group.

The company owns a small vineyard, Quinta da Madelena, in the Rio Torto, although most Smith Woodhouse wines are a deft exercise in blending. Much of the company's production is standard Tawny destined to be sold as own-label wines on the French market. This is not to denigrate the wines sold under the Smith Woodhouse label, for the fact is that these Ports are good, and often extremely good.

Throughout the 1970s and 1980s, Smith Woodhouse Vintage Ports have consistently been among the best, perhaps midway between Dow and Graham in style combining sweetness and muscular strength. When it comes to the 1977, I am tempted to echo Professor Saintsbury and claim that I have never had a better '77 than Smith Woodhouse... Both the 1980 and 1983 from Smith Woodhouse are ample, complete wines with a long life ahead. They certainly count among the top wines of the decade. Without the cachet of some of the big names, Smith Woodhouse Ports are frequently extremely good value, making them wines to drink rather than collect.

Smith Woodhouse was one of the first shippers to revive unfiltered LBV. Unlike many of the more recent so-called 'traditional' LBVs, the wine is not released until it has been aged in bottle for six to ten years. The result is a poor man's Vintage Port!

Taylor, Fladgate & Yeatman SA, Rua do Choupelo, 250, Apartado 1311, 4401 Vila Nova de Gaia

Taylor's has built up the reputation as a 'first growth' among Port shippers. With the notable exception of Quinta do Noval Naçional, their wines consistently fetch the highest prices at auction. Perhaps this is partly due to the accumulated weight of tradition. Partners have come and gone but Taylor's is the only British company to have been handed down through the generations without having been sold, bought or taken over.

The company was founded in 1692 by Job Bearsley, who started out in the Port of Viana do Castelo around 1670. Like so many present-day Port houses, Taylor's began as general traders and the enigmatic 4XX symbol, which continues to form part of the company's livery, originated as a wool mark. It was probably Job Bearsley's son Peter who made the crucial move from Viana to Oporto. By 1709 he was well established as a shipper and is thought to have been the first Englishman to venture up the Douro in search of wine. In 1744 the Bearsleys purchased a property at Salgueiral just downstream from Régua. It is the first recorded British-owned property in the Douro and still belongs to the company.

The Bearsleys left the firm at the end of the eighteenth century and a number of families, Webb, Sandford, Grey and Camo, came and went before the first Taylor entered the partnership in 1816. Joseph Taylor joined a firm known as Campbell Bowden & Taylor but within ten years he was running the firm under his own name. In 1836 he was joined by John Fladgate, and two years later Morgan Yeatman, a wine merchant from Dorset in southern England, became a partner in the firm. Joseph Taylor himself died in 1837 but his name was retained.

In 1844 Taylor Fladgate & Yeatman bought Quinta da Roêda and John Fladgate, ennobled as a baron by the Portuguese, took his title from the property. Due to his daughter's marriage, Quinta da Roêda later went to Croft but Taylor's duly compensated for this by acquiring Quinta de Vargellas in 1893. Having been devastated by phylloxera, the property produced a miserable six pipes but by the great harvests of 1908 and 1912, Vargellas was making up a third of Taylor's 300-pipe Vintage *lote*. Today it serves as one of the company's principal vinification centres as well as the flag-ship estate. Quinta de Vargellas has been joined more recently by Quinta da Terra Feita and in 1998 the company purchased two more properties, Junco and Casa Nova, making up an enviable holding in the Pinhão valley.

Much of Taylor's nineteenth- and twentieth-century expansion was overseen by the Yeatman family who continued to run the firm until Dick Yeatman, great-grandson of the Dorset wine mer-chant, died in 1966. His widow, Beryl, briefly took charge and asked her nephew Alistair Robertson to join the firm as a partner. Alistair admits that he was reluctant at the time and that he had to be persuaded to 'give it a go'. The Port trade was in the doldrums and Oporto was a long way (both literally and metaphorically) from London in the swinging sixties. He has been ably supported by two partners: Huyshe Bower, a cousin of Dick Yeatman, and Bruce Guimaraens, who is a descendant of the Fladgates and of the family who sold Fonseca Guimaraens to Taylor shortly after the Second World War.

This is the team that steered Taylor's through the 1974–1975 revolution and transformed a small old-fashioned concern into one of the most successful of all players in the Port trade. Their not so secret weapon has been LBV, which Taylor's claim to be the first to have introduced as far back as the 1950s. It has to be said that there are many other claimants who go back further but Taylor's deserve the credit for the modern, filtered style of LBV, which they launched in 1970. Removing the need to decant, it immediately proved popular in traditional markets and, taken up by other shippers, LBV has been largely responsible for the growth in the premium Port trade over recent years.

The success of Taylor's LBV has undoubtedly been reinforced by their reputation as one of the leading producers of Vintage Port. For over a century two vineyards, Quinta de Vargellas and Quinta da Terra Feita, have provided the backbone for the blend. In great years like 1927, 1963, 1977 and most recently 1994, Taylor's vintages have had a massive structure with a characteristic 'pea-cock's tail' of powerful tannins on the finish. Few other wines rise to the challenge in comparative tastings although Taylor is sometimes pipped at the post by wines from its sister company Fonseca, which seem to be slightly more opulent in style. There is no question that both Taylor and Fonseca belong in the premier league.

Taylor's were the first of the current generation of shippers to commercialise a single-*quinta* Vintage Port. In good interim years, both Quinta de Vargellas and Quinta da Terra Feita are bottled individually. Whereas Vargellas tends to produce firm, tannic wines that sometimes seem rather reserved when young, the wines from Terra Feita are big and powerful with huge amounts of ripe fruit. The wines are cellared in Gaia for a decade or so until they are considered ready to drink and will continue to evolve in the medium to long term. It is intended that wine from Quinta do Junco will also be bottled as a single-*quinta* Vintage Port. In a recent innovation Taylor's have begun to bottle wine from the old mixed vineyard at Quinta de Vargellas under the name Vinha Velha. The 1995 is as deep, intense and powerful as one would expect from old, low-yielding vines but it remains to be seen whether bottling the wine separately detracts from the overall character and development of Quinta de Vargellas as a single-*quinta* Vintage.

With so much adulation over wines at the top end of the spectrum, it is easy to overlook Taylor's rich, vibrant premium Ruby known as First Estate after the property at Salgueiral established by Bartholomew Bearsley in 1744. Around 20 per cent of the blend is foot-trodden in traditional *lagares*. Taylor's also produce a full range of aged Tawnies culminating in a supremely refined over forty-year-old.

The wine-maker responsible for this exceptional range of wines (and those of Fonseca) is David Guimaraens, who took over from his father Bruce in the early 1990s. The chairman, Alistair Robertson, is gradually handing over the reins to his daughter Natasha and son-in-law, Adrian Bridge. Together they look well placed to sustain Taylor's role as a trend-setter in the Port establishment.

QUINTA DO TEDO

Vincent Bouchard, Vila Seca, 5110 Armamar, and PO Box 2322, Napa, CA 94558, USA
Of Burgundian extraction, Vincent Bouchard has been involved in cooperage both in France and California. In 1992 he purchased

Quinta do Tedo, a small property on an isthmus overlooking the confluence of the River Tedo with the Douro. With initial help from the Bergqvists from Quinta de la Rosa, the Bouchards are producing a single-*quinta* Vintage, LBV and premium Ruby known as Finest Reserve for the US market.

TUKE HOLDSWORTH

(see Hunt Constantino)

QUINTA DO VALE DA MINA AND QUINTA DO VALE DONA MARIA

Lemos & van Zeller Lda, Quinta do Vale Dona Maria, Sarzedinho, 5130 São João de Pesqueira
Since leaving Quinta do Noval when the company was sold in 1993, Cristiano van Zeller has turned his hand to promoting single *quintas*. He has two small properties under his own control, Vale da Mina in the Douro Superior and Vale Dona Maria in the Rio Torto. Since 1995, both properties have been producing some serious single-*quinta* Vintage Ports foot-trodden in *lagares*. Dirk Niepoort, a stickler for traditional quality, has been lending a helping hand with the wine-making.

QUINTA DO VESÚVIO

Sociedade Agricola Quinta do Vesúvio Lda, Numão, Vila Nova de Foz Côa. Correspondence address: Travessa Barão de Forrester, Apartado 26, 4401 Vila Nova de Gaia
Lisbon, Rome and Quinta do Vesúvio all have one thing in common: they cover seven hills. The Symingtons bought this epic, 400 plus-hectare *quinta* from the Ferreira family in 1989 and, rather than attaching it to one of the six Port houses under their control (Dow, Graham, Warre, Smith Woodhouse, Quarles Harris and Gould Campbell) they turned Vesúvio into an independent shipper in its own right. Much had to be done to restore the property, which includes a grandiose twenty-three-bedroom house, the largest in the Douro. The eight granite *lagares*, each with a capacity of twenty-five pipes, remain in place and are now equipped

with a purpose-built stainless-steel cooling system. Quinta do Vesúvio has to be seen to be believed!

Under the legislation, as well as being made on site, all the wine must be aged and bottled on the property. The *armazém* has therefore been restored and the old olive oil bins have been modified to store bottles of Port, with air-conditioning installed to maintain a constant temperature over the summer months. The 80 hectares of vineyard on the property produce around 300 pipes, of which around 3,000 cases are bottled as a Vintage Port in all but the poorest years. The first Vesúvio Vintage Port was 1989 and despite its relatively short track record, the Symingtons have established Quinta do Vesúvio as one of the leading properties in the Douro. It has already earned itself a place in the premier league. Packed with fruit, Vesúvio's Vintage Ports appeal particularly to North American consumers who enjoy drinking their Ports young but have the capacity to age well in bottle.

VISTA ALEGRE

Sociedade Agricola Barros SA, Quinta da Vista Alegre, Covas, 5060 Sabrosa

Not to be confused with Barros Almeida, the Sociedade Agricola Barros sells its wines under the brand name 'Vista Alegre'. This is the name of the company's principal *quinta*, well located near Pinhão in the heart of the Cima Corgo. The group owns a number of other properties in the region, which together supply the greater part of the company's requirements. All the wines are aged in the Douro, which may account for the rustic, baked (even oxidised) character of most of the wines although from my experience handling is more likely to be at fault.

WARRE

Warre & Ca., SA, Travessa Barão de Forrester, 85, Apartado 26, 4401 Vila Nova de Gaia

Established in 1670, Warre (pronounced 'War') is the oldest of the British-owned houses. The first name associated with the company is John Clark, who may have brought the company to Oporto from Viana do Castelo, where it began as a general trader. Certainly by the time the Indian-born William Warre joined the firm in 1729 it was firmly established in Oporto and trading in wine. Warre married Elizabeth Whitehead, sister of John Whitehead who was later British Consul in Oporto and was instrumental in building the Factory House. Warre's eldest son, also named William, followed his father as Senior Partner and went on to become British Consul himself.

A third William Warre, born in Oporto in 1784, had a brief but colourful career in the family firm. He used sealing wax to fix the pigtail of Pedro Alves, then an elderly Portuguese member of the firm, to his desk as he slept – no doubt after a heavy lunch. The ensuing indignation meant that the young William Warre left the company. Having distinguished himself in the Peninsular War, he went on to become Lt.-General Sir William Warre. His portrait hangs in the Factory House.

In the late nineteenth century, the Warre family ceased to be directly involved in the firm. Dr Edmond Warre was the Headmaster of Eton from 1884–1905 and Provost from 1909–1918. George Acheson Warre (nephew of the Lt.-General and Edmond's cousin) was a partner in the firm of Silva & Cosens. It was in 1905 that Andrew James Symington, who had arrived from Glasgow in 1882, became a partner in the firm. He soon took a share in Silva & Cosens as well and established the foundations of the Symington's dominion, which now includes Dow, Graham, Smith Woodhouse, Quarles Harris and Gould Campbell. The Symingtons and the Warres ran the firm of Warre & Ca. in tandem until the Warre family sold out in the early 1960s. William ('Bill') Warre M.W. continued to work for the group in London until he retired in 1991.

Warre has always been on the top tier of the Symington-owned Port houses and produces some of the finest, most elegant of Vintage Ports. The style of the wine is deliberately in between that of Graham and Dow, perhaps without the cast-iron tannins that often penetrate Smith Woodhouse. Warre's Vintage Ports were on the light side in the 1940s and 1950s but regained substance and flesh during the 1960s and 1970s. The wines are characterised by their fragrant, perfumed aromas and opulent fruit and yet, as the 1963, 1966 and 1970 vintages of Warre prove, they have the structure to last. The grapes for Warre's Vintage Ports were traditionally sourced in the Rio Torto but in 1978 the company acquired Quinta da Cavadinha, an 'A' grade property in the upper reaches of the Pinhão valley. In good interim years, wine from

Cavadinha is declared as a single-*quinta* Vintage Port, which shares much of the raspberry and black cherry fruit of Warre's vintage *per se*. Quinta de Cavadinha has a small vinification centre for grapes from the *quinta* and surrounding vineyards but the majority of Warre's Ports are produced either at Quinta do Bomfim or Quinta do Sol.

Like Smith Woodhouse, Warre's LBVs are unfiltered and bottle-matured, released around six years after the harvest. These wines have genuine Vintage Character. Warre also produce a pair of young aged Tawnies, 'Sir William' and 'Nimrod', as well as an excellent premium Ruby known as 'Warrior'. The wines are drawn from the same properties that produce Warre's Vintage Port and 'Warrior' has much more substance and character than nearly all the other wines in this category. In continuous production since the 1750s, it is the oldest brand in the Port business.

Warre also supplies the Cintra brand under which large quantities of standard Ruby and Tawny are sold to France.

WIESE & KROHN

(see under Krohn)

DIRECTIONS IN OPORTO AND VILA NOVA DA GAIA

Most visits to the Douro begin and end in Oporto. The atmosphere of Portugal's second city is encapsulated in the Portuguese saying that while 'Lisbon shows off, Oporto works for a living'. The city has expanded both upwards and outwards in recent years but the central, downtown area with its workaday nineteenth-century atmosphere bears an uncanny resemblance to Manchester in the north of England. Like Manchester, rain is frequent and plentiful so Oporto's soberly dressed commuters carry umbrellas just in case.

Between the Praça de Liberdade, which marks the centre of the city, and the riverfront, there is a maze of medieval streets with sanitary conditions to match. The cathedral, a small but solid thirteenth-century building with later add-ons, surveys Oporto's welter of rooftops and the long, low roofs of the Port lodges in Vila Nova de Gaia beyond. The eighteenth-century Torre dos

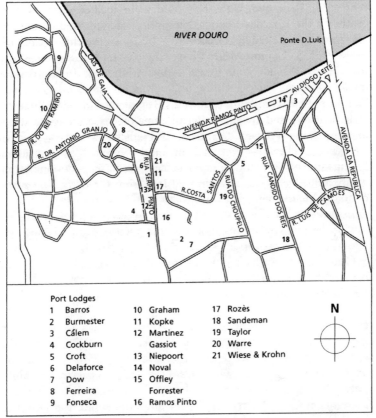

Map 3. The location of Port lodges in Vila Nova de Gaia.

Clerigos, Portugal's tallest church tower, provides the best overall view of Oporto. There are 240 steps to reach the top.

The historic centre of commerce is to be found close to the river along the Rua Infante Dom Henrique (formerly the Rua Nova dos Inglezes – New English Street). The Port Wine Institute occupies a sober granite building on the Rua Ferreira Borges and a portrait of Baron Joseph James Forrester can be seen inside. Close by, the Salão Arabe or Arab Hall of the Oporto Stock Exchange is worth viewing for the ostentatious internal decoration inspired by the Alhambra in Granada. It is completely out of sorts with the staid grey character of the financial district.

The British still have a significant presence in Oporto, with life centred on their own club. This used to be located near the city centre on the Rua das Virtudes, inappropriately named because it also served as the red light district! In the 1960s the club decamped to the Rua do Campo Alegre ('happy field') and became known as the Oporto Cricket and Lawn Tennis Club. The oldest British institution is the Factory House on the Rua Infante Dom Henrique. Behind the austere grey façade is an elegant interior with English-style furniture and some wonderful china. There are two identical dining rooms placed end to end, both of which are used by shippers and guests. The meal is served in one room and then you leave, taking your napkin, and sit at the same place in the adjoining room where Vintage Port can be enjoyed free from the detracting smell of food. Membership is restricted to British-owned Port shippers who meet at the Factory House every Wednesday for lunch. At times when no function is arranged, the Factory House is open by appointment to visitors.

Oporto is connected to Vila Nova de Gaia by a two-tier iron bridge, the Ponte D. Luíz. The lower tier, best approached from the Cais da Ribeira or riverfront, takes you directly to the Port lodges on the opposite side of the river. Some shippers have an enviable location on the waterfront whereas others are hidden up narrow granite alleyways reeking of Port (see map 3). All but the smallest houses conduct regular tours, finishing with a tasting and an opportunity to buy wine (although don't expect a bargain!). Each firm has a different atmosphere. Among the most visible (and therefore most popular) are Cálem and Sandeman, the latter set back from the waterfront in an elegant building that is frequently flooded in the winter. Outdoor bars and cafés sponsored by the shippers look across the river to Oporto, and boat trips are available throughout the summer months.

During the summer the main road along the waterfront, the Avenida Ramos Pinto, is lined with creaking gondola-shaped *barcos rabelos*, mothballed after years of service bringing Port down the Douro. Once a year on the morning of 24 June (the feast day of São João, Oporto's patron saint) they cast off from the quayside and make their way down to the mouth of the River Douro. There is much consternation as these unwieldy craft find an imaginary starting line in front of the huge concrete arch of the Arrábida bridge, which marks the start of a good-humoured race between Port shippers. Many an incident has been recorded as the boats sail slowly upstream to the finish by the Ponte D. Luíz. Many are either blown into the fishing port of Afurada or beached by the sewer outfall upstream on the opposite side. One boat famously sank and a rather corpulent senior shipper was rescued floating down river on an empty Port pipe!

Oporto is reasonably well served by hotels although there are few with any real character. The Hotel Infante de Sagres in the city centre is five star with old-fashioned standards. Built in the 1930s, it has a spacious Edwardian interior and an elegant dining room. The Hotel da Bolsa near the Port Wine Institute is convenient for visiting both the Port lodges and city centre whereas Hotel Boa Vista at Foz overlooks the mouth of the Douro. Both are three star

Barco rabelo

and have a certain amount of local charm although guests at the Boa Vista are often woken by the sound of the fog horn as mist rolls in from the Atlantic during the night.

The inhabitants of Oporto are often called *Tripeiros* (tripe eaters) after the city's staple dish, *Tripas a moda do Porto*. This seemingly unappetising but spicy dish is served in restaurants throughout the city. The trusty *bacalhau* (salt cod) can be seen (and smelt) hanging outside old-fashioned grocers' stores, many of which carry dusty bottles of Port (mostly rather weary *Colheitas*).

Organised by the Port Wine Institute, the Solar do Vinho do Porto is a good place to sample a wide range of Ports. It occupies an eighteenth-century mansion with a fine view across the Douro to Vila Nova de Gaia. Located west of Oporto city centre, it is to be found below the Palácio de Cristal on the Rua Entre Quintas. There is also a Solar do Vinho do Porto in Lisbon at the 'Palace de Ludovic' on the Rua São Pedro de Alcantara in the fashionable Bairro Alto, and the Port Wine Institute has small shops selling wine and books at the main Portuguese airports.

6

Douro Wines

CLARET FOR BOYS, PORT FOR MEN

Alongside Port, unfortified wines from the Douro have long been considered as something of a poor relation. This is partly reflected in the nomenclature. Often dismissed as *consumo* or spoken of misleadingly as 'light wine' or 'table wine' (*vinho da mesa*), no one can quite decide how to distinguish unfortified red and white wines from Port. The task has been made easier since 1979 when the wines of the 'Douro' were officially awarded their own *Denominação de Origem Controlada* (DOC), over two centuries after the region was first delimited for Port.

But unfortified wines are hardly new to the Douro. Until the early years of the eighteenth century, most of the wine produced in the region was fermented dry and occasionally bolstered with a small amount of fortifying spirit to lend stability to the wines for shipment abroad. The evolution of Port into a sweet, fortified wine is covered in some detail in Chapter 1 but even as late as the mid-nineteenth century, the eclectic Joseph James Forrester continued to advocate a return to dry, unfortified red wine considering Port to be 'adulterated' by the addition of *aguardente*. Writing thirty years later Henry Vizetelly refers to 'natural Port' and 'Alto Douro wine made without adventurous spirit' as something of a curiosity. He observes:

> Having consumed all its natural sugar by means of its more perfect fermentation, it has none of the rich fruity flavour of the younger vintage wines, nor the refined liqueur-like character of the older growths to which Port-drinkers have been accustomed, and they naturally refuse to accept it as a substitute for their

favourite beverage. We have tasted at different times numerous wines of the above description made from the best varieties of grapes, and on the manufacture of which unusual care and attention had been bestowed. Undoubtedly they were all wines of some character; still they were not to be compared, either as regards flavour or bouquet, with the highest growths of the Médoc or the Côte d'Or, simply because the Douro vines, with all their advantages of soil, climate, and aspect, are not equal to the carbenet (*sic*) and the cruchinet rouge of the Gironde or the pineau (*sic*) noir of Burgundy. There is no reason whatever why a perfectly fermented and consequently dry Alto Douro wine, which has received no addition of spirit should not find a market in England . . .

The market never materialised and phylloxera finally put paid to these unfortified wines, many of which were distilled to provide *aguardente* for fortification. As Ernest Cockburn records, 'prices in Oporto started to rise all round in view of the position created by the phylloxera and the heavy demand from Brazil for Consumos at a time when the Consumo districts had failed at the vintage. This caused prices of Portugal brandy . . . to rise appreciably'. The shortage continued into the 1890s when Cockburn mentions that 'there had not been enough "Consumo" [Claret type wine of the Douro District] in Portugal to satisfy the demands, and even the price for home consumption in the country constituted a record. The situation existed in the north and south of Portugal, and firms found it necessary to pay excessive prices for wines for "*Beberagem*" for their employees'.

The dismissive tone adopted by Cockburn writing in the 1930s was shared by the majority of Port shippers for much of the twentieth century. 'Consumo', 'table wine' (call it what you will) was accorded the lowliest status in the Douro caste system with the best grapes reserved exclusively for the production of Port. The majority of shippers embraced Samuel Johnson's opinion that 'Claret is for boys, Port for men'. The wine accompanying stately lunches at the Factory House or in the shipper's lodges was usually a parsimonious glass of weedy local red. All the serious talk took place at the end of the meal over a decanter of Vintage Port.

REVIVAL

This macho approach to wine merely served to illustrate the shippers' isolation from the world outside their own. It is all the more remarkable that in 1950 Ferreira's Technical Director, Fernando Nicolau de Almeida, should take himself off to Bordeaux to study production techniques. At first he could not conceive how the Bordelais could possibly tread the grapes in huge wooden vats but Nicolau de Almeida soon found out that they employed softer, more gentle extraction methods. Inspired by this, he returned to his family *quinta* high in the Douro Superior and began to put their ideas into practice using high quality Port grapes. The story (recounted in full on pages 259–60) is a triumph of strength over adversity. Ferreira's Barca Velha was born in 1952 and quickly earned itself the reputation as Portugal's uncrowned 'first growth'. It now commands a price in excess of many Vintage Ports.

Following the success of Barca Velha, other producers slowly began to sit up and take notice and in the late 1970s and early 1980s a flurry of new Douro wines appeared on the market. Initially they were viewed as no more than a by-product of Port, made from grapes left-over after the annual *benefício* or authorisation had been used up (see Appendix III). Thus, in a productive year, perhaps half the region's grapes would be directed into Port with the remainder (mostly from the poorer E and F rated vineyards or young vines) being fermented out to make a dry red wine. Much of the production was concentrated in the hands of down-at-heel co-operative wineries on the higher margins of the region and the quality of the wine did little to enhance the reputation of the Douro. Production techniques were outmoded with vinification (often autovinification) geared towards the extraction of tannin for the production of Port. With a complete absence of temperature control, the resulting wines were hard, mean and astringent. The use of sulphur dioxide as an anti-oxidant was frequently overlooked and the wines deteriorated rapidly. By the time they were bottled many were little better than the rough and ready *agua pé* ('foot water') that used to be doled out to the workers in the vineyard.

There were exceptions. The Symington family has been quietly stashing away a few bottles of Douro red for a number of years.

Made from grapes surplus to the *benefício*, a 1970 Quinta do Bomfim red (tasted in 1998) still retained its deep colour and hugely powerful sinewy tannins. It must have started out as 'black-strap', the derisive term used to describe Douro reds in the early eighteenth century.

Douro wines were given a much-needed fillip by Portugal's accession to the then European Community in 1986. This brought the necessary finance to one of the continent's poorest regions and, from one vintage to the next, wineries were re-equipped with the latest in stainless-steel technology. There remained, however, a lack of technical expertise, not to mention wine-making flair, among producers blinkered by their total commitment to Port. 'Why waste good grapes on *consumo* when you can make them into Port?' was a common cry into the 1990s. Wild fluctuations in yield continued to compound the problem meaning that in one year (e.g. 1996) there was a huge surplus of grapes for making Douro wine whereas in the next vintage there would be a shortage. For an itinerant wine-maker like Peter Bright, it was impossible to plan ahead. Throughout the 1980s and into the mid-1990s, Douro wines continued to be treated as an afterthought.

In the late 1990s, however, there is evidence of a new approach. Prompted by a younger generation of resourceful wine-makers, many with experience abroad, a number of leading Port shippers are according ever greater importance to Douro wines. In fact Douro wines are becoming so serious for some producers that I recently witnessed a *lagar* of premium grapes (originally destined for a potential Vintage Port *lote*) go past the point of no return in order to ferment out as a dry red wine. Financially, Douro wines are also starting to add up. With an increasingly appreciative audience in Portugal and a growing export market, many of the better Douro wines are commanding margins similar to or better than LBV Port. Much of the innovation has taken place at single *quintas* who previously sold their grapes to Port shippers or local co-operatives but which, with a helping hand from the European Union, have been able to break free to make and market their own wines. For a number of growers with C or D rated vineyards in the Baixo Corgo, Douro wines seem to offer a more secure future than the vagaries of Port (see The Future for Port and the Douro on page 272).

RED WINES: TAMING TANNINS

Just as the production of Port is all about the extraction of colour
and tannin, so the successful vinification of red Douro wine
revolves around the need to tame the tannic excesses of the local
grapes. The understanding of this has been increased by the extensive varietal replanting of A and B grade vineyards under the
PDRTIM project in the 1980s. Tinta Roriz, Touriga Francesa and
Touriga Naçional, three of the five varieties sanctioned under the
replanting scheme, have proved to be eminently suitable for Douro
reds. In the case of Tinta Roriz this is not at all surprising. Masquerading under the names of Tempranillo and Tinto Fino, it is the
most widely planted grape in northern Spain, forming the basis for
the finest Riojas and making up a good proportion of Vega Sicilia
upstream where the Douro becomes the Duero. The characteristics
of each of the five main Port grapes are covered in detail in Chapter
2 but in terms of Douro wines Tinta Roriz is appreciated as an
all-rounder for its warm, fleshy, cherry-like fruit. Touriga Francesa
is characterised by colour, natural acidity and fragrance, Touriga
Naçional by colour, tannin and structure; Tinta Barroca is appreciated for its high levels of sugar and potential alcohol and Tinto
Cão (of which there is very little) for fine-grained tannins. Tinta
Amarela (successful in the Alentejo under the name Trincadeira)
clearly has potential to produce fine Douro reds but has an
alarming tendency to rot in the more humid climate of northern
Portugal. Tiny quantities of Cabernet Sauvignon have crept into
the region but its use is only permissible in a second category of
wines bottled under the uninviting name of Trás-os-Montes –
Terras Durienses, which is the title of the local *vinho regional*.
With so many distinctive indigenous grape varieties in the Douro,
it is to be hoped that the near ubiquitous Cabernet will be sidelined.

Most of today's wine-makers seek balance above all else and
therefore tend to source their grapes from more temperate
locations, either downstream from Pinhão or from the so-called
meia encosta (half slope) at altitudes of around 300–400 metres.
Grapes from the Douro Superior and the sheltered tributaries
around Pinhão produce the most robust wines; big but often unbalanced with a pH of around 4. Early picking and/or substantial
acid adjustment are therefore essential. On the other hand, those

from the higher westerly margins of the region on the *altos* around Lamego and Vila Real lack the warmth of the Douro sun and tend to produce thin, rasping wines sometimes akin to Vinhos Verdes. Many of the most successful Douro reds therefore achieve a happy medium by blending wines from a number of different districts within the region. Within single estates like Quinta do Crasto and Quinta de la Rosa, there is a difference in altitude of around 400 metres, which lends balance to the final blend.

Quinta do Crasto

In their concerted endeavour to produce softer, more supple red wines, most producers destalk the greater proportion of the crop once it reaches the winery. A number of notable single *quintas* continue to tread grapes in *lagares* but the majority of producers have abandoned autovinification for Douro wines in favour of pumping over in stainless-steel fermentation tanks. Selected yeast cultures are generally favoured over wild yeasts, which frequently lead to stuck fermentations at higher levels of alcohol. Fermentation temperatures are generally controlled to between 24°C and 28°C (a few degrees lower than for Port) and maceration is increasingly carefully managed. Wines destined for early drinking remain on the skins for the duration of the fermentation (five days on average) whereas those destined for longer ageing generally undergo a period of *cuvaison* on the skins extending to fifteen or twenty days. Pressing has become less extractive and many producers have installed gentle pneumatic presses specially for the production of Douro wines.

Malolactic fermentation (the natural transformation of malic to lactic acid) generally takes place straight after the vintage as ambient temperatures in the Douro remain quite warm to the end of October/early November. Hygiene has improved across the board and most wineries have turned their backs on dirty old wooden vats in favour of stainless steel and/or short ageing in new oak. Portuguese oak from Gerês and Trás-os-Montes was initially favoured, which seemed to contribute a distinctive but not terribly beneficial green-vanilla character to some Douro wines, Barca Velha included. But with no forest management policy to speak of, Portuguese oak is now virtually extinct and producers are gradually turning to either French or American oak. A number are also using oak chips as a cheaper alternative to maturation in cask. Fortunately, most wine-makers have resisted the temptation to view new oak as the ultimate panacea (a tendency in parts of Italy and Spain) and are intent on letting the flavour of the Douro's naturally sweet, ripe cherry and damson fruit come to the fore. Although few Douro wines have much of a track record as yet, the region's heavyweights probably have an in-built twenty- or thirty-year-life span, parallel to Vintage Port! Based on regular comparative tastings, I suggest the following classification (see page 152 for an explanation):

Premier League
Barca Velha (Ferreira)
Quinta do Côtto, Grande Escolha
Redoma (Niepoort)

First Division
Quinta do Côtto
Quinta do Crasto, Reserva
Duas Quintas, Reserva
Evel, Grande Escolha
Quinta da Gaivosa
Reserva Ferreirinha (formerly Reserva Especial)

Quinta de la Rosa, Reserva
Sogrape, Reserva
Vallado
Vinha do Fojo

WHITE WINES: ALL ABOUT ACIDITY

Rather like White Port, the Douro's white wines have mostly been neglected in favour of red. Many of the region's white grapes are interplanted with red varieties and the separation of the two is often too painstaking to be worthwhile. There are, however, promising local grape varieties like Viosinho and Gouveio (Verdelho) which, with careful handling, are capable of producing some fresh, fragrant dry wines. A small amount of Chardonnay and Sauvignon Blanc has also been planted, although the latter has so far met with more success. The best white grapes originate from the higher districts around Lamego, Vila Real, Alijó and São João de Pesqueira where they retain a better acid balance than at lower altitudes. Acid adjustment is nevertheless virtually obligatory but, none the less, many of the Douro's whites have a rather ponderous, fat oily character. They continue to be marred by heavy-handed wine-making. Fermentation temperatures are frequently too high and pressing is over-extractive resulting in phenolic wines that lack charm and elegance. Many wines go through malolactic and are kept for too long prior to bottling so that they lose any trace of their initial freshness. Until 1998 this was enshrined in the local legislation, which stipulated that all Douro whites had to be kept for at least six months before bottling. This is no longer an excuse as white wines may now be bottled at any time from 15 November following the harvest. There are a few notable exceptions where the wine-maker's skill has triumphed over local adversity and some distinctive, rich, warm country whites shine out like beacons above the dull wines that are so often the norm. Quinta do Côtto, Nie-poort, Real Vinicola and Quinta do Valado so far make up the short role of honour.

PRODUCERS OF DOURO WINES

The following list of Douro wine producers is by no means exhaustive but includes all those with a significant presence on export markets. The wines are listed alphabetically by producer with the producer's full name and address immediately below.

BRIGHT BROS.

Correspondence address: Bright Brothers Vinhos (Portugal) Lda, Fornos de Cima, Calhandriz, 2615 Alverca
Every year Australian flying wine-maker Peter Bright scours the Douro for grapes to produce red wine. In productive years like 1996 he succeeds in producing large quantities of vibrant fruity red, softened by a touch of oak, from excess grapes at the Symington family's Quinta do Sol winery. When there is a shortfall he buys *benefício* production from Quinta dos Frades, an impressive property on the south side of the river midway between Régua and Pinhão. Here he makes a bigger, altogether more serious wine named TFN, a solid blend of Touriga Francesa and Touriga Naçional with a distinctly toasty character resulting from short ageing in French oak *barriques*.

BURMESTER

J.W. Burmester & Ca., Lda, Rua de Belmonte, 39, 4050 Oporto
Family-owned Port shippers J.W. Burmester purchased Quinta Nova de Nossa Senhora do Carmo in 1991 and it now serves as the company's vinification centre in the Douro. With 120 hectares, Quinta Nova produces a full range of Ports alongside two unfortified reds. Casa Burmester is a solid blend of Tinta Roriz and Touriga Francesa aged for between six and nine months in wood. Tavedo (named after the rivers Tavora and Tedo) is a lighter style of wines mainly based on Roriz with a small quantity of Touriga Naçional. Given shorter ageing prior to bottling, it qualifies as a Vinho Regional.

CALÇOS DA TANHA

Manuel Pinto Hespanhol, Vilarinho dos Freires, 5050 Peso da Régua

Named after the traditional step-like terraces above the River Tanha, this 35-hectare *quinta* produces both Port and Douro wine from a roadside winery in the village of Vilarinho dos Freires. Like so many properties in the Baixo Corgo, the Port is sold off in bulk to shippers in Vila Nova de Gaia but since 1989 Manuel Pinto Hespanhol, together with his two sons Manuel and António Luís, have successfully built up their own brand of Douro wine. The wines include a clean but neutral dry white and a fragrant, well-balanced red both bottled under the Calços de Tanha label, alongside a firm-flavoured Reserva partly aged in Portuguese and French oak. Quinta da Vila Freire is a second, somewhat lighter red. The property is famous for its granite *lagares* surrounded by thirteen panels of *azulejos* (blue and white tiles) illustrating the viticultural year in the Douro. The *lagares* have sadly been abandoned in favour of stainless steel.

CÁLEM

A.A. Cálem & Filho, SA, Rua da Reboleira, 7, 4050 Oporto

From grapes purchased in the Baixo Corgo, Cálem produces a duo of Douro reds under the names Solar de Sá and Terras de Sá. The wines are aged in new Portuguese oak pipes (subsequently used for Port) and tend to be rather hard and sappy as a result.

COCKBURN

Cockburn Smithes & Ca., SA, Rua das Coradas, 13, Apartado 20, 4401 Vila Nova de Gaia

As Cockburn's Special Reserve Port went from strength to strength on the UK market, Tuella remained a well-kept secret. Named after the company's *quinta* and vinification centre at Tua, the wine is made from surplus grapes high in the Douro Superior at Vila Nova de Foz Côa. Tuella was first produced back in 1972 and until 1990 it languished on the local market. The cleanly made dry white Tuella made from a blend of Malvasia Fina, Codega and Rabigato is much less interesting than the red. Tinta Roriz, Touriga Francesca, Tinta Barroca and Mourisco make up the backbone of the red Tuella, which is fermented at relatively high temperatures in open tanks and subject to *remontage* (pumping over) to extract colour and flavour. Up to a third of the wine is aged in old wood at Cockburn's lodges in Vila Nova de Gaia, resulting in a wine which combines a ripe leathery character with good depth, weight and texture. Tuella has always represented excellent value for money and is worth seeking out.

QUINTA DO CACHÃO

Sociedade Agricola e Commercial dos Vinhos Messias SA, Rua José Mariani, 139, Apartado 1566, 4401 Vila Nova de Gaia
The flagship property belonging to the Messias family produces both Port and unfortified Douro wine (see p. 113). Although the wines have been good in the past, capturing the wild if rather roasted character of the Douro Superior, I have found them to be alarmingly variable over recent years. *Caveat emptor*!

QUINTA DAS CASTAS

Sociedade Agricola Vila Velha da Vilariça, Rua dos Camilos 179, 5050 Peso da Régua
Few wine-makers have yet had the temerity to produce a Douro wine from super-ripe grapes grown up in the Douro Superior. Quinta das Castas, produced entirely from Touriga Naçional grown in the Vilariça valley, is a bruiser of a wine – big, ripe and somewhat ungainly. Vinha das Castras is its rather lighter sibling made from grapes grown at Santa Marta de Penaguião in the Baixo Corgo.

QUINTA DO CÔTTO

Montez Champalimaud, Lda, Cidadelhe, 5040 Mesão Frio
This imposing eighteenth-century property above the Baixo Corgo village of Cidadelhe is much admired as a producer of some of the finest red and white Douro wines. With a history dating back to the fourteenth century, Quinta do Côtto only became known outside the immediate locality as recently as the 1980s when its vociferous owner, Miguel Champalimaud, began to channel his

energy into promoting the concept of single-*quinta* wines. Port now takes second place in the hierarchy with only three vintages having been declared between 1980 and 1998. The cream of the crop from this mainly 'C' grade vineyard is directed towards two Douro wines: Quinta do Côtto and Quinta do Côtto Grande Escolha.

Often referred to as 'normal' (merely to distinguish it from the Grande Escolha), the red Quinta do Côtto is produced nearly every year from a blend of Tinta Roriz, Touriga Francesa and Touriga Naçional. Since the mid-1990s, under the tutelage of wine-maker Carlos Agrellos, the quality of Quinta do Côtto has improved markedly. Whereas in the past the wine had a hard mean streak, it has now grown up to be a refined Douro red characterised by firm ripe tannins and supple plum-like fruit. However, the real acclaim must be reserved for the Grande Escolha. Produced in the most successful years from the oldest vineyards on the property, it undergoes an extended maceration or *cuvaison* followed by eighteen months in new Portuguese oak. The resulting wines are hugely tight and concentrated when young, without any of the green 'sappy' character that sometimes originates from Portuguese casks. With age Grande Escolha retains its extraordinary colour, fruit and structure, gaining character and complexity. To date Quinta do Côtto Grande Escolha has only been produced in the following years: 1980, 1982, 1985, 1987, 1990, 1994 and 1995.

Quinta do Côtto also makes one of the few genuinely interesting white Douro wines from a blend of Malvasia Rei, Malvasia Fina, Avesso (a Vinho Verde grape) and a small amount of Sémillon. Bottled young without any ageing in wood, it perhaps suffers like so many of its peers from a slight lack of acidity. Nevertheless for a Douro white it has real concentration of flavour with ripe, sub-tropical overtones. (See page 199 for details on Ports from Quinta do Côtto.)

QUINTA DE COVELOS

José Carlos de Morais Calheiros Cruz, Canelas, 5050 Peso de Régua, Portugal
Port comes first at this hill-top property at Canelas near Régua with 30 hectares of vineyard. With a well-equipped stainless-steel winery, Covelos began making Douro wines in 1996 from a blend

of Tinta Roriz, Touriga Francesa, Touriga Naçional and Tinta Barroca, aged in a combination of French, American and Portuguese oak pipes. The reds produced to date are not made for long keeping, but combine sappy Douro fruit with new oak. Quinta do Redolho is a second label attached to a simple, lightweight red.

QUINTA DO CRASTO

Sociedade Agricola da Quinta do Crasto, Rua da Gondarem 834, 4150 Oporto
One of the most beautifully situated properties in the Douro (see page 98), Quinta do Crasto produces some of the region's most alluring red wines. Ever since dynamic Oporto financier Jorge Roquette took control of the family property in the 1980s, Crasto has been at the cutting edge. Nearly 50 hectares of vineyard are split between mixed plantings of old vines up to seventy years old and newer varietal planting which began in 1986. Port tends to play second fiddle to Douro wine and Crasto's duo of Australian wine-makers, David Baverstock and Dominic Morris, often have the pick of the crop. A proportion is still foot-trodden in traditional *lagares* but most of the wines are fermented in an impressive purpose-built stainless-steel winery and finished in new oak. Starting out in 1994 with just one wine, Crasto's range has widened to include a Reserva based on low-yielding old vines and varietal wines selected from among Tinta Roriz, Touriga Naçional, Touriga Francesa and Tinto Cão according to the year. All Crasto's wines succeed in capturing the quintessence of Douro fruit tempered by judicious use of French or American oak. A combination of carefully chosen fruit and thoughtful, even handed wine-making yields wines that are well structured and supple without being over-extractive, hard and tannic. Quinta do Crasto combines the best of the old and new worlds!

FERRERIA

A.A. Ferreira, SA, Rua da Carvalhosa, 19–103, 4400 Vila Nova de Gaia
The late Fernando Nicolau de Almeida was indisputably the father of modern-day Douro wines. Inspired by a visit to Bordeaux in 1950, Ferreira's former chief taster and technician returned to the

family's Quinta do Vale do Meão in the Douro Superior with the intention of making a first-class red wine. There was no electricity in the early 1950s (ironically there is now a hydro-electric station nearby) so Nicolau de Almeida had to be inventive. In order to combat the raging heat, he rigged up a Heath Robinson system of temperature control using blocks of ice insulated with sawdust that had to be brought up by train from Oporto. 'We made good wine by mistake,' declared Nicolau de Almeida some years later after the 1952 red christened Barca Velha became a rapturous success. In the 1980s, the responsibility for the wine passed to José Maria Soares Franco, but long before he died in 1998 Fernando Nicolau de Almeida had become a legend in his own lifetime.

D. Antónia's gates

To date only twelve vintages of Barca Velha have been produced (1952, 1954, 1958, 1964, 1965, 1966, 1978, 1981, 1982, 1983, 1985 and 1991) but over the years it has become much less of a hit and miss affair. The wine is still made at Quinta do Vale do Meão although vinification will shortly be transferred to a purpose-built winery at nearby Quinta da Leda. Grapes will continue to be sourced from both Meão and Leda along with properties at higher altitudes that contribute more acidity. Tinta Roriz has traditionally formed the backbone of the blend, let out with smaller amounts of Touriga Francesa, Tinta Barroca and Tinta Amarela. With the shift to Quinta da Leda, more Touriga Naçional is entering the blend. The grapes are destemmed and fermented in stainless-steel vats at around 25°C. Regular, carefully managed pumping over ensures that extraction is controlled according to the character of the grapes and vintage. After going through malolactic in the Douro, the wine is transferred to Ferreira's lodges at Vila Nova de Gaia where it spends around eighteen months in new, formerly Portuguese, now French oak.

Adopting something of the philosophy of Vintage Port, Barca Velha is the product of an exceptional harvest and the wine is only released after spending seven or eight years maturing in bottle. It starts out with the in-house designation of 'Douro Especial' and the wine is continually reassessed before a decision is taken as to whether or not it should be launched under the Barca Velha label. Since 1962, wine that is not considered to be quite up to Barca Velha standards is declassified as Reserva Especial (renamed Reserva Ferreirinha in 1989). The two wines share an affinity with each other, combining open, sweet, fragrant aromas with suave tannins, often a touch of eucalyptus and dense, concentrated, almost minty fruit. Sometimes a slightly sappy undertone creeps in from Portuguese oak. After an apparent dip in quality in the 1980s, Barca Velha returned to form in 1991 with a tight, powerful wine that has the capacity to develop in bottle like earlier vintages for twenty or thirty years. The 1966 (tasted in 1998) is an extraordinary wine, still upright and concentrated with a touch of tobacco box and the long sinewy finish that has become Barca Velha's hallmark. Reserva Ferreirinha from years like 1980 and 1989 (nearly 'declared' as Barca Velha) can be almost as impressive, showing similar build without the 'first growth' cachet or price.

Owned by Sogrape since 1987, Ferreira has released a number of other Douro reds. Of these Callabriga and Vinha Grande are the most impressive, both of which are firm, fruit-driven wines having been released much earlier than Barca Velha and Reserva Ferreirinha. Departing from tradition, Ferreira has also bottled a concentrated varietal Touriga Naçional from grapes grown at Quinta da Leda. At the bottom of the pile, Esteva (named after the gum cistus that fills the Douro air with its heady smell) is a much lighter red wine made at Quinta do Seixo from grapes grown at higher altitudes above Pinhão. Accessible and early maturing, in poor years it can be rather weedy and insipid.

VINHA DO FOJO

Quinta do Fojo, Vale de Mendiz, 5070 Alijó
Brother and sister Jorge and Margarida ('Gui') Serôdio Borges took over the running of two prime *quintas*, Fojo and Manuela, deep in the Pinhão valley, from their grandfather in the early 1990s. The family has been selling Port to shippers in Vila Nova de Gaia for nearly 200 years, recently supplying wine of potential vintage quality to both Churchill and Morgan. Without any newfangled varietal plantings to rely on, the quinta's *omnium gatherum* of grapes from old, low-yielding vines (principally Touriga Francesca and Tinta Roriz) are foot-trodden and fermented in traditional granite *lagares*. Initially the wines suffered from a lack of temperature control and in 1997, a proportion of the crop was spoiled. This has now been overcome by the installation of a heat exchanger in the *lagares*. Reflecting the local *terroir*, Vinha do Fojo is a bruiser of a wine with hefty yet supple tannins, offset by vibrant berry fruit. Without a track record as yet, Fojo could turn out to be one of the Douro's most distinguished reds.

FONSECA GUIMARAENS

Fonseca Guimaraens – Vinhos SA, Rua Barão de Forrester, 404, Apartado 13, 4401 Vila Nova de Gaia
Sometimes referred to in a self-deprecatory manner as 'Dom Pior' ('*pior*' means 'worse' in Portuguese), Fonseca's Dom Prior is a cleanly made, refreshing dry Douro white served well chilled at the end of a long hot day.

QUINTA DA GAIVOSA

Domingos Alves de Sousa, Apartado 15, 5031 Santa Marta de Penaguião
Descended from a family of Douro growers, Domingos Alves de Sousa has subsequently added to his holdings to become one of the largest vineyard owners in the Baixo Corgo, with five properties amounting to over 100 hectares. Since giving up his profession in

civil engineering in 1987, he has established a production centre at Quinta da Gaivosa, a large C rated property at Santa Marta de Penaguião in the heart of the Baixo Corgo facing the Serra do Marão. Over the intervening period, Alves de Sousa has gradually been retreating from the production of Port sold in bulk to a number of major shippers, making his first Douro wines in 1992. Greatly helped in this task by Anselmo Mendes, producer of some of the best Alvarinho Vinhos Verdes, Quinta da Gaivosa has quickly established a reputation as one of the leading Douro reds. Rather like Quinta do Côtto Grande Escolha (see page 257), it is only made in the best years. Produced from old mixed vineyards, some of which were planted more than seventy years ago, Quinta da Gaivosa is a solid, structured red given short ageing in new French oak. Sensing the growing interest in Douro varieties, Alves de Sousa has launched a series of red wines from Tinto Cão, Tinta Roriz and Touriga Naçional. Of these, Gaivosa's Tinto Cão is certainly the most fascinating with a suave elegance that is unusual in the Douro. At the time of writing, it is one of just two wines in Portugal made from this low-yielding but high quality grape.

A second wine, Quinta do Vale da Raposa, named after the adjoining property, is lighter and fresher in style. Alves de Sousa has recently begun to age a proportion of this wine, which is made from younger vines, in second-year wood, a practice that tends to mask the character of the ripe damson-like fruit. Since 1996 another property, the B rated Quinta das Caldas above the spa town of Caldas de Moledo, has begun to produce a firm-flavoured, spicy red, and Alves de Sousa intends to launch wines from his other *quintas*, Estacão and Aveleira, in due course. A partly barrel-fermented white wine blended from Gouveio, Malvasia Fina and Viosinho grown at Quinta da Gaivosa is, to my mind, much the least successful of Domingos Alves de Sousa's ever-expanding range of innovative Douro wines.

NIEPOORT

Niepoort (Vinhos) SA, Rua Infante D. Henrique, 39, 4050 Oporto Making the most of a network of long-established contacts in the Douro, Dirk Niepoort has begun to produce remarkable Douro wines. After a few years of trial and error in the early 1990s, Niepoort's Redoma has settled down as a potential challenger to the hegemony of Barca Velha. The two wines are very different in style. Redoma is based on a blend of Tinta Amarela, Touriga Francesa and Tinta Roriz grown at the company's own property, Quinta do Carril in the Tedo Valley midway between Pinhão and Régua. Mostly aged in French *barriques*, the wine belongs to the old school with broad, burly fruit backed by big, strapping tannins. Niepoort has also produced one of the Douro's most promising dry white wines blended from Gouveio and Rabigato growing in an old, low-yielding vineyard near Celeirós in the upper margins of the Pinhão valley. Fermented in new oak followed by a year spent on the lees, Niepoort's white Redoma has tropical weight and richness but, like so many Douro whites, it lacks sufficiently incisive acidity.

Niepoort is also responsible for a solid, foursquare red made at Quinta do Passadouro from grapes from old vineyards in the Pinhão area. The wine is made entirely in *lagares* and aged, like Redoma, in French *barriques*.

QUINTA DO NOVAL

Quinta do Noval – Vinhos, SA, Avenida Diogo Leite, 256, Apartado 57, 4401 Vila Nova de Gaia
Noval began experimenting with Douro reds when Cristiano van Zeller was at the helm in the 1980s. Having made some 'blackstrap' reds that were never released, Noval (under new management and ownership) has settled on a lighter, more approachable red named Corucho. The grapes (predominantly Tinta Roriz, Touriga Francesa and Tinta Baroca) are sourced from a number of neighbouring A grade properties near Pinhão. Vinified in stainless steel, Corucho is a firm, focused red, which captures the vibrant fruit of the Douro.

QUINTA DA PACCHEA

Eduardo M. Freire de Serpa Pimentel, Quinta de Pacheca, 5100 Lamego
The Serpa Pimentel family have attracted plenty of attention by planting Riesling, Gewürztraminer, Sauvignon Blanc and Cabernet Sauvignon alongside traditional Douro varieties. Although they achieve good distribution in Portugal, personally I have always

found the wines from this estate somewhat variable and disappointing.

POÇAS

Manoel D. Poças Junior – Vinhos SA, Rua Visconde de Devesas, 186, Apartado 1556, 4401 Vila Nova de Gaia
Family Port shippers Poças Junior have a duo of Douro wines, which are the brainchild of their Bordeaux-trained wine-maker Jorge Pintão. Both are well made but lack flair. The white wine made from Malvasia Fina, Codega, Rabigato and Viosinho is soft but flat, and the red (a blend of the five main varieties) has a firm, ripe, dusty character from heavy tannin extraction. In a pun on words, the wines have been christened Coroa d'Ouro (meaning 'Crown of Gold').

QUINTA DO PORTAL

Sociedade Quinta do Portal, SA, Rua Guilharmina Suggia, 200, 4200 Oporto
Formerly part of the Sandeman empire, the Branco/Mansilha family from Favaios bought Quinta do Confradeiro at Celeirós and renamed it Quinta do Portal. Huge amounts of capital have been sunk into a well-planned modern winery equipped with all the hi-tech toys needed to produce a modern, quality wine. The range is eclectic to say the least and includes a white with a proportion of barrel-fermented Moscatel and a light red called Beijo d'Uva ('Kiss of the Grape') made by carbonic maceration followed by two months in wood! Sadly, the investment is not reflected in the quality of the wines, which tend to be extractive and stretched but there is clearly potential here for something better.

RAMOS PINTO

Adriano Ramos Pinto (Vinhos) SA, Avenida Ramos Pinto, 380, Apartado 1320, 4401 Vila Nova de Gaia
João Nicolau de Almeida seems to be taking over from where his father, Fernando (of Barca Velha fame), left off. Their backgrounds could hardly be more different. Whereas his father learnt about

wine on the hoof, João studied oenology at Bordeaux University and joined the family Port shipper Ramos Pinto in 1976. Sometimes betraying the countenance of a mad professor, João Nicolau de Almeida has an insatiable thirst for experimentation having been one of the principal brains behind the Douro's red varietal breakthrough in the early 1980s (see page 79). Nicolau de Almeida has now turned his attention to white varietals like Viosinho, Gouveio and Rabigato. Although on granite soils just outside the Douro demarcation, Quinta dos Bons Ares is a crisp blend of local white varietals lifted by grassy Sauvignon Blanc. A red from the same property combines Touriga Naçional with Cabernet Sauvignon. Both wines are classified as *Vinho Regional* Trás-os-Montes – Terras Durienses.

The Douro is better represented by the red Duas Quintas. First produced in 1990, it combines the fruit of two very different properties (hence the name 'Two Quintas'). The wild and remote Quinta da Ervamoira in the Côa valley (Douro Superior) provides the ballast and richness that is offset by a firmer more structured character from fruit grown at Quinta do Bom Retiro in the lower reaches of the Torto valley. Duas Quintas has already established a good track record as a supple, balanced Douro red that even performs well in weaker years like 1993 and 1996. It is reinforced by a Reserva, which manages to capture a hint of the New World with its intensely ripe, almost minty fruit and ripe but dense tannic structure. Both wines evolve well in bottle.

REAL VINICOLA

Real Companhia Vinicola do Norte de Portugal, Rua Azevedo Magalhães, 314, 4400 Vila Nova de Gaia
Real Vinicola has the longest continuous history of any of today's producers of Douro wines. Founded in 1889 under contract with the Portuguese government, it was entrusted with the task of selling wines from various regions in northern Portugal. With brands spanning Vinho Verde, Bairrada and Dão and a decidedly patchy record in the 1980s, Real Vinicola is increasingly concentrating on wines from the Douro. In 1996 Real Vinicola created a Fine Wine Division, accompanying this with a substantial revamp of its huge *adega* at Granja near Alijó. Under the combined direction of Pedro da Silva Reis and Californian wine-maker Jerry Luper, Real Vini-

cola has begun to produce some impressive Douro wines. White wines made from Douro varieties grown on the *planalto* around Alijó are fresh, clean and aromatic without being anything to write home about in an international context. The exception, however, is the white Quinta do Sidró made from 10 hectares of low-yielding Chardonnay planted at the eponymous C/D-rated *quinta* near São João de Pesqueira. Fermented and aged (with regular *batonage*) in new Portuguese oak, it combines a richly textured concentration of flavour with unusually good natural acidity. Chardonnay does not qualify as a permitted Douro variety and the wine is therefore sold as a Vinho Regional Trás-os-Montes.

The scope of Real Vinicola's red wines has been greatly increased by a new winery at Granja equipped with a battery of small stainless-steel fermentation tanks and corresponding storage vats. With so many tiny plots of old vines in the Douro, many of which undoubtedly have the potential to produce wines of excellent quality, Luper has seized on the idea of vinifying selected batches of grapes on a Burgundian scale. This also enables him to look seriously at some of the Douro's so-called 'exotic' varieties: grapes like Rufete and Tinta Francisca, which are found in tiny quantities, often in older mixed vineyards. Real Vinicola's principal Douro reds are Evel and Porca da Murça, both of which started out as respected brands when they were conceived in the 1920s and 1930s but began to look rather lacklustre half a century later. Since the creation of the Fine Wine Division, both have received a much-needed make-over so that they are now well-accepted, reliable reds with plenty of sappy, spicy Douro fruit softened by short ageing in oak. The pride of the range is Evel Grande Escolha. Produced since 1996 from small plots of old vines growing at lower altitudes around Pinhão, it combines ripe berry fruit and well-integrated new oak. At this rate Real Vinicola will soon be among the premier league of Douro wine producers.

QUINTA DO RORIZ

Quinta do Noval – Vinhos, SA, Avenida Diogo Leite, 256, Apartado 57, 4401 Vila Nova de Gaia
Belonging to a branch of the van Zeller family, Quinta do Roriz has long been associated with Noval. After Quinta do Noval was bought by the AXA insurance group in 1993, the van Zellers

entered into a long-term contract whereby Noval guarantees to buy and vinify all the grapes from Roriz at the same time as promoting the property as a single-*quinta* wine. A Port from the estate has now been joined by a Douro red. Made from a blend of Tinta Roriz, Touriga Naçional and Touriga Francesa, the wine is dense with plenty of substance but without the hard, over-extractive tannins that characterise so many Douro reds. Short maturation in new French oak lends a gentle toasty note to the finish.

QUINTA DE LA ROSA

Quinta da Rosa (Vinhos do Porto) Lda, 5085 Pinhão

Port clearly has pride of place at this prime A grade *quinta* near Pinhão but, with the help of Australian David Baverstock, the Bergqvist family is also producing a range of increasingly good Douro reds. It began back in 1990 using grapes from a newly planted vineyard and the wines seem to have gained in substance in succeeding vintages. La Rosa lacks the weight and structure of some Douro reds but the wines are approachable at a relatively early age having been exposed to short ageing in 600-litre oak casks. In particularly successful years like 1995, a small quantity of wine is kept back and bottled as a more serious Reserva. Second wines are bottled without recourse to oak under the names Amarela and Vale de Clara. Both manage to capture the essence of ripe Douro fruit.

SANDEMAN

Sandeman & Ca., SA, Largo Miguel Bombarda, 3, Apartado 1308, 4401 Vila Nova de Gaia

Despite the sale of the *quinta* to the Branco family (see Quinta do Portal on page 265) Sandeman retained the brand name 'Confrad-eiro'. This well-made, solid, dependable Douro red is mainly seen on the Portuguese market.

QUINTA DE SANTA JULIA

Eduardo Francisco da Costa Seixas, Quinta de Santa Julia de Lour-eiro, Loureiro, 5050 Peso da Régua

Eduardo Seixas is both taster and blender for Sandeman as well as one of the pioneering producers of Douro wines at his own *quinta* overlooking Régua in the Baixo Corgo (see page 233). He began making Douro wine in the mid-1980s with only the most rudimentary technology. A couple of portable stainless-steel tanks were adapted as fermentation vats, cooled by water from garden sprinklers! The enterprising and fastidious Seixas has since built a new *adega* at the *quinta*. His Douro reds are well made but, perhaps due to the altitude of the property, tend to be on the light side. The best grapes from there are made into Port for Sandeman.

QUINTA DE SEARA D'ORDENS

Sociedade Agricola Quinta de Seara d'Ordens, Lda, Vila Seca de Poiares, 5050 Peso da Régua
Resembling a hamlet rather than a *quinta*, Seara d'Ordens has been in the same family since the eighteenth century. It is now run by three brothers who produce their own Port as well as Douro wine. Situated at an altitude of between 400 and 500 metres above the village of Vila Seca de Poiares, this 60-hectare C/D rated vineyard is ideally suited to producing dry white wines. Batch-planted Malvasia Fina, Fernão Pires, Gouveio and Codega combine to form a concentrated yet balanced Colheita Especial (first produced in 1997), which is among the best white wines in the Douro. The reds, aged in French and Portuguese oak, are less impressive.

SOGRAPE

Sogrape Vinhos de Portugal, SA, 4430 Avintes
Portugal's largest wine-making concern, owners of Ferreira and Offley Port shippers with interests throughout the country and in South America, began life in the Douro. The Sogrape winery at Vila Real was originally constructed in the 1950s to produce Mateus Rosé from grapes growing in small vineyards on the surrounding *altos* (high land). Production of Mateus has gradually shifted to Anadia in the Bairrada region and the Vila Real plant (not much more than a stone's throw from the famous Palace of Mateus) has been thoroughly updated to make the most of the surplus grapes growing on the northern margins of the Douro region.

Sogrape's diversification began with the revival of the Planalto brand, a crisp blend of Viosinho, Malvasia Fina and Gouveio from the high plains above the Douro. Other wines have followed including the rather disappointing Vila Regia (the Roman name for Vila Real) and an extremely good red and white Douro Reserva. The white is barrel-fermented in new French and Portuguese oak and has gained a rich, creamy texture from a further six months in cask. The red Reserva has vibrant yet supple berry fruit flavours softened by a hint of new wood. The Mateus 'Signature' name has been ascribed to a pair of lighter, rather insubstantial red and white Douro wines.

VALE DONA MARIA

Lemos & van Zeller Lda, Quinta do Vale Dona Maria, Sarzedinho, 5130 São João de Pesqueira

Helped by both Quinta do Crasto and Niepoort, Cristiano van Zeller (ex-Quinta do Noval) has launched a red wine from his family's property in Torto, Quinta do Vale Dona Maria. The grapes are foot-trodden in *lagar* and the wines are finished in new French oak casks. Bottled without fining or filtration, Vale Dona Maria is a firm, well-structured red with fine-grained tannins. It reflects the high quality of the fruit emanating from the Torto valley.

QUINTA DO VALADO

Jorge Viterbo Ferreira, Herdeiros, Vilarinho dos Freires, 5050 Peso da Régua

Quinta do Valado is by no means a newcomer. This property upstream from Régua has been producing wine since at least the beginning of the seventeenth century and has been in the hands of the Ferreira family for six generations. But it was as recently as 1995 that the present representatives of the family, Maria Antónia Ferreira and Guilherme Alvares Ribeiro, decided to divert about half the crop towards a pair of excellent Douro wines under the 'Vallado' label. With 64 hectares of vineyard spanning an altitude of 47 to 325 metres above sea level, Valado has the capacity to make a range of wines, from Port (for Ferreira) to a delicious, dry Douro white (made mainly with Fernão Pires, Malvasia Fina, Viosinho and Rabigato), which succeeds in being ripe, but not over-ripe. Wine-making is in the skilled hands of Francisco Olaz-abal (son of Vito Olazabal, who manages Ferreira) and the day-to-day running of the *quinta* is overseen by Francisco Ferreira (son of the late Jorge Maria Cabral Ferreira). Their greatest achievement is undoubtedly the red Vallado based on a blend of Tinta Roriz, Tinta Barroca and Tinta Amarela. Made without recourse to oak, Vallado combines supple tannins with naturally sweet fruit taking the wine to an alcohol level of around 14 per cent by volume. Quinta do Valado represents the best of the new wave of Douro wines. With three centuries of history, an exciting future lies ahead.

A number of other producers located outside the Douro region also buy up and bottle Douro reds, often from local co-operative wineries:

Caves Aliança: Foral
Aveleda: Charamba
Caves Primavera
Caves Velhas: Lagar Velho

Although sound, the wines are never as successful as those from producers based in the region.

Postscript
The Future for Port and the Douro

The Port trade has never been very good at clairvoyance. In the years that followed the Second World War many shippers fully expected a return to the boom years of the 1920s when in fact the trade lapsed into a deep depression. It was under the cloud of closures, mergers and acquisitions in the 1960s and 1970s that the present structure of the Port trade came about with multinationals vying alongside established family firms.

At the start of a new century, the prospect for Port seems brighter than at any time over the past hundred years. Shipments continued to grow through the early 1990s and have stabilised at around ten million cases, just below the all-time high. Port continues to buck the trend set by other fortified wines. Whereas Sherry and Madeira linger in the doldrums and once-great wines such as Malaga and Marsala face near extinction, Port has made remarkable progress. On established markets like the UK and (more recently) North America, consumers continue to trade up from standard Ruby and Tawny to premium styles. From accounting for just 5 per cent of the world market in 1990, the so-called 'special categories' have increased their share to 11 per cent in 1997, representing 25 per cent of the total value of Port shipments. Much of this is due to astute marketing men who have given so-called 'Vintage Character' and LBV the cachet of a GTi or GTV car. Far from being the fuddy-duddy, gout-provoking drink that some like to depict, in the UK over 40 per cent of Port drinkers are in the 25–44 age group.

In the meantime Vintage Port remains on a roll, fuelled by the seemingly insatiable demand from the US for wines with gobs of vibrant fruit. In drinking the wines young – thereby turning the established vintage ethos on its head – the Americans have unwittingly created an entirely new market. The rapid turnover in declared Port vintages must have left some Port shippers examining their consciences whilst making straightway to the bank.

As the competition hots-up at the top end of the market, there is an increasing demand for quality grapes from the A and B grade vineyards in the Cima Corgo and Douro Superior. This is further exacerbated by the growing number of Douro wines that are starting to pay their own way on domestic and international markets. A number of blue-chip shippers who once looked down with disdain on Douro reds are likely to test the market with their own unfortified wines before long.

The healthy outlook for Port and the shippers in Vila Nova de Gaia is not without its perils. With Portugal running headlong into the European mainstream, production costs are certain to increase. Given the labour-intensive character of agriculture in the Douro, mechanisation is sure to proceed apace. Replanting will continue with this in mind, focusing on the best sites for the production of high quality wines. It is hard to envisage how smallholders (who still account for over 60 per cent of production in the Douro) will keep up. Most of these properties are in the Baixo Corgo where returns are considerably lower than in the Cima Corgo and Douro Superior. As the younger generation is increasingly attracted by bright lights and a sedentary urban life, the future for these small farmers looks increasingly bleak.

Over 90 per cent of Port finds its way to just seven markets, with France and Holland currently leading the way. Unlike the UK and US, these countries have proved largely unreceptive to con- certed encouragement to trade up from standard to premium styles. They remain blisteringly price-sensitive and it is hard to see how this can be reconciled over the medium term with sharply increased production costs. Something, somewhere will have to give. Although it flourishes for the moment, the US market is notoriously fickle. No other country in the world responds quite so readily to fashion, medical opinion or the power of the media. The North American Port miracle could so easily come to a sticky end.

If the Port industry should dip into recession, the small growers will be hit first and foremost as the shippers retreat to their own carefully consolidated holdings. It happened to a limited extent in the early 1990s when a number of major shippers hurriedly changed their purchasing strategies, forcing hundreds of farmers to seek alternative buyers for their grapes. The Douro has been led for centuries by just one crop. Whereas Jerez went over to cereals and Madeira to bananas, in these days of industrialised agriculture and European food surpluses it is impossible to conceive how the Douro could adapt to a collapse in the market for Port. If the bottom should ever fall out of the bargain basement in France, Holland and Belgium, it would bring suffering to the Baixo Corgo not seen since phylloxera swept through the region in the 1870s. Emerging Port markets like Spain or eastern Europe may help to mop up in the process but a sharp increase in both the quantity and quality of Douro unfortified wine may be the only long-term solution.

With the region more accessible than at any time in its history, one Douro industry is sure to flourish. Tourism has already begun to creep inexorably into the valley. It is to be hoped that this will be undertaken with some sympathy. Glancing down at the Algarve the portents are not good, but so-called Turismo de Habitacão has already helped to give a lease of life to some of the crumbling manor houses in the Douro.

In an international context, the Port industry is still relatively small. In volume terms total world-wide sales of Port only amount

Oporto

to just over half that of Smirnoff, the single most popular international brand of vodka. Within the multinational groups who own some of the leading global food and drink brands, Port is so small as to be almost insignificant. Pick up one of their annual reports to shareholders and it is difficult to find a single mention of Port in spite of the fact that they control some of the leading Port brands. Having ridden in like white knights in the 1960s and 1970s when many firms were on their uppers, there can be little doubt that some of the multinationals want to sell up and go. Their exodus would be hugely destabilising and leave a void that would be hard to fill. Perhaps another era of consolidation, merger and acquisition is already in prospect.

Although Port is often unfairly perceived as a badge of tradition, it has already shown a remarkable capacity for renewing its appeal. The trade is much less isolated than it was and the new generation of thirty-something wine-makers and viticulturalists have more experience of the wine-world outside the Douro than their forefathers could possibly conceive. With over three centuries of tradition and twenty-first century technology in tandem, of one prediction I can be certain. The Douro will continue to be one of the world's most captivating wine regions and Port will remain among the greatest of all wines.

Bibliography

Chapter 1

Andrade Martins, C., *Memoria do Vinho do Porto*, Lisboa 1990
Bradford, S., *The Story of Port*, London, 1983
Carvalho, M., *A Guide to the Douro and Port Wine*, Porto, 1995
Cockburn, E., *Port Wine and Oporto*, London, 1949
Corte Real, M, *England and Portugal over the Centuries*, London, 1986
Delaforce, J., *The Factory House at Oporto*, London, 1979
Fletcher, W., *Port – an Introduction to its History and Delights*, London, 1978
Fonseca, Alvaro Moreira da. et al. *Port Wine: Notes on its History, Production and Technology*, Oporto, 1998
Liddell, A. and Price, J., *Port Wine Quintas of the Douro*, London, 1992
Livermore H.V., *A New History of Portugal*, Cambridge, 1976
Macaulay, R., *They Went to Portugal*, London, 1946
Macauley, R., *They Went to Portugal Too*, Manchester, 1990
Martins Perreira, G., *O Douro e O Vinho do Porto de Pombal a João Franco*, Porto, 1991
Martins Perreira, G; Olazabal, Maria Luisa, Almeida, J. Nicolau de, *Dona Antónia*, Portugal, 1996
Mayson, R.J., *Portugal's Wines and Wine-Makers*, San Francisco, 1998
Mayson, R.J., *The Story of Dow's Port*, London, 1998
Oliveira Marques, A.H., *History of Portugal*, New York, 1976
Ordish, G., *The Great Wine Blight*, London, 1987
Robertson, G., *Port*, London, 1992
Sellers, C., *Oporto Old and New*, London, 1899
Suckling J., *Vintage Port*, San Francisco, 1990
Villa Maior, Visconde de, *O Douro Illustrado*, Porto, 1876
Vizetelly, H., *Facts About Port and Madeira*, London, 1880

Chapter 2

Bravo, P. and Oliveira, Duarte de, *Viticultura Moderna*, Porto, 1916
Fonseca, Alvaro Moreira da et al., *Port Wine: Notes on its History, Production and Technology*, Oporto, 1998
Liddell, A. and Price, J., *Port Wine Quintas of the Douro*, London, 1992
Magalhães, N. and Almeida, J. Nicolau de, in *O Vinho do Porto e os Vinhos do Douro*, Lisboa, 1998
Villa Maior, Visconde de, *O Douro Illustrado*, Porto, 1876
Vizetelly, H., *Facts About Port and Madeira*, London, 1880

Chapter 3

Fonseca, Alvaro Moreira da et al. *Port Wine: Notes on its History, Production and Technology*, Oporto, 1998
Mayson, R.J., *Portugal's Wines and Wine-Makers*, San Francisco, 1998
Reader, H.P. and Dominguez, M., 'Fortified Wines: Sherry, Port and Madeira', in *Fermented Beverage Production*, (edited by A.G.H. Lea and J.R. Piggott), Glasgow, 1998
Vizetelly, H. *Facts About Port and Madeira*, London, 1880

Chapter 4

Cockburn, E., *Port Wine and Oporto*, London, 1949
Fonseca, Alvaro Moreira da. et al. *Port Wine: Notes on its History, Production and Technology*, Oporto, 1998
Guimaraens, D. F., *Ageing Gracefully*, a paper to accompany a Tawny Port Tasting held in London, 1997
Reader, H.P. and Dominguez, M., *Fortified Wines: Sherry, Port and Madeira*, in *Fermented Beverage Production*, (edited by A.G.H. Lea and J.R.Piggott), Glasgow, 1995
Robertson, G., *Port*, London, 1992
Suckling, J., *Vintage Port*, San Francisco, 1990
Vintage Reports from Bruce Guimaraens (Taylor/Fonseca), João Nicolau de Almeida (Ramos Pinto), Alistair Robertson (Taylor/Fonseca), Port Wine Institute, Peter Symington, Michael Symington and James Symington

Chapter 5

Fletcher, W., *Port: an Introduction to its History and its Delights*, London, 1978
Mayson, R.J., *Portugal's Wines and Wine-Makers*, San Francisco, 1998
Mayson, R.J., *The Story of Dow's Port*, London, 1998
Ray, C., *The House of Warre: a Three-Hundred-Year-Old Tradition*, 1970
Spence, G., *The Port Companion: a Connoiseur's Guide*, London, 1997

Chapter 6

Mayson, R.J., *Portugal's Wines and Wine-Makers*, San Francisco, 1998

Soares Franco, José Maria, in *O Vinho do Porto e os Vinhos do Douro*, Lisboa, 1998

Vizetelly, H., *Facts About Port and Madeira*, London, 1880

Glossary of Portuguese Terms

ABAFADO (as in *vinho abafado*): a general term for a fortified wine where the fermentation has been arrested by the addition of *aguardente* (q.v.) leaving residual sugar. From *abafar*, meaning to choke, smother or stifle.

ADEGA: winery.

ADEGA CO-OPERATIVA: co-operative winery.

AGUE PÉ: (literally 'foot water'); the name of a local drink made by adding water to *bagaço* (q.v.), which is then trodden and fermented for a second time.

AGAURDENTE: brandy. It is also the name of the white grape spirit (77 per cent alcohol by volume) used to fortify Port.

ALMUDE: a liquid measure determined by the quantity of Port a man might reasonably be able to carry on his head: 25.44 litres. Twenty-one *almudes* make up a *pipa* (q.v.) or pipe.

ALOIRADO: the Portuguese expression used to signify 'Tawny' (from the words *loira/loura* meaning 'blonde' or 'fair').

ALTOS: colloquial expression referring to the high plateau north and south of the Douro valley.

ARMAZÉM (plural *armazéns*): warehouse, store or wine lodge.

ARTISTAS: skilled employees on a *quinta* (q.v.).

AZENHA: the building on a *quinta* (q.v.), which houses the olive press.

AZULEJOS: panels of decorative tiles, so-called because they are traditionally blue (*azul*) and white.

BACALHAU: dried salt cod, a staple dish in the Douro and throughout Portugal.

BAGA: elderberry.

BAGACEIRA: *marc* distilled from the *bagaço* (q.v.).

BAGAÇO: skins, stalks and pips left over after fermentation and pressing.

BAIXO: low/lower (as in Baixo Corgo: Lower Corgo).

BALÃO (plural *balões*): literally 'balloon'; large concrete storage vessel

279

for Port. Also known colloquially as *mamas or ginas* (after Gina Lollobrigida) because of their distinctive shape.

BALSEIRO: large upstanding wooden vat used for storing and maturing Port prior to bottling.

BARCO RABELO: traditional Douro boat used for bringing Port downstream.

BENEFICÍO: literally meaning 'benefit', it signifies the annual authorisation of must which may be fortified to produce Port in any one year. Intended to keep supply in line with demand, the *benefício* system is complex and is explained in detail on pages 67–8.

BICA ABERTA: fermentation off the skins.

BRANCO: white (as in White Port, vinho do porto branco).

CADASTRO: register of vineyards (see page 67).

CÂMARA: town hall or town council.

CANADA: liquid measure (2.12 litres), which has now fallen from regular use. There are 252 *canadas* in a *pipa* or pipe (q.v) and twelve *canadas* in an *almude* (q.v.).

CARDENHO: dormitory building for the pickers during vintage.

CASAL: the couple who manage a *quinta* (see also *caseiro*).

CASEIRO: the farmer-manager of a *quinta* who lives permanently on the property. The *caseira* is his wife.

CASTA: grape variety.

CEPA: an individual vine (see also *pé*).

CESTO DA VINDIMA: the traditional baskets used to carry grapes during vintage, sometimes referred to as a *gigo*.

CIMA: top or upper (as in Cima Corgo; Upper Corgo).

COLAGEM: fining to clarify wine with potentially unstable material remaining in solution.

COLHEITA: literally 'harvest', it also signifies a style of Port.

CONCELHO: municipal district.

CONTO: one thousand escudos.

CORTE: literally 'cut', it signifies the first stage in the treading of a *lagar* (q.v.).

COSTA: bank or slope.

CUBA: vat (as in *cuba de inox*: stainless-steel vat; *cuba de cimento*: cement vat).

DESAVINHO: uneven development of individual berries within a bunch of grapes provoked by cold, wet weather at the time of flowering. Known as 'hen and chickens' in English or *millerandage* in French.

DOCE: sweet (see also *lagrima*).

DORNA: a large steel hopper with a capacity for up to 1,000 kg of grapes.

ENCARREGADO: the foreman on a *quinta* (q.v.).

ENGAÇO: stalks, stems.

ESCOLHA: choice, selection.

ESTUFAGEM: the heating process used in Madeira to advance ageing. Ports can also be subject to natural *estufagem* if they are left for an extended period in the Douro. From the word *estufa* meaning 'stove' or 'greenhouse'.

FREGUESIA: parish.

GALLEGOS: a collective term for the itinerant Galicians (Spanish) who built many of the stone-walled terraces in the Douro in the nineteenth century.

GENEROSO: literally 'generous', also meaning fortified as in *vinho generoso*, fortified wine.

GEROPIGA: grape must prevented from fermenting by the addition of *aguardente* (q.v.). Sometimes used in blending.

GIGO: see *cesto da vindima*.

GRANEL: bulk (as in *vinho de granel*, bulk wine).

GRAU: degree of temperature, sugar or alcohol.

INOX: the colloquial word for stainless steel (from *aço inoxidavel*).

JEROPIGA (occasionally spelt *geropiga*): grape must prevented from fermenting by the addition of spirit or *aguardente*. It is commonly used for sweetening fortified wines. The South Africans commercialise an intensely sweet wine known as *jerepigo*.

LAGAR: stone (usually granite) or concrete tank for treading and fermenting grapes.

LAGRIMA: literally 'tears'; depending on the context *lagrima* signifies free-run grape juice or a very sweet unctuous White Port.

LEVE: light (as in the category of White Port known as *leve seco* – light dry).

LOTE: a 'lot' or parcel of wine.

MACACO: literally 'monkey', it also denotes the spiked plungers that are used to keep the floating *manta* (q.v) in contact with the fermenting *mosto* (q.v.).

MANTA: literally 'blanket'; in the context of Port vinification it means the 'cap' of grape skins and stalks that floats to the surface during fermentation.

MIRADOURO: a vantage point to admire the view.

MORTÓRIOS: literally 'mortuaries', the term signifies the terraces abandoned during the phylloxera epidemic of the 1870s and 1880s.

MOSTO: grape juice, must.

OBRAS: works or alterations. The word has entered the Anglo-Portuguese lexicon because of the seemingly continual *obras* and the disruption that they cause!

PATAMAR: vineyard terrace without a retaining wall.

PATRÃO (plural *patrões*): the owner of a *quinta*; the boss!

PÉ: literally 'foot' but often used to refer to an individual vine or *cepa* (q.v.). *Pisa a pé* means to tread by foot.

PILHEIRO: hole in a vertical terrace wall formerly used for planting vines.

PIPA: a 'pipe' or cask used for ageing wine. A *pipa* is also a unit of measurement: 550 litres in the Douro, 620 litres in Vila Nova de Gaia and 534.24 litres for export purposes.

PLANALTO: the high plains on the northern and southern margins of the Douro.

PODA: pruning.

PRENSA: press (as in *vinho da prensa*, press wine).

PROVA: tasting.

QUINTA: literally a farm, estate or landed property (see page 89 for a fuller definition in the context of the Douro).

RAMADA: overhead pergola system used for training vines in the Vinho Verde region and for table grapes/decorative purposes in the Douro.

RAMO: literally a branch, it also signifies the festooned palm or bamboo branch that is traditionally presented to the wife of the *patrão (q.v.)* by the *roga* (q.v.) at the end of the harvest (see page 140).

REI: literally 'king' but also a common unit of currency in the seventeenth and eighteenth centuries representing a thousandth of an escudo. One *milrei* therefore equals one escudo.

REMONTAGEM: pumping over (see page 134).

RIBEIRA: riverside/quays.

RIBEIRO: a small river.

RIO: a river.

ROGA: the gang of pickers who work on a *quinta* (q.v.) for the duration of the vintage.

ROGADOR: the leader of the gang of pickers who acts as drill sergeant in the lagar (q.v.).

ROLHA: a cork.

SACA-ROLHAS: corkscrew.

SECO: dry (as in *vinho branco seco*, dry white wine).

SOCALCO: a walled terrace.

SOLAR: a manor house.

TANOARIA: cooperage.

TANOEIRO: cooper, barrel maker.

TINTO: red (as in *vinho tinto*, red wine).

TONEL (plural *toneis*): a large wooden cask with a capacity of between twenty and sixty *pipa* (q.v.) used for storing and ageing wine.

TURISMO DE HABITACÃO: guest accommodation in private houses found in the Douro and throughout rural Portugal.

UVA: grape.

VINAGRINHO: literally 'a touch of vinegar'; descriptive term for a wine that is 'high toned' with noticeable but not necesarily detrimental levels of volatile acidity.

VINDIMA: vintage or harvest.

VINHA: vineyard or plot of vines.

VINHA VELHA: an old mixed vineyard.

VINHO: wine.

XISTO: schist.

Glossary of Acronyms

Portugal has a wearisome number of different acronyms. These are the initials of organisations, institutions and projects most closely involved in the day-to-day life of the Douro:

ADVID: Associação para o Desenvolvimento da Viticultura Duriense (Douro Viticultural Development Association).

AEVP: Associação das Empreseas do Vinho do Porto (Port Wine Shippers Association).

AVEPOD: Associação dos Viticultores Engarrafadores dos Vinhos do Porto e Douro (Port and Douro Wine Growers and Bottlers Association).

CD: Casa do Douro.

CIRDD: Comissão Interprofissional do Região Demarcada do Douro (Interprofessional Commission for the Douro Demarcated Region).

IVP: Instituto do Vinho do Porto (Port Wine Institute).

IVV: Instituto do Vinho e da Vinha (Institute of Vines and Wine – formerly the Junta Nacional do Vinho).

PDRITM: Projecto de Desenvolvimento Rural Integrado de Trás-os-Montes (Trás-os-Montes Integrated Rural Development Project).

UTAD: Universidade de Trás-os-Montes e do Alto Douro (University of Trás-os-Montes and the Alto Douro).

Glossary of Technical Terms

Anthocyanins: the principal member of a complex group of organic chemicals responsible for the red/purple hue in wines.

Baumé: a measure of dissolved compounds in grape juice and therefore its approximate concentration of sugars. The number of degrees baumé is a rough indicator of percentage alcohol by volume (i.e. grape juice with 12o baumé will produce a wine with about 12 per cent alcohol by volume). Its inventor was Antoine Baumé (1728–1804), a French pharmacist.

Cuvaison: a French term that applies to red wine-making for which there is no English translation. It signifies an extended period of maceration on grape skins following fermentation, resulting in the greater extraction of both colour and tannin.

Elevage: a French wine-making term which defies translation into English. It literally means 'rearing' or 'raising' as it might be applied to either young livestock or humans, but in the context of wine it is the term applied to the series of operations between the end of fermentation and bottling. At this stage in the process, the wine-maker's role is analogous to that of a parent and there is much that can go wrong before a wine is finally bottled, shipped and consumed.

Ethyl Acetate: the most common ester in wine formed by the reaction of acetic acid with ethanol. At low to moderate concentrations, ethyl acetate contributes to the aroma and flavour of the wine but at high concentrations a wine will be unacceptably vinegary. Many old Tawny Ports have relatively high levels of ethyl acetate.

Fining: the process where microscopic particles are removed from a wine by the addition of a fining agent. The most commonly used fining agents are bentonite, casein, egg white, or gelatin, which adsorb or coagulate with potentially unstable colloidal material suspended in the wine, causing it to precipitate more quickly. The fining of Port is discussed on p. 147.

Pectolitic Enzymes: used by wine-makers to break up natural pectins in the grape skins and by some Port shippers to aid colour and flavour extraction.

pH: hydrogen power; a measure of the concentration of the acidity. Low pH indicates high concentrations of acidity and vice versa. All grape must is acidic registering pH values between three and four. The scale is logarithmic so a wine with a pH of three has ten times as much hydrogen ion activity as one whose pH is 4. Most Douro grape musts are naturally at the upper end of the spectrum (occasionally in excess of pH 4) and have to be corrected by the addition of tartaric acid (see also Total Acidity).

Phenolics: a large group of reactive chemical components responsible for the tannins, pigment (anthocyanins) and many of the flavour compounds found in wine. Most of the phenolics come from the skins of the grape.

Sulphur Dioxide (SO_2): a disinfectant and anti-oxidant used by wine-makers. The efficacy of sulphur dioxide is influenced by the wine's pH.

Total Acidity: a measure of both fixed and volatile acids in wine usually expressed in Portugal as grams per litre tartaric. The ideal range for grape musts is between 7 g/l and 10 g/l with wines varying between 4.5 g/l and 8 g/l. Port naturally tends to be towards the lower end of the spectrum with musts registering as little as 5 g/l expressed as tartaric acid. The addition of tartaric acid is therefore commonplace.

Volatile Acidity: a measure of the naturally occurring organic acids in a wine that are separable by distillation. The most common volatile acid in wine is acetic acid, which imparts a vinegary character if present in excessive concentrations. The Portuguese use the term *vinagrinho* ('little vinegar') to describe a wine with noticeable but not detrimental levels of volatile acidity (usually found in old *Colheita* and Tawny Ports).

Appendix I

Institutions Promoting and Regulating Port

Instituto do Vinho do Porto (IVP)
Rua Ferreira Borges, 4050, Porto
Formed in 1933, the Port Wine Institute is a public body under the direct
supervision of the Ministry of Agriculture but with its own financial
autonomy. The IVP is responsible for controlling the quantity and quality
of Port by regulating production and certifying the wine after a rigorous
quality control process. All Port has to be submitted to the IVP for
analysis and tasting before seals of origin are granted to the wine in
question.

The IVP is also responsible for the generic promotion of Port world-
wide, defending the region and using every available means to combat
fraud. It acts alongside the Portuguese government in European Union
negotiations with third countries to restrict the use of the name 'Port'.

Comissão Interprofissional do Região Demarcada do Douro (CIRDD)
Instalações do Casa do Douro, Rua dos Camilos, 5050 Peso da Régua
Established in 1995, the Interprofessional Committee for the Douro
Demarcated Region is a public body under the supervision of the
Ministry of Agriculture. Its main responsibility is to promote a
convergence of interests between growers and shippers, determining
and regulating the total amount of grape must that may be fortified to
produce Port in any one year (the benefício).

Casa do Douro
Rua dos Camilos, 5050 Peso da Régua
Created in 1932, the Casa do Douro has lost much of its statutory power
since it purchased 40 per cent of the Real Companhia Velha in 1990.
It operates today as a federation purporting to represent the interests of

growers and co-operatives in the demarcated Douro region. All growers are obliged by law to register with the Casa do Douro.

Associação das Empresas do Vinho do Porto (AEVP)
Rua Barão de Forrester, 412, 4400 Vila Nova de Gaia
The successor to the former exporters' guild or *grêmio*, the Port Wine Shippers Association is a voluntary body to which nearly all of the major shippers belong. The main object of the AEVP is to promote and defend the interests of the exporting companies both at home and overseas.

Associação dos Viticultores Engarrafadores dos Vinhos do Porto e Douro (AVEPOD)
Rua Vilarinho de Freire, 5050 Peso de Régua
The Association of Port Wine Growers and Bottlers was formed in 1986 to represent and promote those producers based in the Douro region who are making and marketing their own Ports.

Confraria do Vinho do Porto
Rua Barão de Forrester, 412, 4400 Peso de Régua
The Port Wine Brotherhood was established to diffuse, promote and consolidate the prestige of Port world-wide. One of its activities is the organisation of the annual boat race between *barcos rabelos* that takes place each year on 24 June to commemorate Oporto's patron saint, São João. The author of this book is a *Cavaleiro* of the *Confraria do Vinho do Porto*.

Gabinete da Rota do Vinho do Porto
Rua dos Camilos, 90, 5050 Peso da Régua
Co-ordinating office of the Port Wine Route with information available on *quintas* open to visitors.

Appendix II
Douro Sub-regions

Sub-region	Total area (ha)	%	Area under vines (ha)	% of Total area
Baixo Corgo	45,000	18	13,492	29.9
Cima Corgo	95,000	38	17,036	17.9
Douro Superior	110,000	44	8,060	7.2
Total	250,000		38,588	18.33 (average)

Source: Institute do Vinho do Porto/Casa do Douro

Sub-region	Number of growers	Area under vines/grower (ha)	Average number of plots/grower	Total number of plots under vine
Baixo Corgo	13,338	1.01	4.7	62,111
Cima Corgo	13,690	1.24	4.1	55,753
Douro Superior	6,052	1.33	3.5	21,198
Total	33,080	1.17	4.2	139,062

Source: Institute do Vinho do Porto/Casa do Douro

Distribution in % of plots by size (ha)

	<0.5	0.5–1	1–3	3–5	5–10	10–20	20–30	>30
Baixo Corgo	83.52	10.95	4.28	0.72	0.40	0.11	0.02	0.00
Cima Corgo	85.57	8.45	4.68	0.74	0.38	0.14	0.02	0.01
Douro Superior	79.37	12.55	6.39	0.97	0.53	0.16	0.01	0.02
Total	83.71	10.19	4.76	0.76	0.12	0.12	0.02	0.01

Source: Casa do Douro 1996

Vineyard gradients in the Douro by sub-region (areas in hectares)

Sub-region	Area of vineyard with gradients up to 5%		Area of vineyard with gradients between 5–30%		Area of vineyard with gradients between 30–50%		Area of vineyard with gradients over 50%	
Baixo Corgo	382	2.9%	4,126	31.6%	8,032	61.4%	535	4.1%
Cima Corgo	648	3.9%	7,198	43.0%	8,330	49.8%	551	3.3%
Douro Superior	484	6.3%	5,460	71.2%	1,712	22.3%	8	0.1%

Source: Instituto do Vinho do Porto/Casa do Douro

Appendix III
Port Benefício/Total Production
1989–1998

	Benefício/ authorisation[1]	Amount of must fortified	Total amount of Port produced[2]	Total production in the Douro[3]	Percentage of total made into Port wine
1998	135,000	118,281	141,654	164,489	86.1
1997	131,500	130,288	165,334	214,121	77.2
1996	130,000	129,997	164,651	365,670	45.0
1995	127,500	129,350	163,528	257,192	63.6
1994	110,000	107,831	136,818	198,435	68.9
1993	90,000	85,550	108,184	168,494	64.2
1992	85,000	80,054	101,333	234,481	43.2
1991	110,000	117,192	147,456	298,794	49.4
1990	115,000	153,966	193,194	392,665	49.2
1989	145,000	172,867	216,825	258,460	83.9

[1] Amount of grape must authorised for fortification.
[2] Grape plus *aguardente*.
[3] Total production of Port and Douro wine.
Units: pipes of 550 litres.

Appendix IV

Port Grape Varieties
(Recommended and Authorised)

Recommended varieties

White		Red	
Min. 60%	Max. 40%	Min. 60%	Max. 40%
Esgana Cão	Arinto	Bastardo	Cornifesto
Folgasão	Boal	Mourisco Tinto	Donzelinho
Gouveio	Cercial	Tinta Amarela	Malvasia
(Verdelho)	Côdega	Tinta Barroca	Periquita
Malvasia Fina	Malvasia Corada	Tinta Francisca	Rufete
Rabigato	Moscatel Galego	Tinta Roriz	Tinta da Barca
Viosinho	Donzelinho	Tinto Cão	
	Branco	Touriga Francesa	
	Samarrinho	Touriga Naçional	

Authorised varieties

White		Red	
Min. 60%	Max. 40%	Min. 60%	Max. 40%
Alvaraça	Jampal	Alicante	Preto Martinho
Avesso	Malvasia Parda	Bouschet	Santarém
Borrado das	Malvasia Rei	Alvarelhão	São Saúl
Moscas	Medock	Aramont	Sevilhão
Branco Especial	Moscadet	Carinhana	Sousão
Branco Sem	Mourisco	Carrega Tinto	Tinta Aguiar
Nome	Branco	Casculho	Tinta da
Branco Valente	Pedernão	Castelã	Bairrada
Caramela	Praça	Concieira	Tinta Carvalha
Carrega Branco	Rabigato	Gonçalo Pires	Tinta Lameira
Chasselas	Francês	Grand Noir	Tinto Martins
Dona Branca	Sarigo	Grangeal	Tinta Mesquita
Fernão Pires	Touriga Branca	Mondet	Tinta Miuda de
Formosa	Trincadeira	Moreto	Fontes
		Mourisco de	Tinta Pereira
		Semente	Tinta Pomar
		Nevoeira	Tinta Roseira
		Patorra	Tinta Valdosa
		Petit Bouschet	Tinta Varejoa
		Português Azul	Touriga
			Brasileira

Appendix V
Port Wine Trade

Principal markets	1998		1997		1996		1995		1994	
	hl	%	hl	%	hl	%	hl	%	hl	%
France	299,448	31.70	283,995	31.43	288,129	31.16	328,768	35.58	297,769	34.96
Holland	151,825	16.07	143,112	15.84	136,194	14.73	115,816	12.53	123,539	14.51
Portugal	128,481	13.60	127,920	13.60	117,281	12.69	116,114	12.57	80,633	9.47
Belgium/Lux	120,660	12.77	116,815	12.93	138,588	14.99	142,524	15.43	139,186	16.34
UK	88,153	9.33	92,772	10.27	92,291	9.98	92,408	10.00	84,417	9.91
Germany	33,171	3.51	24,340	2.69	33,954	3.67	28,886	3.13	27,650	3.25
USA	32,381	3.43	32,074	3.55	27,977	3.03	18,178	1.97	17,244	2.02
Denmark	16,910	1.79	18,473	2.04	18,774	2.03	18,615	2.01	20,128	2.36
Italy	11,655	1.23	11,531	1.28	16,617	1.80	15,720	1.70	18,095	2.12
Canada	11,556	1.22	8,892	0.96	6,822	0.74	4,773	0.52	5,408	0.64
Spain	11,035	1.17	8,839	0.98	8,441	0.91	6,587	0.71	6,472	0.78
Brazil	7,307	0.77	9,745	1.08	7,321	0.79	6,472	0.70	3,156	0.37
Switzerland	4,493	0.48	3,590	0.40	7,783	0.84	4,614	0.50	4,893	0.57
Ireland	4,244	0.45	4,138	0.46	4,626	0.50	3,584	0.39	4,010	0.47
Sweden	4,057	0.43	3,632	0.40	4,222	0.46	3,842	0.42	4,974	0.58

Special categories (Vintage Character, LBV, aged Tawny, Vintage Port, Light Dry White)

Principal markets	1998		1997		1996		1995		1994	
	hl	%	hl	%	hl	%	hl	%	hl	%
France	10,533	10.72	11,684	11.50	9,511	11.47	9,178	12.40	8,523	11.88
Holland	5,843	5.95	5,975	5.88	4,496	5.42	3,823	5.16	4,275	5.96
Portugal	10,359	10.54	7,828	7.71	6,093	7.35	5,734	7.75	5,241	7.30
Belgium/Lux	3,548	3.61	2,289	2.78	2,740	3.30	3,219	4.35	3,272	4.56
UK	34,560	35.17	40,410	39.78	32,466	39.16	33,527	45.29	33,652	46.89
Germany	1,905	1.94	1,538	1.51	1,025	1.24	819	1.11	784	1.09
USA	14,900	15.20	16,203	15.95	13,674	16.49	6,956	9.40	6,558	9.14
Denmark	2,620	2.67	2,763	2.72	3,021	3.64	2,475	3.34	1,922	2.68
Italy	411	0.42	322	0.32	325	0.39	332	0.45	275	0.38
Canada	7,432	7.56	5,703	5.61	4,487	5.41	2,782	3.76	3,148	4.35
Spain	459	0.47	347	0.34	203	0.24	265	0.36	325	0.45
Brazil	313	0.32	357	0.35	257	0.31	255	0.34	160	0.22
Switzerland	557	0.57	523	0.51	413	0.50	373	0.50	444	0.62
Ireland	524	0.53	526	0.52	485	0.58	427	0.58	433	0.60
Sweden	687	0.70	699	0.69	425	0.51	503	0.68	336	0.47

1993		1992		1991		1990		1989		1988	
hl	%	hl	%	hl	%	hl	%	hl	%	hl	%
281,037	32.90	250,216	34.63	248,887	34.20	248,852	39.39	286,512	44.00	272,117	41.26
100,850	11.81	81,478	11.28	81,345	11.18	63,123	9.99	60,686	9.32	60,859	9.23
142,537	16.69	112,187	15.53	112,764	15.50	116,719	18.47	103,326	15.87	106,426	16.14
130,286	15.25	127,877	17.70	126,377	17.37	155,442	24.60	128,307	19.70	142,129	21.55
80,883	9.47	48,843	6.76	48,868	6.72	52,824	8.36	55,182	8.47	65,460	9.93
31,538	3.69	25,009	3.47	28,540	3.92	28,378	4.49	28,330	4.35	32,159	4.88
12,282	1.50	6,890	0.95	6,632	0.91	6,914	1.09	7,602	1.17	5,487	0.83
18,663	2.19	18,210	2.52	18,715	2.57	19,143	3.03	18,593	2.84	17,651	2.68
17,496	2.05	19,530	2.70	23,874	3.28	22,715	3.60	30,723	4.72	30,385	4.61
3,578	0.42	1,961	0.27								
4,637	0.54	2,878	0.40	3,447	0.47	4,231	0.67	5,172	0.79	5,090	0.77
2,070	0.24	1,015	0.14								
5,995	0.70	6,173	0.85	6,498	0.89	6,162	0.98	6,451	0.99	7,169	1.09
3,316	0.39	3,286	0.45								
4,334	0.51	4,495	0.62	4.225	0.58	4,866	0.77	4,945	0.76	5,159	0.78

1993		1992		1991		1990		1989		1988	
hl	%	hl	%	hl	%	hl	%	hl	%	hl	%
9,650	16.31	9,090	16.59	8,512	16.48	11,708	21.53	9,757	18.93	11,285	19.18
3,386	5,72	2,902	5.30	2,776	5.37	2,544	4.68	2,164	4.20	2,226	3.85
4,673	7.90	4,744	8.66	4,982	9.64	5,439	10.00	4,568	8.86	6,154	10.46
2,688	4.54	2,751	5.02	2,752	5.33	2,684	4.93	2,774	5.38	2,881	4.90
26,696	45.12	23,903	43.62	23,036	44.59	25,083	46.12	24,811	48.13	29,360	49.89
848	1.43	1,035	1.89	967	1.87	1,331	2.45	1,107	2.15	1,264	2.15
4,596	7.77	3,559	6.49	2,620	5.07	4,523	8.32	4,441	8.62	6,114	10.39
1,084	1.83	1,261	2.30	888	1.72	583	1.07	773	1.50	976	1.66
362	0.61	392	0.72	466	0.90	738	1.36	894	1.73	578	0.98
1,779	3.01	1,856	3.39								
203	0.34	263	0.48	262	0.51	337	0.62	334	0.65	277	0.47
167	0.28	44	0.08								
345	0.58	329	0.60	366	0.71	442	0.81	449	0.87	400	0.68
236	0.40	269	0.49								
343	0.58	222	0.41	185	0.36	164	0.30	168	0.33	426	0.72

Appendix VI

Vintage Declarations since 1960 (excluding single quintas)

1997 (at the time of going to press): Barros, Burmester, Cálem, Churchill, Cockburn, Dow, Feist, Ferreira, Fonseca, Gould Campbell, Graham, Hutcheson, Kopke, Martinez, Messias, Niepoort, Noval, Noval Naçional, Offley, Osborne, Poças, Quarles Harris, Ramos Pinto, Romariz, Royal Oporto, Rozès, Sandeman, C. da. Silva, Skeffington, Smith Woodhouse, Taylor, Warre

1996: Barros, Kopke, Noval Naçional, Poças

1995: Barros, Borges, Burmester, Constantino, Duff Gordon, Feist, Ferreira, Gilberts, Hutcheson, Kopke, Krohn, Noval, Offley, Osborne, Poças, Ramos Pinto, Rozès, C. da Silva.

1994: Barros, Borges, Burmester, Delaforce, Cálem, Churchill, Cockburn, Constantino, Croft, Delaforce, Dow, Duff Gordon, Ferreira, Fonseca, Gould Campbell, Graham, Kopke, Martinez, Morgan, Niepoort, Noval, Noval Naçional, Offley, Osborne, Poças, Quarles Harris, Ramos Pinto, Romariz, Royal Oporto, Rozès, Sandeman, Smith Woodhouse, Taylor, Warre

1992: Burmester, Cálem, Delaforce, Fonseca, Kopke, Niepoort, Osborne, Taylor

1991: Barros, Burmester, Cálem, Churchill, Cockburn, Croft, Dow, Feist, Feuerheerd, Ferreira, Gould Campbell, Gilbert, Graham, Hutcheson, Kopke, Krohn, Martinez, Morgan, Niepoort, Noval, Noval Naçional, Osborne, Poças, Quarles Harris, Ramos Pinto, Rozès, C. da Silva, Smith Woodhouse, Warre

1989: Barros, Borges, Burmester, Feist, Hutcheson, Kopke

1988: Borges

1987: Barros, Constantino, Feist, Ferreira, Kopke, Martinez, Niepoort, Noval, Noval Naçional, Offley, Rozès, Royal Oporto, C. da Silva

1985: Andresen, Barros, Borges, Burmester, Cálem, Churchill, Cockburn, Croft, Delaforce, Dow, Ferreira, Feist, Feuerheerd, Fonseca, Gilberts, Graham, Gould Campbell, Krohn, Kopke, Martinez, Messias, Morgan, Niepoort, Noval, Noval Naçional, Offley, Osborne, A. Pinto dos Santos, Poças, Quarles Harris, Ramos Pinto, Robertson's Rebello Valente, Romariz, Royal Oporto, Rozès, Sandeman, C. da Silva, Smith Woodhouse, Taylor, Van Zeller, Vieira de Sousa, Warre

1984: Krohn, Messias, Royal Oporto

1983: Barros, Borges, Cálem, Cockburn, Dow, Feist, Fonseca, Gould Campbell, Graham, Hooper, Kopke, Martinez, Messias, Niepoort, Offley, Poças, Quarles Harris, Ramos Pinto, Robertson's Rebello Valente, Royal Oporto, Rozès, C. da Silva, Smith Woodhouse, Taylor, Van Zeller, Warre

1982: Barros, Borges, Churchill, Croft, Delaforce, Feist, Ferreira, Hopper, Kopke, Krohn, Martinez, Messias, Niepoort, Noval, Noval Naçional, Osborne, Offley, A. Pinto dos Santos, Poças, Ramos Pinto, Royal Oporto, Rozès, Sandeman, C. da Silva

1980: Barros, Burmester, Borges, Dow, Feist, Ferreira, Feuerheerd, Fonseca, Gould Campbell, Graham, Hooper, Kopke, Messias, Niepoort, Noval Naçional, Offley, A. Pinto dos Santos, Quarles Harris, Ramos Pinto, Robertson's Rebello Valente, Royal Oporto, Smith Woodhouse, Sandeman, Taylor, Vieira de Sousa, Warre

1979: Andresen, Barros, Borges, Feist, Hutcheson, Kopke

1978: Barros, Feist, Ferreira, Kopke, Krohn, Niepoort, Noval, Noval Naçional, Poças, Royal Oporto, Rozès, C. da Silva, Vieira de Sousa

1977: Barros, Burmester, Cálem, Croft, Delaforce, Diez Hermanos, Dow, Feist, Ferreira, Feuerheerd, Fonseca, Graham, Gould Campbell, Kopke, Messias, Morgan, Niepoort, Offley, Poças, Quarles Harris, Robertson's Rebello Valente, Royal Oporto, Rozès, Sandeman, C. da Silva, Smith Woodhouse, Warre

1975: Andresen, Barros, Butler & Nephew, Cálem, Cockburn, Croft, Delaforce, Dow, Feist, Ferreira, Fonseca, Graham, Gould Campbell, Kopke, Krohn, Martinez, Niepoort, Noval, Noval Naçional, Offley, Poças, Quarles Harris, Ramos Pinto, Robertson's Rebello Valente, Sandeman, Taylor, Warre

1974: Barros, Feist, Kopke

1972: Dow, Offley, Robertson's Rebello Valente

1970: Butler & Nephew, Barros, Borges, Burmester, Cálem, Cockburn, Croft, Delaforce, Dow, Feist, Ferreira, Feuerheerd, Fonseca, Gould Campbell, Graham, Gonzalez Byass, Hutcheson, Kopke, Krohn, Martinez, Messias, Morgan, Niepoort, Noval, Noval Naçional, Offley, Osborne, Poças, Sandeman, C. da Silva, Smith Woodhouse, Poças, Quarles Harris, Ramos Pinto, Robertson's Rebello Valente, Royal Oporto, Taylor, Vieira de Sousa, Warre

1967: Cockburn, Krohn, Martinez, Noval, Noval Naçional, Offley, Royal Oporto, Sandeman

1966: Barros, Cálem, Constantino, Croft, Delaforce, Dow, Feist, Ferreira, Fonseca, Graham, Gould Campbell, Kopke, Messias, Morgan, Niepoort, Noval, Noval Naçional, Offley, Quarles Harris, Robertson's Rebello Valente, Rozès, Sandeman, Smith Woodhouse, Taylor, Warre

1965: Barros, Kopke, Krohn

1963: Barros, Borges, Burmester, Cálem, Cockburn, Croft, Delaforce, Dow, Feist, Ferreira, Fonseca, Gonzalez Byass, Gould Campbell, Graham, Kopke, Krohn, Martinez, Messias, Morgan, Niepoort, Noval, Noval Naçional, Offley, Poças, Quarles Harris, Ramos Pinto, Robertson's Rebello Valente, Royal Oporto, Rozès, Sandeman, C. da Silva, Smith Woodhouse, Taylor, Warre

1962: Noval Naçional, Offley

1961: Krohn

1960: Barros, Borges, Burmester, Cálem, Cockburn, Constantino, Croft, Dow, Feist, Ferreira, Fonseca, Gould Campbell, Graham, Kopke, Krohn, Martinez, Messias, Noval, Noval Naçional, Offley, Osborne, Poças, Ramos Pinto, Robertson's Rebello Valente, Sandeman, Smith Woodhouse, Taylor, Warre

Index

Figures in bold indicate main references
to shippers and producers.

Dias, Bartolomeu, 4
diatomaceous earth, 148
Dickens, Charles: *Nicholas Nickleby*,
  217
Diez Hermanos, 222
Diniz, King of Portugal, 3
diseases, 75–6
Disnoko, 219
distillation, 68
'Dixon's Double Diamond', 217
DOC (*Denominação de Origem
  Controlada*), 247
Donzelinho Branco, 88
dornas (steel bins), 127, 132
double *guyot* training, 73
'Douro', the term xiv–xv
'Douro bake', 145, 160
Douro region
  directions in the, 117–24
  during the Second World War, 45
  expansion of, 17–19
  first grafted vineyard, 34
  Forrester and, 25, 26, 121, 221
  hive of activity, 36
  the kitchen, 90–91
  oidium, 30
  phylloxera, 30, 33
  railway construction, 30, 31–3
  shippers lose interest in, 12, 13
  statistics, 56
  storage of port, 145
  sub-regions, 62–3, 78
  tobacco, 39–40
  upheaval in, 23–4
  and wine export bans, 16
  wine list, 255–71
  in winter, 142–4
Douro River, 2, 3, 33, 40, 111, 119,
  245, 251
  the bar, 40, 41, 46
  the *barcos rabelos*, 32, 244
  and cereals, 7
  dams, 29, 49–40, 59, 123, 144
  flooding, 10, 49–50, 115
  Forrester and, 25–6, 28
  navigability, 18, 25–6
  Romans, 1
Douro, S.S., 49
Douro Superior sub-region, 9, 18, 28,
  30, 49, 63, 65, 66, 81–4, 86, 89,
  92, 107, 113–17, 122, 160, 198–9,
  206, 222, 226, 249, 251, 273
  alcohol levels, 126

diseases and pests, 75
  harvest-time, 125, 126, 127
  Port vintage, 167, 168, 173
  vineyard classification, 199
Douro Wine Shippers and Growers
  Association, 192, 213
Dow, James Ramsey, 204
  *An Inquiry into the Vine Fungus
    with Suggestions as to a
    Remedy*, 30
Dow (Silva & Cosens Ltd), 47, 97,
  109, 113, 115, 121, 131, 154, 159,
  161, 162, 169, 170, 173, 174, 175,
  176, 177, 178, 179, 180, 181, 183,
  184, 185, 203–5, 224, 235, 239, 241
  see also Silva & Cosens Ltd
Dow & Co., 204
Dow's Port, 21, 204
Dow's Trademark, 157, 205
Dow's Vintage Port, 46, 204, 205
drip irrigation, 77
drought, 77
dry red wines, 148, 250
Ducellier system, 48, 131
Duckinfield, near Manchester, 38n
Duero River, 251
Duff, James, 231
Duff Gordon, 222, 231
Dutch, the *see* Netherlands

EDP, 49, 50
Edward I, King, 3
Edward II, King, 3
Edward III, King, 3, 4
egg white, 147
eggs, 41–2
elderberry *see baga de sabugueiro*
élevage, 145
Elizabeth II, Queen, 1
encuba, 138
England
  antipathy towards Spain, 6
  and the Battle of Aljubarrota, 3
  drinking habits, 8
  Portuguese communities in, 20
  preference for stronger wines, 18
  textiles, 10
  trade with Portugal, 1, 3, 4–5,
    10, 16, 19–20, 27, 29, 37–8
  trade war with France, 7
  treats Portugal like a colony (17th
    C.), 11–12
  the Treaty of Windsor, 1, 4

INDEX

oidium, 30, 31, 32, 75, 87, 167
Oidium tuckeri, 30
Olazabal, Francisco, 116, 271
Olazabal, Vito, 206, 268, 271
Oliveira, Duarte de, 78
Oporto, 55, 118, 194, 209, 231, 232,
    237, 240
  bottling, 46
  British community, 6, 9, 10, 11,
    20, 21-2, 29, 37, 40-41, 45,
    50, 52, 243-4
  civic buildings, 58
  civil war, 23, 25
  Colheitas in, 163
  and the *coup d'état* (1974), 50
  described, 36, 242-6
  during the Second World War, 45
  the Dutch and, 9
  at the end of the nineteenth
    century, 36-9
  English Factories, 6, 14
  Factory House, 21, 22, 23, 37, 53,
    156, 165, 189, 241, 244, 248
  fidalgos, 20, 24
  fierce fighting (1927), 43
  Gaia competes, 3
  the Harris family, 10
  Kopke & Co. founded, 9
  Port lodges, 242, 244, 245, 248
  and Portucale, 2
  Portuguese nobility, 20
  production crisis, 35
  radical politics, 23
  recaptured by Wellesley, 22
  and 'Red Portugal', 7
  republican revolution attempted
    (1891), 39
  rioting (1910), 40-41
  Rua Nova dos Inglezes (now Rua
    Infante D. Henrique), 21, 23,
    25, 36-7, 244
  'sanitary cordon', 39
  siege of, 23, 24
  Soult in, 21, 22
  time warp in, 46-7
  'Tippler's Revolt', 14
  tripe, 5-6, 23, 246
Oporto Cricket and Lawn Tennis Club,
  244
Oporto Stock Exchange, 243
Ordish, George: *The Great Wine
  Blight*, 30
organic material, 76

organic Port, 76
Organic Vintage Character Port, 213
Osborne, 168, 222-3
Osborne, Thomas, 222
over-production, 12, 29, 44, 81
Oxford, 29
oxidation/oxidative character, 19, 144,
    145, 147, 152, 157, 158, 160, 163,
    164, 215, 240

Pacheco & Irmcos Lda, 102
paciência (steam train), 31, 123
Padernã, 88
Padrela, 60
Palace of Mateus, 122-3, 269
Pálacio dos Carrancas, Oporto, 22, 37
Panascal, 108
parque archeologico, 50, 117
passing the Port, 189
pasteurisation, 148
patamares (terraces), 53, 70, 71, 73,
    76, 98, 99, 101, 102, 107, 114, 116
patrão (owner), 91, 125
PDRITM (Projecto de
    Desenvolvimento Rural Integrado
    de Trás-os-Montes), 53, 71, 79, 83,
    251
Pé-agudo, 77
pectolytic enzymes, 135, 138
Pedro IV (previously Pedro I, Emperor
    of Brazil), 23, 207
Pedro VI, 24
Pénajoia, 17
Peninsular War, 22, 23
pergolas, 65, 119
Perignon, Dom, 11
Periquita, 78
pessoal (staff), 91
pests, 75-6
pH, 125, 126, 132, 251
Phayre & Bradley, 9, 10, 200
phenolic wines, 254
phenolics, 127, 137
pheromones, 76
Philip II, King of Spain, 6
Philippa of Lancaster, 4
Phoenicians, 1
phosphorous, 76
photosynthesis, 73, 75
phylloxera, 30-34, 36, 39, 53, 68, 70,
    71, 72, 77, 91, 104-5, 184, 204,
    236, 248, 274
Pierce's Disease, 75